To Ron & his dogs — enjoy!
Best wishes —
Deborah, Anadyr
(& Natasha).

THE
SIBERIAN HUSKY
Joan McDonald Brearley

TS-148

THE
SIBERIAN HUSKY
Joan McDonald Brearley

Contents

CONTENTS

ACKNOWLEDGEMENTS

Much time is spent and many people are called upon before a book gets published as worthy tribute to a breed. I am especially grateful to Jean Fournier for all her help and support. With this book, as with my first book on our breed, she was always available to answer questions or supply needed and essential materials to make this book a reality. To all others who submitted photographs of their beautiful dogs and told the stories of their involvement in the breed I also owe sincere thanks. As always I must thank my veterinarian, Robert Shomer, DVM, for his expert counsel and support on this book and all my others over the years. I hope everyone will get enjoyment out of what I hope will be a permanent tribute to the breed we all love so much.

Joan Brearley
Sea Bright, New Jersey

PREFACE

It is not the purpose of this book to name each and every Siberian Husky, breeder, owner, or exhibitor that ever lived. That would be virtually impossible. Nor is it the purpose to chronicle a complete history of the breed since its beginning. This also, would be next to impossible. It is, however, the intention of this book to educate or instruct those who have not been in the breed as yet, or are new and eager to learn, or who wish to improve and perpetuate the breed and to preserve some facts and information about it.

It is also the purpose of this book to reach those who are drawn to the breed as it exists today, and who wish to know the highlights of its history and background and to have photographs of many of the great dogs that have appeared on the scene over the years in the show rings. Our Siberian

Huskies have become so much a part of the dog fancy that anything new that is said or written about them can be of value if it enhances our knowledge and admiration of their place in our lives.

Some of the material in this book was written originally for my first book on the breed, *This is the Siberian Husky*, published in 1974. That material which is contained here I believe to be of importance to those who did not, or cannot now, purchase the first book, and is of much value to those in the breed today.

The author would like to believe that this book is yet another entry in our library of dogs that have served mankind well, and as her personal tribute to a wonderful breed.

ABOUT THE AUTHOR

Joan Brearley is the first to admit that animals in general—and dogs in particular—are a most important part of her life. Since childhood there has been a steady stream of dogs, cats, birds, fish, rabbits, snakes, alligators, turtles, etc., in her own personal menagerie. Over the years she has owned over thirty breeds of purebred dogs as well as countless mixtures, since the door was never closed to a needy or homeless animal.

A graduate of the American Academy of Dramatic Arts, where she studied acting and directing, Joan started her career as an actress, dancer, and writer for movie magazines. She studied ballet at the Agnes DeMille Studios in Carnegie Hall, and was with an Oriental dance company which performed at the Carnegie Recital Hall. She studied journalism and creative writing at Columbia University and has written for radio, television and magazines, and was a copywriter for some of the major New York City advertising agencies, working on the accounts of Metro-Goldwyn-Mayer movie studios, Burlington Mills, *Cosmopolitan* magazine, White Owl Cigars, and *World-Telegram Sun* newspapers.

While a television producer-director for a major network, Joan worked on "Nick Carter, Master Detective"; "Did Justice Triumph"; and news and special feature programs. Joan has written, cast, directed, produced, and, on occasion, starred in television commercials. She has written special material or programs for such personalities as Dick Van Dyke, Amy Vanderbilt, William B. Williams, Gene Rayburn, Bill Stern, and many other people prominent in the entertainment world. She has appeared as a guest on several of the nation's most popular talk shows, including Mike Douglas, Joe Franklin, Cleveland Amory, David Susskind, and the "Today Show," to name just a few. Joan was selected for inclusion in the *Directory of the Foremost Women in Communications* in 1969 and the book *Two Thousand Women of Achievement* in 1971.

Her accomplishments in the dog fancy include breeding and exhibiting top show dogs, being a writer and columnist for various magazines, and author of over thirty books on dogs and cats. She is a contributor to *World Book Encyclopedia* and the *Funk and Wagnalls Encyclopedia* as well. For five years she was executive vice president of the Popular Dogs Publishing Company and editor of *Popular Dogs* magazine, the national prestige publication for the fancy at that time. Her editorials on the status and welfare of animals have been reproduced as educational pamphlets by dog clubs and organizations in many countries of the world.

Joan is almost as active in the cat fancy, and in almost as many capacities. The same year her Afghan Hound, Ch. Sahadi Shikari won the Ken-L Ration Award as Top Hound of the Year, one of her Siamese cats won the comparable honor in the cat fancy. She has owned and/or bred almost every breed of cat. Many of her cats and dogs are Best in Show winners and have appeared in magazines and on television. For several years she was editor of the *Cat Fancier's Association Annual Yearbook,* and her book *All About Himalayan Cats* was published in 1976.

In addition to breeding and showing dogs since 1955, Joan has been active as a member and on the Board of Directors of the Kennel Club of Northern New Jersey, the Afghan Hound Club of America, the Stewards Club of America, and the Dog Fanciers Club. She has been an American Kennel Club approved judge since 1961. She has appeared as a guest speaker at many dog clubs and humane organizations, crusading for humane legislation, and has won several awards and citations for her work in this field. She is one of the best-known and most knowledgeable people in the animal world. Joan is proud of the fact that her Ch. Sahadi Shikari was top-winning Afghan Hound in the

The author, Joan McDonald Brearley.

history of the breed for several years, and remains in the top three even today. No other breeder to date can claim to have bred a Westminster Group winner in his first homebred litter. She has also bred champion Yorkshire Terriers.

Joan is a former trustee, and still an active member, of the Morris Animal Foundation, does free-lance publicity and public relations work, is a Daughter of the American Revolution and member of the New York Genealogical Society. In her "spare" time she exhibits her needlework (for which she has also won prizes), haunts the art and auction galleries, is a graduate auctioneer with the full title of colonel, and is a realtor associate. At the same time she is working toward her degree in Criminal Justice and Law at Brookdale Community College.

This impressive list of activities doesn't include all of her accomplishments, since she has never been content to have just one interest at a time, but manages to dovetail several occupations and avocations to make for a fascinating career.

Joan lives with her dogs, cats, hamsters, guinea pigs, and over twenty tropical birds in a townhouse on the oceanfront in Sea Bright, New Jersey, where she also serves as councilwoman, secretary, and active member of the First Aid Squad, and Trustee of both the Sea Bright Village Association and the Sea Bright Partnership. On a county level she is a director, assistant recording secretary, and publicity chairwoman of the Monmouth County Federation of Republican Women and has been appointed to the Monmouth County Heritage Committee by the Board of Chosen Freeholders.

EARLY HISTORY OF THE DOG

"In the 1950s in an excavation in Pelegawra, Iraq, a canine fossil was discovered that is said to date back 14,500 years; it was appropriately labeled the Pelegawra dog. Siberian remains are said to go back 20,000 years."

Many millions of years ago, dinosaurs and other strange-looking creatures roamed the earth. As "recently" as 60 million years ago, a mammal existed that resembled a civet cat and is believed to have been the common ancestor of dogs, wolves, and coyotes. Miacis were long-bodied, long-tailed, short-legged beasts that stalked and chased their prey, grasped it in their long, powerful, fanged jaws, and gnashed their food with their teeth. Just 15 million years ago, *Tomarctus* evolved from the earlier *Miacis* and provided an even truer genetic basis for the more highly intelligent prototype of the domesticated dog.

It is only 15 to 20 thousand years since the first attempts were made to domesticate the direct ancestors of dogs. Archaeologists have uncovered the skeletal remains of dogs that date back to the age of the cavemen and must have coexisted with them as members of their families in several ancient civilizations.

There are several schools of thought among scholars and scientists on the exact location of the very first creatures to live with man. Some contend that the continent of Africa was the original locale. Ancient remains unearthed near Lake Baikal, Russia, date back to 9000 years BC. In the 1950s in an excavation in Pelegawra, Iraq, a canine fossil was discovered that is said to date back 14,500 years; it was appropriately labeled the Pelegawra dog. Siberian remains are said to go back 20,000 years. The Jaguar Cave dogs of North America have been dated circa 8400 BC.

Others claim the Chinese wolf to be the ancestor of the dog. Advocates of the theory of the

Chinese wolf point out that the language barrier was responsible for the Chinese wolf's not being known or acknowledged in earlier comparisons. Because scientists could not translate Chinese writings, they could not study or authenticate the early Oriental findings. Their theory is also based on the presence of the overhanging bone in the jawbone of both the Chinese wolf and the dog. This is believed to be significant in the change from strictly carnivorous creatures to creatures that eventually became omnivores.

The general concensus of opinion among scientists dealing with prehistoric and archaelogical studies seems to settle on the likelihood that dogs were being domesticated in many parts of the world at approximately the same period of time. Since dogs were to become so essential to man's very existence, they were naturally absorbed into family life.

Climate, geography, and other environmental conditions all played a part in the evolution of the dog.

The three most primitive types originated in three parts

Aurora's Sparks A'Flyin', CD, and his mother, Aurora's Sienna Fleetfoot, two beautiful sable Siberian Huskies, owner-bred by Sharlene Lawson of Phoenix, AZ.

of the globe, as we see it now. While all bore certain very exact characteristics, the wolf-type (Dingo) seemed to evolve in southern Asia (and later entered Australia), the Pariahs in Asia Minor and Japan, and the Basenjis in Africa.

The Dingo found its way north to Russia and Alaska, across what is now the Bering Straits, into North America. The Pariahs moved far north, learned to pull sleds, and developed into the various northern breeds in the Arctic regions. The Basenjis and Greyhounds coursed the desert sands, climbed mountains, and hunted in the jungles of Africa when they weren't guarding royal palaces in Egypt. As dogs found their way across Europe, they served as guard dogs in the castles, rescue dogs in the Alps, barge dogs on the canals, and hunting dogs in the forests. The smaller dogs were bred down even smaller and became companions and pets for the aristocracy, or served their masters as rodent-killers in the fields or in the homes. But the kings and queens of the world have always maintained their own personal kennels for their favorite breeds. Perhaps the most famous of all dog lovers was Queen Victoria. Adventurers and world travellers brought back specimens of various breeds from countries all over the world, hoping to please and win the seal of approval on yet another breed.

BREED DEVELOPMENT

While the caveman used dogs primarily as hunters to help provide meat and to be used as meat themselves, he also made use of the fur as clothing and used the warmth from the dogs' bodies when sleeping. Dogs were to become even more functional as time went by, obeying the dictates of the climates and geographical regions. Definite physical changes were taking place that would eventually distinguish one dog from another, even within the same area. Ears ranged in size from the little flaps that we see on terriers to the large upright ears on the Ibizan Hound. Snouts either flattened greatly, as they did with the Pekingese, or grew to amazing lengths, as we see in the Borzoi. Tails grew to be long and plumy, such as those we see on our Siberian Husky, or doubled up into a small curl, such as we see on the Bulldog and Pug. Legs grew long and thin for coursing Greyhound, or were short and bent for the digging breeds such as the Dachshund and the Bassett Hound. Sizes went from one extreme to the other, ranging from the tiniest Chihuahua all the way up to the biggest of all breeds, the Irish Wolfhound. Coat lengths became longer or shorter. There were thick woolly coats for the northern breeds and smooth, short coats for the dogs that worked in the warm climates.

As dogs changed in physical

appearance, their instincts and sensory perception also developed. In some breeds, the German Shepherd Dog for instance, the sense of smell is said to be 20 million times keener than in his human counterpart, allowing him to pick up and follow the scents of other animals miles away. Dogs' eyes developed to such a sharpness that they could spot moving prey on the horizon far across desert sands. Their hearing became so acute that they were able to pick up the sounds of the smallest creatures rustling in the leaves.

All things considered, it becomes easy to comprehend why man and dog became such successful partners in their fight for survival, and why their attraction and affection for each other are such wondrous things.

Lovely head study of Margaret Cook's AmCan Ch. High Country's Hyper Holly.

EARLY HISTORY OF THE SIBERIAN HUSKY

"The term husky is a corruption of 'esky,' a slang word for Eskimo; it covered all the sled-pulling breeds that had tough, shaggy coats, pointed faces, and plumy tails."

Alaska and Siberia, separated by only 55 miles of Bering Sea—with some of the smaller islands in the straits as close to each other as only two miles—have all through the ages shared their ancestry, a way of living, and their life-preserving dogs.

Some 35,000 years ago, the people of Central Asia migrated farther and farther north to the most extreme regions of Siberia and the Arctic, and brought with them their jackal-type dogs (Canis aureus). Crossbred with the Arctic wolves (Canis lupus), these animals developed over the centuries into what later came to be referred to as the Northern breeds, including the Malamute, Samoyed, Spitz, Keeshond, Elkhound, the Nootka dogs of Iceland, and the Russian Laikas.

By the Neolithic age (3500 to 2000 BC), the Northern dogs had become established with their own type and characteristics which, with periodic breedings to the wolf, managed to endure down through the ages. All of these dogs were referred to as "huskies." The term husky is a corruption of "esky," a slang word for Eskimo; it covered all the sled-pulling breeds that had tough, shaggy coats, pointed faces, and plumy tails. Their coats were thick and woolly to protect them from the elements, and they came in almost every color: solids, brindles, white with spots, black with white, white with black patches, reds, yellow, yellow spotted, red spotted, etc.

From the first days of the Eskimos' existence on earth,

the dogs had been there at their sides, living with them and hunting with them, thousands of years before sleds were thought of or necessary to their existence. As far back as Mesolithic times, men travelled on skis, and there are also evidences that they used the travois for ages before they got around to building the more practical sleds.

As the Eskimos continued their northward migration across the Arctic Circle, eventually coming to Greenland, some of the natives moved in behind them and established tribes along the foothills of the Cherski Mountains at the basin of the Kolyma River. One of these tribes was the Chukchi people who were to develop the Siberian Husky. The early association of dog and tribe led

Above: **Shalimar's Arctic Joe of Snoden as a puppy; bred by Shalimar Kennels, owned by Gerry and Nanci Sevigny.** *Right:* **Judith Russell and a 7-dog team in a 1979 race. Notice the depth of the snow, which doesn't stop the dogs at all.**

to the dog's being sometimes referred to as the Siberian Chukchi.

All of these tribes consisted of three divisions: the marine or maritime people, who were largely fishermen and lived along the river where the Huskies were used to pull the umiaks, or large skin boats, along the shore; the sedentary people, who remained in one place and traded to make a living; and the nomadic tribes, which wandered far and wide following the huge herds of reindeer. Travelling by reindeer became less and less satisfactory to the nomads, who became more and more dependent on their dogs, not only to help them hunt and herd, but also to get them from village to village to trade.

As the wilderness opened up before them, and as their numbers grew, they began to develop a dog bred to meet the requirements of their specific needs. The Husky became the dog with the necessary conformation to provide speed and endurance over great distances with the least expenditure of energy and food.

While many of the tribes were hostile toward one another, there were times when the tribes depended upon one another and their dog teams for their very survival. When food was scarce, they would join their dogs to one sled when it became necessary to move entire villages, and all their belongings, from one location to another. At times, the

women and children would get into harness and pull right along with the dogs to facilitate the move. Their dogs were held in such high esteem that only the babies, the sick, or the elderly were allowed to ride on the sleds.

Drivers led or walked behind the teams, guiding their worldly goods to a new, less hostile location. In heavy snow or bad weather, the drivers would often blaze the trail with their snow shoes ahead of the lead dog, and the teams would follow in his footsteps along the man-made trail. These Northern dogs were seldom fast runners, as it was more important that they maintain

Marcia Hoyt's team in the foreground at the Skwetna checkpoint at the 1985 Iditarod Race. This is the all-Siberian team of Earl Norris's kennels.

the long pull from one village or camp to the next by moderate speed, to assure their arriving with their cargo in tact. Today, as well, the Siberian Husky is at his best when he can cover great distances with a comparatively light load at a moderate speed. Under these conditions he has no peer. Pound for pound, the Siberian Husky is the strongest draft dog of them all!

STONEHENGE ON THE ESQUIMAUX DOG

One of the most famous writers on the dog in England was a man who used the pen name of Stonehenge. Actually, he was the editor of *The Field*, a major dog publication in England in the 19th century. He wrote books about individual breeds and enormous editions covering all breeds as they were known up to that time.

In the preface to *The Dog In Health and Disease*, dated July 1859, he expounds at great length about his extensive and reliable sources and, with this in mind, it is fascinating to read the account of The Esquimaux Dog, which states: "This dog is the only beast of burden in the

Sire and dam of one of the Quirin's litters: Ch. Sikisha's Para-Trouper and Fra-Mar's Cree of Scoqui.

Kolyma Team photograph contributed by Stu Galka. A breathtaking view of the High Sierras near Sonora, CA.

northern parts of the continent of America and adjacent islands; being sometimes employed to carry materials for hunting or the produce of the chase on his back, and at others he is harnessed to sledges in teams varying from seven to eleven, each being capable of drawing a hundred weight for his share. The team are harnessed to a single yoke-line by a breast-strap, and being without any guide-reins, they are entirely at liberty to do what they like, being only restrained by the voice of their master and urged forward by his whip. A single dog of tried intelligence and fidelity is placed as leader, and upon him the driver depends for his orders being obeyed. In the summer, they are most of them turned off to get their own subsistence by hunting, some few being retained to carry weights on their backs; sledges are then rendered useless by the absence of snow; and as there is a good subsistence for them from the offal of the seal and the walrus which are taken by the men, the dogs become fat at this season of the year. The Siberian and Greenland dogs are nearly similar to those of Kamtschatka, but somewhat larger, and also more manageable, all being used in the same way. The Esquimaux dog is about 22 or 23 inches high, with a pointed, fox-like muzzle, wide head, pricked ears, and wolf-like aspect; the body is low and strong, and clothed with long hair, having an under-coat of thick wool; tail long, gently curved, and hairy; feet and legs strong and well formed; the colour is almost always a dark dun, with slight disposition to brindle, and black muzzle."

Stonehenge went on to include brief mention of other Northern dogs in a one-sentence paragraph entitled *Iceland and Lapland Dogs:*

"These are nearly similar to the Esquimaux, but rather larger, more wolf-like, and far less manageable."

THE SOCIAL HIERARCHY

All descendants of either the wolf or the jackal are dogs which belong to a group which adheres to communal family living. In other words, they lived in packs, and each pack had its leader.

It was the function of the leader not only to protect his position but also to guide, keep order, discipline, and excel in every way over all the rest of the pack. The leader, therefore, was always the strongest, most intelligent, and certainly the

AmCan Ch. Sunset Hill's Bella Donna, owned by Grawyn Siberians of Deanna and Lou Gray, Woodstock, IL.

Top: Ch. Princess Omi of Troika is a multi-Group winning bitch out of Karnovanda's Troika Kavik ex Ch. Setting Sun's Miss Parashinka. Bred by Vearl and Patty Jones; owned by Gene and Gail Corfman. *Bottom:* Troika's Twist of Fate taking Best of Winners. The judge is Vic Clemente.

Top: The 1977 Hartford Show under Henry Stoecker finds Carol Nash's Ch. Toko's Twenty Four Karat Gold winning Best of Opposite Sex with Jean Fournier handling, and Ch. Marlytuk's Kiska Trey finishing for her championship. *Bottom:* Ch. Snoking's Snowdrift winning Best of Breed at a 1985 show judged by Peggy Adamson. Bred by the MacWhades; owned by Dick and Beth McClure of Milford, MI.

bravest and most aggressive of the lot and had to take on all comers at all times, since other males were constantly challenging his position. Since the leaders were first with the females as well, it assured the breeding of the best and strongest specimens within the pack. This "law of the jungle" is as old as time.

While there seems to be little doubt that the ancestors of domestic dogs were the wolves, there is good reason to believe that there was also jackal blood introduced through the centuries. This supposition is based on research in observance of the Asian wolves. The

Right: **Innisfree's Impresario, owned by Joe and Brenda Kolar, Astoria, OR. The sire was Ch. Innisfree's Red Roadster ex Innisfree's Gabney.** *Opposite:* **Saroja's Skyhope Sorcerer, bred by Doris Anne and Bryant Dussetschleger and co-owned by Deanna Gray and Sandra James.**

Northern wolf, for instance, blends into the Tibetan wolf, the Tibetan wolf in turn shades into the pale-footed Asian wolf, and the Asian wolf shades into the Mesopotamian desert wolf, and so on...and all of them are most similar to the jackal.

There is also a supposition among a number of historians that jackals and wolves were actually the same, that jackals were merely wolves which went off in an opposite geographical direction and to a different way of life, developing qualities and characteristics necessary to survive in a particular region.

Those which migrated toward the North developed into shaggy, wolf-like creatures able to withstand the colder climates and made conformation adjustments accordingly. When they became domesticated by the Eskimos they were regarded as the Northern breeds of dogs. The wolf-jackal-dog species all can interbreed and produce fertile get, so it was not an impossibility.

Hutchinson's Encyclopedia offers the theory that while the wolf coloration of the Husky may bear out the general impression that Huskies were

Opposite: Head study of Alice Watt's Ch. Kossok's Patch of Bleu. *Left:* The call of the wild! AmCan Ch. Tandara's Che Kodiak singing into the air. Bred and owned by Lynne Patterson of Washington State.

frequently wolf-crossed, if that were the case most Huskies would be all white, because the Arctic wolf is white. Also, the Arctic wolf is a much larger animal than the Husky, often weighing 150 pounds. They also carry their tails down while the Husky dogs carry them up and over their backs. And strangely enough, the Arctic wolf is the only animal a Husky is afraid to attack.

Additionally, purebred wolves have been trained and used to a limited extent as sled animals. They proved most unsatisfactory since they did not have the endurance so necessary for a good sled dog! The only conclusion can be that while the Husky may have originally descended from wolves, there has since been only what could be considered as occasional crossbreedings.

According to Dr. Edward Moffat Weyer, Jr., one of the foremost students of the Eskimo, "It seems altogether likely that the dogs have crossed to some extent with wolves. The skeletal similarity points to a relationship."

Perhaps the most obvious difference seems to be in behavioral pattern of the wolf and of the jackal. While both the wolf and the jackal packs recognize a leader, the wolf packs support a graduated order of superiority from the leader down, in a one, two, three "pecking order." The jackals, on the other hand, are said to recognize a leader, but the rest of the pack share

"In spite of the virtually complete domestication of the Husky today, they observe the 'leader of the pack' social pattern, which is one of the reasons they fit in so nicely with our family living."

equally in rank, with no dog taking second place to any other dog in importance.

With this comparison in mind, and going beyond the wolf-like physical appearance of today's Siberians, and knowing that they have been interbred with the wolves over the centuries, we must also note that their social behavior resembles that of the jackal. In spite of the virtually complete domestication of the Husky today, they observe the "leader of the pack" social pattern, which is one of the reasons they fit in so nicely with our family living. The dog joins the family "pack" and recognizes the dominant member of the family as his "leader." This is the person to whom obedience is paid and to whom his allegiance belongs. But he also upholds the jackal social behavior pattern in that he gets along equally well with all other members of the family "pack," a trait attributed to animals descending morphologically from the jackal.

MYTHS AND LEGENDS

We have all at one time or another heard a fantastic story about the part animals play in various rites and ceremonies. Whether they are true stories or mere legends, we do know that some of the people of the North put great stock in these tales. They have been passed down from generation to generation and have never lost their fascination.

For instance, many Eskimos believe that there are dog guards at the gates to paradise. Dog-lover tales are prominent with the Eskimo women, who tell of unknown lovers who are dogs by day, men by night. Many Eskimos also tell us that Indians and Europeans are descended from a dog. The way the story goes is that, at the beginning of the world, a woman had ten children by a dog, five of which became inlanders, and the other five she set afloat on a raft to become Europeans! Lapp women would offer dog sacrifices to the goddesses of childbirth just before they delivered to insure a healthy baby.

Brian Kenney of Bow, NH, with his dog Marco.

THE SACRIFICIAL DOG

There is little doubt that vast numbers of Husky dogs were sacrificed to the gods, although there does seem to be some discrepancy as to what was done with the remains once the sacrifice had been offered. We are well aware that the dogs' skins were used for clothing and that, in times of famine, the flesh was eaten by man and dog alike. There are written records which state that the Koryak did not eat dog meat, except when there was famine. There are also reports that the Chukchi kill dogs for food, but do not eat those which are sacrificed. We do know, also, that while the dogs were bred in great numbers, each family seemed to have fewer dogs than they bred. Over the years this could have been a disaster to the family, as well as the tribe!

The Museum of Natural History in New York City has on file a series of photographs of what was referred to by villagers as the most perfect specimen of a Husky dog ever seen until that time. It was to have been sacrificed on the very day it was photographed, but was literally snatched from the arms of death by an explorer who purchased him for a bottle of whiskey! This dog, whelped at the turn of the century, is noticeably more like a brindle Chow Chow than any Siberian Husky, Malamute, Spitz, or Samoyed that we have seen in this century.

Not always were the dogs sacrificed to the gods— sometimes they were offered to ward off the evil spirits. On the Western Union Telegraph Expedition, September, 1865, members of the Kamchadals tribe seized one of the dogs from their team; after knifing it to death, they offered its body up to the evil spirits.

Opposite: A lovely sylvan setting for William Creamer's Arahaz Kristi and Arahaz Ciara.
Below: An Alaskan 11-dog team on the run over a typical trail. Photo taken in the early 1970s.

EARLY EXPLORERS AND EXPEDITIONS

Opposite:
Mrs. Lorna Demidoff and her team blazing a trail near her Monadnock Kennels in Fitzwilliam, NH, in the 1950s.

It was the Northern type husky dog which the Russians used during the 17th century when they succeeded in charting the Siberian coastline. All the dogs were described to be merely domesticated wolves and had the same instincts and characteristics as the sled dogs used and described by the members of the Western Union Telegraph Expedition of 1865, 1866, and 1867.

Apparently they did not differ from any of the dogs found along the entire route of the expedition, which extended from its starting point at the lower Kamchatka Peninsula to the top northeastern tip of Siberia. We can be sure that the colonization of the northeastern part of Siberia by Czarist Russia during the last few centuries played a part in improving the lot and expanding the uses of these native dogs, even though breeding between the dogs the Cossacks brought with them and the Northern dogs they encountered along their way disputes the claim that the Chukchi dog was a purebred for over two thousand years!

In actuality there is no different description of the Northern sled dogs in the diaries of Marco Polo, written in the thirteenth century while describing their use in relay teams as a means of rapid transportation in the Arctic.

As late as 1900, only slight superficial differences could be discerned among the Northern breeds. They were all described by the early explorers as having

long, shaggy coats and very definite wolf or fox-like appearances. The very earliest photographs and drawings of these dogs, and writings by explorers such as Olaf Swenson, Vilhjalmur Stefanson, Waldemar Jochelson, Valdemar Borgoras (writing on the Jessup North Pacific Expedition in 1904), George Kenner, Washington B. Vanderlip, Irving Reed, and the rest seemed to have a single picture in mind of the breed.

THE PEARY-COOK CONTROVERSY

Hutchinson's Encyclopedia pays tribute to the Husky as helping to make the remarkable strides in exploration at both the North and South pole regions, declaring that it was indispensable to its owner as no other breed. The same holds true with the explorer. Every expedition had to depend largely on the use of the sled dogs, and therefore it is very probable that no other breed has had such a wide natural distribution.

Two creditable, adventurous men claimed to have reached the North Pole—Navy Commander Robert E. Peary and Dr. Frederick A. Cook. Peary was steadfastly backed by the Peary Arctic Club, composed of 21 millionaire sportsmen who all secretly yearned to have accomplished the feat themselves. Dr. Cook, backed by a notorious gambler, John R. Bradley, lost the honor in the raging controversy which ensued.

Dr. Cook was discredited, ridiculed, and on the verge of a breakdown, as all his previous accomplishments were placed in doubt and he was dubbed the "prince of losers." The

The 1971 Fairbanks North American with Roger Reitano's Ch. Tucker in the lead with Mr. Chips, an Igloo-Pac-registered Siberian Husky. In fact, all leaders of this 10-dog team are registered Siberians.

campaign waged against him by Peary's wealthy backers led him to despair to the end of his days.

Cook returned to civilization first to announce his achievement. Cook was a loner and made the journey with two Greenlanders, doing all the charting and navigating himself. Peary had 25 men go along to support his claim. It worked. Years of trying to clear his name of the Peary accusations, and a prison sentence for stock fraud, all took their toll on Dr. Cook. The sentence was commuted by President Franklin D. Roosevelt on Cook's deathbed. He rallied upon hearing this news, but it was mild consolation to this dedicated explorer.

The paths of Peary and Cook had crossed before. In 1892 Cook had been signed on as medic on one of Peary's expeditions to Greenland. During the journey Peary sent Cook and another man back, while Peary and a few of the others went on with three sledges and 14 dogs until they reached 82 degrees north latitude. Peary believed he had proven that Greenland is an island, and when he and his party reached a great body of water he proclaimed it Peary Channel. In 97 days Peary had travelled 1130 miles. In 1915, however, Peary Channel was removed from the maps, as Danish explorers proved that Greenland went a great deal beyond Peary's calculations. His first expedition thus discredited, his second was also a failure. In 1893-1895 they tried again, but were forced to return, having to eat some of the dogs on the return journey. In 1898, he made another

> *"During the journey Peary sent Cook and another man back, while Peary and a few of the others went on with three sledges and 14 dogs until they reached 82 degrees north latitude . . . In 97 days Peary had travelled 1130 miles."*

unsuccessful attempt to reach the Pole and met the famous Norwegian explorer Otto Sverdrup when their ships both became frozen in the ice about 700 miles south of the Pole.

Before sailing, Peary said good-bye to President Theodore Roosevelt, who said to him, "I believe in you, Peary, and believe in your success—if it is within the possibility of man." At this time news of Dr. Cook's departure reached him.

Dr. Cook had come up with a new way to reach the Pole and had written, "There will be game to the 82 degree point and there are natives and dogs for the task, so here is for the Pole." On March 18, 1908, he reduced his party to two 20-year-old Eskimos, two sleds, and 26 dogs and started for the North Pole.

When Peary arrived at Etah, the starting-off point in the North, he claimed it was difficult to get Eskimos and dogs because Cook had gotten there first. This simply was not true, since Peary left Etah with 49 Eskimos and 246 dogs. A pair of dogs could be had in a trade for a tin cup and saucer.

The cold was excruciating for Cook and his group. The dogs' tails, ears, and noses drooped and perspiration froze and coated their bodies with ice. A hundred miles from the Pole, Etukishook and Ahwelah, the Eskimos, decided they did not want to go on. The knife and gun each was to receive as payment no longer seemed enough. But they trusted Cook, who convinced them to go on.

On April 21, 1908, Cook and his two Eskimos reached the Pole. Cook later said, "I strode forward with undaunted glory in my soul…The desolation was such that it was almost palpable…What a cheerless spot this was, to have aroused the ambition of man for so many years."

He buried a short note, mentioning the good health of the men and dogs, and part of a flag in a metal tube. He later admitted that he felt a "sense of the utter uselessness of this thing, of the empty reward of my endurance," which had followed his exhilaration at his accomplishment.

Peary on his last assault had with him four Eskimos and his Negro servant Matthew Henson, along with five sledges and 40 dogs. Peary also expressed almost the same disappointment in the face of his success. He recorded in his diary, "The Pole at last. The prize of three centuries. Mine at last! I cannot bring myself to realize it. It all seems so simple and commonplace."

Peary also buried a jar with a piece of the flag in it and took possession of the territory in the name of the President of the United States. The route back was aided somewhat by following the urine stains left by the forty dogs which accompanied him to the North Pole.

MACMILLAN ON THE HUSKIES

Lieutenant-Commander Donald B. MacMillan, an Arctic explorer whom Peary referred to as an excellent dog man, made several trips to the North Pole. In 1908-1909 he went with 250 dogs, during 1913-1917 with 400 dogs, 1923-1924 with 60 dogs. His 1927-1928 journey to Northern Labrador gives us considerably more information regarding the part the dogs played in these expeditions. He definitely claimed that the dogs from Labrador were better looking and the best of all the Northern dogs he had seen. MacMillan, who is accredited with running an authentic trip of 100 miles in less than 18 hours, had nothing but good to say about the ability and endurance of the dogs.

He noted that for fast travelling they limited the load to approximately the combined weight of all dogs in the team. For ordinary hauls they limited it to one-and-a-half times the team's total weight, and for heavy hauling the limit was double the weight. When the going was good, and with a light load, the team made six to eight miles an hour.

He further stated: "The usual gait is a fast, steady trot, which they keep up hour after hour. Some dogs will frequently shift from this trot to a pace, evidently as a measure of rest. Occasionally too, they will gallop, probably for the same reason." He also made the same observation that most of us have—once a lead dog is trained, he never forgets. Photographs of all expeditions show pie-balds, solid blacks, and all variations of colors and color combinations. The Husky type dog is evident—they are Husky dogs! Their value is further evidenced by a paragraph contained in

Primed and ready to go. These dogs are awaiting the word from Edward P. Clark to get on their way. This photo taken several years ago before sledding became popular within the fancy.

A famous dog man from the 1930s, Felix A. Leser of Saranac Lake, NY. Mr. Leser was the judge of Eskimo Dogs, Siberian Huskies and Whippets at the 1935 Morris and Essex Dog Show. Photo by E. Gockeler.

Hutchinson's Encyclopedia which reads: "As poor Captain Scott and his brace companions were struggling to their death after reaching the South Pole (in 1911), Amundsen was riding back in comparative comfort with his team of 11 Greenland Eskimo dogs."

THE GREAT SERUM RUN

One of the greatest tales of heroism ever to come out of the frozen North is the story of the great Serum Run of 1925, when a group of drivers and their stalwart sled dogs fought their way through 50° below-zero weather and an 80-mile-an-hour blizzard to get serum to the inhabitants of Nome to halt the march of diphtheria.

In spite of the waist-high drifts and the mountainous crags of the pack ice, they covered the distance of 655 miles in five-and-a-half days under the most excruciating circumstances, safely delivering the 20-pound package containing the precious units of antitoxin serum. On the morning of February 2, 1925, Gunnar Kasson and his half-frozen team of dogs with bloody, torn feet pulled into Nome and handed over the serum to Curtis Welch of the US Public Health Service. Welch was Nome's only doctor, and together with a handful of nurses in an area containing 11,000 inhabitants, stretching one thousand miles to the east and as far north as the Arctic Ocean, they got busy putting the serum to work. The epidemic *had* to be halted, since diphtheria is certain death to Eskimos.

Prayers of thanks were echoed throughout the area and all over the world, for this crisis was big news everywhere. Newspapers had carried the progress reports of the relay teams of Eskimo Pete Olsen, Leonhard Seppala, Gunnar Kasson, and the rest of those involved in the run; and everyone seemed to realize instinctively the icy terror in the black Alaskan night these brave men were facing. The names of Titus Nicolai, John Folger, Jim Kalland, Tom Green, and Bill Shannon became household words as the journey proceded to Nome by the Bering Sea.

Not only did the names of the drivers remain foremost in the minds of the people, but so did the names of the dogs which led and pulled on the teams. There were Togo and Scotty, Seppala's two lead dogs, and the most famous of all, Balto, the dog which pulled into Nome with Kasson. The moment the team halted at the end of the 60-mile run, Kasson fell into the snow beside his dog and began pulling the ice splinters from Balto's torn and bloody paws. Exhausted, Kasson still paid tribute to his lead dog. Newspapers all over the world carried his works of praise for Balto: "Damn fine dog! I've been mushing in Alaska since 1903. This was the toughest I've ever had on the trails. But Balto, he brought us through."

Kasson was referring to Balto's scenting the trail when Kasson had gotten lost on the bare ice and had run into an overflow while crossing the Topkok River. Balto had proved his worth before on more than one occasion. He had led Kasson's team in 1915 when they won the Moose race, and two years before had led the team which carried explorer Roald Amundsen north from Nome when he planned an

Siberians of the Ricker-Seppala Kennels, the winning team at the finish of a 3-day race in Laconia, NH, many years ago.

SEPPALA AT THE FINISH QUIMOY DRUG LACONIA

airplane flight over the North Pole. He well earned and deserved his title of the best lead dog in Alaska.

Seppala's dogs had also come through for him on many occasions. Togo and Scotty were the leads on his team and were known throughout Alaska as the very fastest dogs. At the start of the run, Seppala had been warned by officials not to cut across Norton Sound, since weather officials had reported that the ice was breaking up and drifting out to sea. There was a storm raging over the area at the time as well. He was urged to take the longer distance around which circled Norton Bay, but Seppala preferred to throw caution to the wind to gain speed. He felt his dogs were in good condition to make it, although they had already mushed 80 miles.

The crossing of Norton Bay was hazardous and stormy, but once they reached the other side they headed for Isaac's Point. Seppala pulled the sled into a cabin and by a roaring fire, undid the wrappings around the package containing the serum and warmed it as best he could. His instructions said that the serum had to be warmed up at intervals and the wrapping could be removed down to a certain seal which could not be broken. Once the heat had penetrated the last wrapping, Seppala once again rewrapped the package in its canvas coverings, several thicknesses of reindeer skin, and a final wrapping of a fur

sleeping bag. Then, once again, he started on his way.

Seppala delivered the precious cargo into the hands of Charlie Olson at Golofnin. Olson then with his team of seven Huskies ran the twenty-five miles from Golofnin to Bluff, where he turned over the package to Kasson. Every one of Olson's dogs pulled into Bluff frozen in the groin. They could not have gone on much farther, but true grit made them run on until their mission was completed, even though they all pulled up stiff and sore.

Olson lived in Bluff. He owned a quartz mine and stamp mill there and when he and Kasson met, they took the package into a cabin and warmed it before Kasson struck out in the 28 degree below zero temperature and a raging wind. They had waited two hours for the storm to abate, but Kasson finally decided to buck the snow rather than lose the trail or have it become impassable. He was advised not to attempt it, but he was adamant. The ice was in constant motion from the ground-swell, and it was at this point that he ran into trouble crossing the Topkok River. They hit an overflow, and the winds and snow had become so severe that he could not see even as far as the wheel dogs. His right cheek became frozen and he lost the trail completely. But Balto came to the rescue. He kept to the trail and ploughed on through snow and over ice, allowing nothing to alter his direction. Kasson recalls that he himself did not even know when they passed right by Solomon, where they were to have picked up a message from Nome which would advise him not to go on until the weather improved.

When Kasson finally pulled into Port Safety, Ed Rohn was waiting to take off as relay; but Kasson felt his dogs were doing so well that he decided not to awaken Rohn and drove the

at Fairbanks for the shipment of serum when the dog-teams went through. They knew, however, that weather conditions were so bad that the planes would never get through. Governor Scott C. Bone of Alaska, in a special dispatch to the *New York Times,* stated that any attempt to fly would have been a hazardous undertaking because the flying equipment was

final 21 miles from Port Safety to Nome. The trail ran along the beach of the Bering Sea, and it was at this point that two of the dogs, who had been frozen on another trip, began to stiffen up. Kasson had rabbit-skin coverings for them, but the cold was so severe that it still penetrated.

Three volunteer flyers were standing by with their airplanes

inadequate and only unskilled flyers were available.

Once again, the mushers and their legendary sled dogs came through. Man and animal had fought a bitter battle against the elements—and had won! Another epic tale has become part of the history of the vast Yukon country in which dogs played a major part.

In New York City's Central

With the Appalachian Mountain Club camp on the shore of Lonesome Lake in the White Mountains, Edward P. Clark's dog team is poised and ready to go.

Florence Clark of North Woodstock, NH, with a team of white Eskimo Dogs with black heads, photographed many years ago, in the days when crossbreeding was quite a common practice.

Park there is a magnificent bronze statue of Balto with a trace hanging over his back; it bears the inscription:

"Dedicated to the indomitable spirit of the sled dogs that relayed anti-toxin six hundred miles over rough ice, across treacherous waters, through arctic blizzards from Nenana to the relief of a stricken Nome in the winter of 1925. Endurance–fidelity– intelligence."

THE SAGA OF ADMIRAL BYRD

Rear Admiral Richard E. Byrd, USN, was the first man to fly over the North Pole and the South Pole and the only man to fly over both. He gazed upon more square miles of unknown, uncharted territory than any other human being in history. During his wartime duties he was decorated four times, receiving the Congressional Medal of Honor,

the Congressional Lifesaving Medal, three specially voted Congressional medals, and many others.

In an article in *National Geographic* magazine in October, 1947, Rear Admiral Byrd wrote extensively about his 1946-1947 return to the Antarctic. Entitled "Our Navy Explores Antarctica," the article refers only briefly, but no less significantly, to the role of the Husky dog in that exploration.

Over 4,000 men and 13 ships played a part in this particular expedition, Operation Highjump, which was the largest polar expedition Admiral Byrd had undertaken up to that time; it even was accompanied by an aircraft carrier, the *Philippine Sea*. The objective was to sail as far as possible around the 16,000-mile coast of the continent, since most of the coastline up until that time was mostly conjectural. Expedition leaders proposed to send seaplanes to explore the coast and make inland flights, and to have their ships establish a base for ski-equipped land planes which would make photo-reconnaissance flights across the unmapped interior of the continent.

On this trip, all the aircraft were equipped with the latest inventions which World War II had provided: new weapons, photo-reconnaissance tools, and aerial cameras which could

True spirit of the North. Roger Reitano sharing a tender moment with his dog Shang, taken in Tok, AK, in 1969.

photograph about 100,000 square miles of territory in one shot. All this equipment, plus the wide use of snow tractors, produced remarkable information. But there was still a "dog town" in Little America! The marvelous Husky dogs were still useful and very necessary on the rough, crevassed terrain, where no mechanical equipment could function to full advantage.

Large dogs were usually chosen, because it was thought they could better withstand the ardors of the Antarctic climate. But for Byrd's latest expedition, Milton Seeley chose fifty dogs of the smaller, faster type represented by the Siberian Husky. Upon their return, the explorers reported that the smaller dogs got them farther per pound of dog food,

and that their speed and smaller appetites more than made up for their lower pulling power. While the Husky at that time had an average weight of about 50 pounds to the Malamute's 75, the Husky could still travel at about 13 miles an hour under regular conditions, whereas the heavier dogs could manage only nine or ten. Subsequently, the Siberian Husky became the favorite racing dog of the Northern varieties by offering both speed and endurance.

ED MOODY AND ADMIRAL BYRD

Ed Moody, prominent racer and sled-maker, had accompanied Admiral Byrd on his 1933 expedition, during which the sled dogs played an important part. They took along nine dog sled teams, as

A legend in the breed. Ch. Marlytuk's Ahkee of Huskywood, owned by Janet Peckhamand; bred by Peggy Grant. He was the sire of the first Marlytuk Best in Show winner, Jean Fournier's Ch. Toko's Mr. Chip of Yago, CD.

well as 50 tons of Purina Dog Chow to feed them. Admiral Byrd later referred to the dog teams as the backbone of the expedition. At that time they could not have done without the dogs. Here again, mechanical equipment broke down while the dogs did not.

Weather, claimed Moody, was, even for the dogs, the biggest problem they had to overcome on the trip. Blizzards, crevasses, ice breaks—all played havoc with their progress—but the crucial point in the journey came in the Bay of Whales. The dog teams were hauling 1000 pounds a load and finally, even they

could not work when the temperature dropped to 60 degrees below zero. Below that their lips and foot pads froze. But there is, there was, and there always will be a place for dog teams among the inhabitants of the extreme frozen lands of the Arctic and Antarctic, where even snowmobiles can freeze up!

THE KARLUK

Much has been said over the years about the expeditions of Admiral Byrd, the Peary-Cook affair, and the great Alaska Serum Run, but little has been said about another adventurer who took off into the farthest

Roger Reitano with his Ch. Tucker of Chilkat, winner of the SHCA Racing Trophy two years running. Tucker was an AmCan champion, CD, Canadian Best in Show winner and lead dog for 8 years.

The nicely matched team of Felix A. Leser, ready to move when photographed many years ago.

National Geographic Society in 1920 for this last great Arctic expedition made without benefit of either airplane or wireless while charting more than 100,000 square miles to the maps of that polar region.

The *Karluk* was the leading ship of the expedition and when it got caught in an Arctic ice pack before being crushed and sinking, Stefansson's captain, Robert Bartlett, set off on the ice by dog sled with an Eskimo on the 700-mile journey across Siberia to seek help. It was six months before rescue arrived and when it did, eight of the men had died while the rest were near death.

Both men lived to write books about their experiences. Stefansson, ironically, wrote *The Friendly Arctic* (published in 1921), and later *The Adventure of Wrangel Island*. Captain Bartlett wrote *The Last Voyage of the Karluk*.

The author of *Karluk* (McKinlay) spent his retirement in Glasgow, Scotland, and eventually wrote his book, feeling there was more story to be told by someone who had actually been there. He was the one to reveal that Captain Bartlett had been given the Hubbard Medal for the rescue, and had also been recognized by the Royal Geographical Society of London. He believed the expedition to be "ill-conceived, carelessly planned, badly organized, haphazardly manned and almost totally lacking in leadership." This was because

reaches of the Arctic aboard the *Karluk*. Back in the early 1970s, William Laird McKinlay, survivor of the 1913-1918 Canadian Arctic Expedition organized by the Icelandic anthropologist Vihjalmur Stefansson, wrote *Karluk*.

In the foreword, Magnus Magnusson tells of the expedition and a little of the part that dogs and dog sleds played in it. He describes Stefansson as one of the last of the old school, who believed in "the worker with the dog and the sledge, among whom he easily holds a place in the first rank." It was Admiral Robert Peary himself who personally handed the Hubbard Medal to Stefansson awarded him by the he felt that Stefansson's theory that the Arctic was a friendly place "where a man with a gun, a sledge and a dog team could survive indefinitely" was erroneous—it was not land but miles of drifting ice floes.

Unfortunately, the ship's doctor, Alistair Mackay (who had accompanied Shackleton on his Antarctic expedition), was one of the first to die. He described the crew as "a motley collection of scientists and sailors, with the usual crop of human frailties. One man was even a drug addict!"

This haphazard attitude was born out by Norwegian explorer, Roald Amundsen, in his autobiography, *My Life as an Explorer*, published in 1927, who expressed his concern over Stefansson's explanation of the Arctic as being "friendly." He stated that if he believes that all one needs to survive there is a gun and some ammunition, certain death awaits him.

In spite of the fate that befell the Karluk, Stefansson sent another expedition to Wrangel Island in 1920 to prove his theory that white men could survive there.

William Lair McKinlay obtained the papers and/or diaries of the men with whom Stefansson had associated, including his own log book, and wrote *Karluk*. Captain Bartlett died in 1946, Stefansson in 1962, so neither got to see this finished work, but the book is to be placed in Canadian Archives. As McKinlay explains it: "I do not

wish to detract in any way from the achievements of Vihjalmur Stefansson, but the record must be put straight." He felt he owed that much to those who had died during their mission and to Captain Bartlett, who has saved his life.

The only member of the expedition to survive fit and unfettered was the ship's cat, Nigeraurak. The cat had been carried, during part of the journey, in a bag around one of their necks.

Mrs. Earl Nagle's Kabloona, photographed several years ago. Mrs. Nagle's kennels were in Tokoma Park, MD.

THE BREED IN THE UNITED STATES

"It was in the years before 1910 when Goosak brought the first dogs to Alaska for races, which caught the keen interest of Leonhard Seppala, John Jonson, Fox Maule Ramsey and Olaf Swenson."

The Siberian Husky during the first decade of the 20th century rested in the good hands of some very important and dynamic people. They had no idea then, but they were establishing the breed for future generations of dog lovers and racing and obedience enthusiasts, and would carry the breed to unbelievable heights of popularity that would touch almost every corner of the world.

It was in the years before 1910 when Goosak brought the first dogs to Alaska for races, which caught the keen interest of Leonhard Seppala, John Jonson, Fox Maule Ramsey and Olaf Swenson. Seppala maintained his kennels in Nome from 1909 until 1926, racing and winning with his dogs along the way. Shortly after the Serum Run he took off for Canada and New England, where his friend Elizabeth Ricker (later Mrs. Nanson) had a kennel of Siberian Huskies in Poland Springs, Maine, which included the last dogs brought out of Siberia by Olaf Swenson, the American fur trader, in 1929.

Swenson had put in over 40 years trading and hunting in northern Siberia. He had nothing but good things to say for the great shaggy dogs of the desolate northern wastelands. He felt it was impossible to name a price for a good one, comparing this to buying a person with whom you would undertake a perilous journey, and to whom you would entrust your life. In those days the Eskimo tribesmen would trade one dog for another, but never their lead dogs.

While in New England, Leonhard Seppala entered just about every race that was run, breaking records and continuing to make a name for himself as the world's top racing driver.

Around this same period, Frank Dufresne, formerly head of the Alaska Game Commission and an avid racing enthusiast, had a magnificent team of all-white Siberian Huskies. It was from these white Alaskan dogs that Julian Hurley purchased his first dogs, from a breeding of Dufresne's Jack Frost and Snow White. Hurley, a Fairbanks lawyer and judge,

sold many dogs to New England and Michigan, but unfortunately the line stopped there, though the second Bench Show Champion (1932) from the breed in the United States was Northern Light Kobuk, sold by Hurley to Oliver Shattuck in New England. Hurley's kennel (Northern Light) was in operation from approximately 1926 to 1947. It was Hurley who registered some of the first Siberian Huskies (over a dozen), and most of them were white.

In the late 1920s we see the appearance of Arthur Walden, with his still famous Chinook Kennels in Wonalancet, New Hampshire. It was Walden who

Valeskamo's Palo, Best of Breed winner and proven sire, bred and owned by Eleanor Grahn, Florissant, MO.

was directly responsible for bringing Eva (also known as "Short") and Milton Seeley into the breed. They purchased the Chinook Kennels from Walden and kept the name Chinook in addition to their own Alyeska and Wonalancet names on their dogs. Short Seeley maintained this most extraordinary kennel for many years. The Chinook stock came originally from Seppala and direct Alaskan imports.

This same period saw the start of another major kennel which remained active for many decades, the Monadnock Kennels of Mrs. Lorna Demidoff in Fitzwilliam, New Hampshire. Even in the 1980s, Mrs. Demidoff was an active judge of the breed and her Monadnock dogs are gracing

Judith Russell's 14-month-old Karnovanda's Storm Czar. This future champion was later sent to a kennel in South Africa.

the pedigrees of today's top winners in the breed.

Mrs. Demidoff's original stock also came from some of the Seppala dogs and a few Alaskan imports.

Doctors Alex and Charles Belford appeared on the scene in 1928, and both members of the prominent father and son team had been in racing for years. Their Belford's kennel in Laconia, New Hampshire, was active for many years and will be remembered in the breed.

Roland Bowles' Calivali Kennels were also in New Hampshire and formed in the late 1920s. They were active until the 1970s and were based on stock which came from White Water Lake, Foxstand, and Gatineau lines.

THE 1930s

In the 1930s, the Seppala dogs were still behind most of the breeding in this country. Some of the Seppala dogs were the basis for William Shearer's Foxstand Kennels in New Hampshire; Shearer was active in the breed from 1936 through 1956.

In 1938, Earl and Natalie Norris established their Anadyr Kennels in Anchorage and still keep up with the breed today.

They also used the Alyeska kennel name on some of their dogs, which go back to the Milton and Short Seeley lines. The Norrises transferred to Alaska from Lake Placid, New York, taking with them two registered Siberians from Chinook. Chinook's Alladin of Alyeska became the top stud

dog in Alaska. Red dogs were first bred by the Norrises in 1948, and they believe the red dog that went to Austin Moorecroft provided the coloration behind so many of the red dogs in the Eastern United States. Natalie Norris was active in club work in

Kiok's Pride of Shon, by Shon-Yak of Kiok, CD, ex Ch. Kiok's Sweet Kitu, CDX. Owners, Joe and Brenda Kolar.

Alaska, and in March 1973, she was invited to judge the breed at the Bronx County Kennel Club show in New York.

Charles and Kit McInnes and their Tyndrum Kennels in Alaska began in the 1930s; they were active until 1961. Their stock is behind the S-Komo lines.

From the 1930s to the 1950s, the names of Major John Rodman and Lowell Fields sprang up in Montana. They did not have an official kennel name, but their stock was founded on Monadnock breeding and the McFaul dogs. Their breeding was behind many Siberian Huskies found in the midwest in earlier times.

It was also during the 1930s when Dr. Roland Lombard and his Igloo-Pak dogs, based on Chinook lines, began making their mark.

Nomad

Robert Dickson Crane of Vienna, Virginia, established his kennel in 1935 with the purchase of his first Siberian Husky. She was a handsome bitch from the first Foxstand stock, with litters going back to the 1930s and 1940s. After a hiatus during the 1950s, Bob Crane reactivated his kennel in 1963 under the Nomad prefix. His major achievement has been to highlight the importance of breeding for the natural qualities of the original Siberian Chukchi sled dog.

Mr. Crane believes that, as he puts it, "The breed's strongest point is the still outstanding uniformity of the natural or primitive behavioral characteristics in the gene pool, which evolved during 3000 years of ecological adaptation in the Siberian Arctic."

One of Robert Crane's outstanding show dogs was Ch. Nomad's Chuchanka, a bitch whelped in October 1965 and shot as a suspected wolf in October 1967. His Ch. Nomad's Shane is a lead dog on Lynne Witkin's team in New York.

Robert Crane has done an enormous amount of research on the breed over the past years and considers the breed's important qualities today to be AKC conformation, the inherited desire to run long

Magnificent head study of the Fultons' famous Storm King of Siberia, first OTCH Siberian Husky in the breed. Stormy and the Fultons live in Big Bear Lake, CA. Photo by Country Photo Studio.

Perfect image? Kortar's Kranberry Kaptain, CD, is memoralized in the snow at the Bow, NH, home of James and Maureen Kent.

distances, and the ability to build rapidly from endurance training.

THE 1940s

The Nagles' Kabkol Kennels in Washington, DC, started in the 1940s and continued until the late 1950s. They left their mark on the breed in only a decade.

The 1940s also saw Harold Frendt and his Little Alaska Kennels in New York and Pennsylvania, where they were active until 1967. Their lines were based on the Gatineau and Bow Lake.

Jean Bryar (formerly Jean Lane) got her start in New Hampshire in the late 1940s; she was active until 1968 with her Mulpus, Bryar's, and Norvik lines, which stemmed from the early McFaul,

Seppala, Gatineau, and Monadnock lines.

Earl Snodie and Leonhard Seppala had the Bow Lake Kennels in Seattle, Washington from the late 1940s until 1960. Their kennel contained some of Frendt's breeding plus representatives of Monadnock, Lombard, and Little Alaska bloodlines.

While the Hulens of Washington, DC, did not have an official kennel name, their Ch. Monadnock's Echo was well known. Mr. Hulen bought his first Siberian in 1944—it was one of only 14 registered with the AKC at the time. Mrs. Hulen wrote for the *Gazette* and other publications over the years. Echo lived as a part of a stakeout team for four years, was "crash campaigned" to championship, and then became a house pet.

Another name that comes to mind from the forties is that of the Sylvan Dell Kennels of Doris Cassady in New Hampshire. Her kennel was built on stock from several of the northeastern lines.

Kennels also continued to spring up in Alaska. They include those of Donald and Virginia Clark and Jack and Sid Worbass; Koiri Koti Kennels of Orville and Doris Lake; Nikohna Kennels of Roger and Reta Gidney; Lakota Kennels of Joe and Gladys Traversie; Hank Buege's Kennel; and Darrell and Angie Reynolds' Kossa Kennels.

Dichoda

The kennel prefix Dichoda combines letters from the first three Huskies owned by Frank and Phyllis Brayton, who established their kennel in 1946. (Di)ngo, E(cho) and Gou(da) were the first Siberian Huskies shown in California and were among the first west of the Mississippi. They had their first litter in 1948, when only 105 Siberian Huskies were registered with the AKC.

Dichoda is located in Escalon, California, in the San Joaquin Valley, but the 25° temperature in winter and up to 108° temperature in the summer is of little concern to their dogs. All dogs and litters have done nicely in their location. The Braytons show their dogs and use them for pleasure driving with a three-wheel training rig as a "sled."

Siberian Huskies of their breeding can be found in teams from Alaska to New England.

In 1948, Ch. Dichoda's Aurelia, CD, from their first litter, became the third Husky in the US to earn both her championship and her Companion Dog title. She did it in three shows with all scores above 190. Their Ch. Noho of Anadyr was never defeated in breed competition in the five years he was shown. The second copper champion was Ch. Dichoda's Roja, a championship which did not come easy, for it was accomplished at a time when "reds" were rare.

Ch. Monadnock's Rurik of Nanook was added to their kennel in 1961 and was owner-handled. He won Best of Breed at the Siberian Husky Club of America Specialty Show in Long Beach (California) in 1964. It was at this same show that his daughter, Dichoda Rurik Tika, was Best of Opposite Sex and his son, Czar Nicholas, was Winners Dog to complete his championship. Judge Lorna Demidoff also awarded him first in the stud dog class when eight of his get appeared in the ring with him.

Ch. Czar Nicholas won Best of Breed at the 1966 Siberian Husky Club of America Specialty in Santa Barbara under judge Alice Seekins and was the first Siberian Husky owner-handled at Dichoda to place in the Working Group.

The greatest achievement of all was attained by the copper-coated, blue-eyed Ch. Dichoda's Yukon Red. Shown to his championship by Frank Brayton, he was turned over to handler Tom Witcher, and after being shown just 14 times he was rated top-winning Siberian Husky in the United States, Phillips System, in 1967. Competition in California is very keen, and this record was a fine achievement.

For the next five years after his 1967 rating, he remained on the list of Top Ten Huskies although never heavily campaigned. Yukon was also the third Dichoda Siberian to win Best of Breed at a parent club Specialty Show. This win was under judge Lorna Demidoff in 1969 at Beverly Hills, where he went on to Group Second under judge Maxwell Riddle.

THE 1950s

The decade of the 1950s saw the beginning of some remarkable kennels that would enhance the breed's reputation for many decades to come.

One of the most prominent was the Alakazan kennel (originally called Kazan) of Paul and Margaret Koehler in Gill, Massachusetts. They were active, since 1954, not only in the breed but in the establishment of the Siberian Husky Club of America.

Paul served for three years as club president and Peggy was on the board of directors starting in 1967. They published the club's newsletter for several years, and Peggy was editor from 1968 to 1971. She has also written the breed columns for the *AKC Gazette* and *Popular Dogs* magazine.

Legacy of the Midnight Sun, bred by Janis Church of Nathrop, CO. Sire was Knega's Heritage ex Chamisha of the Midnight Sun.

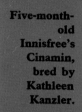
Five-month-old Innisfree's Cinamin, bred by Kathleen Kanzler.

They were active in both showing and racing, and won National Specialties, as well as many other honors with their dogs, through the 1970s.

The Koehlers finished ten champions themselves, and several others finished with other owners. Their Ch. Monadnock's Konyak of Kazan was the sire of ten champions plus a Best in Show winner in Finland.

Their foundation bitch, Kameo of Kazan is dam of five champions including Ch. Dudley's Tavar of Innisfree, the Best in Show winner in 1972. Their Ch. Monadnocks Serge, Ch. Kronprinz of Kazan, Ch. Monadnock's Konyak of Kazan, and Ch. Kandia of Kazan comprised their top racing team, which won the parent club Racing Trophy in 1964.

1954 also was the year for Charlotte and Earl Reynolds, Arctic Kennels, in Dryden, Michigan. They had Huskies in all colors and were active in showing and racing, but they specialized in the silver dogs. Their best known dog was AmCan Ch. Arctic's Storm Frost.

Runaway Farm

Runaway Farm Kennels is owned by Dr. and Mrs. Daniel Rice III in Shrewsbury, Massachusetts. The Rices bought their first Husky, Mulpus Brooks The Reno, in 1955, and started breeding nine years later with their original bitch, Monadnock's Czarya.

Active in racing, all the Rice team dogs are descendants of this bitch, Czarya, and all are bred for sled use and pleasure racing teams. Mrs. Rice believes she is the only competitor who breeds, raises, trains, and races her own dogs. All the dogs are matched, black and white, and wear bright red padding and pompons on their harness.

Her lead dogs have been Czarya's Kier, Czarya's Valeska, and Gilena's Lara, leading with her son Lara's Vodka.

Along with New England Sled Dog class trophies, her team has won the following special trophies: 1970, Siberian Husky Club of America Racing Trophy; 1971 and 1972, Monadnock Racing Trophy; 1972, Gaines Racing Trophy; and 1971, the Douglas Fairbanks Racing Trophy.

Sno-Dak

Lillian Peitzman of Mapleton, North Dakota, boasts that her first Siberian Husky was a great one! It was all white and brown-eyed and because AmCan Ch. Little Sepp's Story of Sno-Dak, CDX. Whelped in September, 1955, this beautiful bitch was one of the few Huskies to attain a CDX title; she died August 1968.

SnoMound

J. Jack Bean, owner of the SnoMound Kennels in Minnetonka, Minnesota, began in 1958 with a brood bitch named Marina of Mulpus Brook Farms and a stud dog, Ch. Inuk. Over the years he has sold puppies to most of the states in the USA and to Canada.

Ch. Frosty Aire's Inuk of

Kryska's Khokolate Khipokate, owned by the Kents.

SnoMound was the second highest-winning Husky in 1963, Phillips System, and many of his offspring are Group and Group Placement winners. Many are also lead and team dogs in the Colorado, Oregon, and Illinois areas, and he is the sire of American and Canadian champions.

One of the SnoMound dogs became the mascot for Northern Illinois University.

Marlytuk

The Marlytuk Kennels of Mr. and Mrs. Lyle Grant go back to 1958. The original Marlytuk stock came from the Cold River Kennel, whose dogs had been purchased from Harry Wheeler in Sainte Jovite, Quebec, who had purchased his dogs from Leonhard Seppala when Seppala came east in the 1920s.

Peggy Grant has always felt it important to have a sled team, and the Grants have raced with the New England Sled Dog Club and have done well. Their Ch. Loonah's Red Kiska became a champion at just nine months of age and is the dam of Ch. Marlytuk's Red Sun of Kiska, who has over 60 Best of Breed awards and several Group Placings to his credit. She is part of a brace with her son, and they have won five Best Brace in Show awards.

Red Sun for two years was the No. Two Siberian Husky, and he is winner of two Specialty Shows at the Philadelphia event in 1970 and in 1971, when the show was held in Cleveland. The Grants have finished ten champions since 1956.

The name Marlytuk can be found on many of the important pedigrees in the breed today as both show winners and foundation stock. A testimonial dinner was given for Peggy Grant, lauding her as one of the most important people in the breed.

Fra-Mar

One of the oldest and most famous kennels in the breed is Marie Wamser's Fra-Mar Kennels in Valley City, Ohio, begun in 1954. Marie has produced a long line of top show and racing dogs over the years.

The name Fra-Mar is a combination of husband Frank and Marie's names and it was actually a Pug with which they started. In March 1959, the Chicago show, Marie saw Ch. Monadnock's Pando, owned by Lorna Demidoff, and was determined to have a Siberian. Lorna had no puppies at the time, and Marie was referred to the Frosty Aires Kennels, owned by Jack and Donna Foster. There she purchased an eight-week-old, the future Ch. Frosty Aires Alcan King. Her next show quality Siberian was Ch. Fra-Mar's Miserah, also purchased at eight weeks of age.

Miserah was purchased with the promise to breed back to her father, Ch. Frosty Aire's Beau Tuk. This gave Marie three lines to work with, which

"The name Marlytuk can be found on many of the important pedigrees in the breed today as both show winners and foundation stock."

"Ritter"

LOUISVILLE K.C.
WORKING

Top: AmCanBda Ch. Fra-Mar's Soan Diavol, Top Siberian in the USA for 1966, 1968 and 1969. Top Siberian in Canada for 1970; finished his Bermudian championship in 1968. Soan was a Best in Show winner in 1969 and is the sire of 13 champions. Owner-bred by Marie Wamser, Valley City, OH.
Bottom: Ch. Marlytuk's Red Sun of Kiska and 2 of his "winningest" offspring take the Stud Dog Class at the 1978 Rocky Mountain SHC Specialty Show. Ch. Marlytuk's Red Noho with owner Linda Livingston and Ch. Toko's Twenty Four Karat Gold, CD, handler-bred by Jean Fournier. Judge was Virginia Hampton.

she still holds dear today.

Alcan Kin was the Fourth Best in Show winner in the breed; this was the second Best in Show for the Fra-Mar Kennels (Soan also won a BIS).

Top: Ch. Karnovanda's Aurora Felena, future Specialty winner, pictured here winning at a 1985 show with owner-breeder-handler, Judith Russell. *Bottom:* Ch. Karnovanda's Zarya, whose sire was Brz Ch. Karnovanda's Boris Groznyi ex Ch. Innisfree's Morning Mist. Pictured winning at a 1985 show with Russell handling.

Marie feels that with her relatively small kennel, she has proven herself with her winnings, and she also counts among her most important dogs: Best in Show Ch. Lo-Bo

Rey Rayle Diavol and Moon Glow, Tadzhik Tango Zhuliak of Siber, and Nikolai Diavol.

Marie is a charter member of the Greater Cleveland club and is active in all phases of the breed.

Karnovanda

Judith M. Russell has maintained her Karnovanda Kennels since 1959, and during that time has finished over 100 champions and several UD dogs. Dogs bearing her kennel name have also won many ISDRA racing awards and the Siberian Husky Club of America Race Show Award five times.

Judith has always loved animals, especially horses and dogs, and has won numerous championships and world championships with her American Saddlebreds from 1949 through 1960. As a graduate student at the University of California, she began training and showing dogs. Today, she teaches high school math and computer science.

Judith's children have always been interested and active in the dog fancy and continue to

Ch. Gre To-Da's Gesha Moon Glow, whelped in 1970, and pictured here winning the Working Group under judge Henry Stoecker in the 1970s. The sire was Ch. Fra-Mar's Rising Sun Dancer ex Fra-Mar's Mide Noel. Bred and owned by Marie Wamser of Valley City, OH.

Top: Ch. Karnovanda's Care Bear at 11 months winning his first Best of Breed. Handled by Brian Still for owner-breeder Judith Russell. The sire was Ch. Karnovanda's Some Kind of Hew ex Ch. Innisfree's Morning Mist.

Middle: Best Puppy in Group at the 1983 Bermuda KC Show was Phyllis Castelton's White Fox's Sik-Sik. This was a championship win for Sik-Sik.

Bottom: Ch. Bunda's Boston Moon Shadow, owned by Dr. Gabriel Mayer and Carol Mayer, and handled for them by Paul Willhauck to this 1981 win under judge Braithwaith.

Top: A 1984 Group win for Totempole's Shaun at the Wampanoag KC Show. As always, Shaun is handled by Tracy Brosque, Totempole Kennels, New Ipswich, NH. *Bottom:* Ch. Yeti's Copper Curry, sire of 3 champions, is from an all-champion bloodline, and is owned by Robert and Joy Messinger, Yeti Kennels, Verona, NJ.

show, breed, and race the Siberians. They have actively participated in sled dog races since 1974.

Karnovanda is located on thirty acres in Davisburg, Michigan, and there are many other animals that are involved in 4-H projects, along with the continuation of 14 generations of Karnovanda dogs. Twenty to 30 dogs are kept at any given time, with which they pursue the goal of breeding Siberian Huskies that are both sound in mind and body, and conform to the breed standard as closely as possible.

Judith claims it is impossible to list all of the dogs that she considers outstanding, but two of the latest are her Ch. Karnovanda's Twilight Time, and Ch. Karnovanda's Care Bear. Among the racing and obedience dogs are The

Replica, Wolfgang, Ivan Groznyi, and Sasha Groznyi.

Wolfden

The late 1950s saw the establishment of Beryl Allen's Wolfden Kennels in Jaffrey, New Hampshire. Ch. Tosca of Monadnock and Ch. Wolfden's Copper Bullet are two of the outstanding show dogs which have brought fame to Wolfden. While they have been breeding and showing only since the late 1960s, their success has been great, with Ch. Wolfden's Copper Bullet winning the 1972 Siberian Husky Club of America Specialty Show over 42 Specials and an entry of 240—the largest to date at that time. He was No. Five Siberian Husky, *Kennel Review* System, and has several Group Placings to his credit, after finishing for his championship at 18 months of age.

AmCan Ch. Karnovanda's Bartholomew, pictured at 9 years of age and finishing for Canadian championship in September 1982. Bred, owned and handled by Judith Russell.

THE 1960s

By the time the 1960s came along the breed was literally and figuratively "booming," if you can say that about dogs. And it couldn't have gotten off to a better start than it did with the 1960 establishment of Kathleen Kanzler's Innisfree Kennels. Little did anyone know at that time that Mrs. Kanzler would, just a quarter of a century later, make breed history when one of her dogs won the prestigious Westminster Kennel Club Best in Show award!

Innisfree

While Kathleen Kanzler has had a kennel since 1947, she first got into Siberians in 1960. While in Alaska she started Innisfree Kennels with two brood bitches from racing stock there. Since then her main objective has been to breed Huskies with the workability of the breed in mind, and with sound, correct type. Therefore, she is interested in show, obedience, racing, sledding, and packing.

After many years of breeding and raising the dogs and

Ch. Innisfree's Marakesh, a very important bitch at Kathleen Kanzler's Innisfree Kennels. Her sire was Ch. Innisfree's Pegasus ex Ch. Innisfree's Goldilocks. She is pictured here winning Best of Breed at a 1981 show with Trish Kanzler handling.

Top: Camelot's Lil Red Corvette pictured winning Reserve at her first show, at 6 months of age, under judge Frank Burch. Owner-handled and bred by Dr. William Miranda, Camelot Siberians, El Paso, TX. *Bottom:* Ch. Talocon's Nova's Calypso, going Best of Winners at a 1979 show for owners Gail and John O'Connell. Gail handled to this win at the Greater Philadelphia Dog Fanciers' Show.

Top: Ch. Snokomo's Commander in Chief winning 5-point major on the Florida circuit. Judge, M.Sgt. H.B. Cox. "The Kool-Aid Dog" is by Setting Sun's Ring Commander ex Snokom's Black Sabbath. *Bottom:* Yeso Pac's Charlie's Angels, multiple winner of the Sled Dog Class and retired co-lead dog, owned by Leonard Bain and A.D. Reynolds. Handled by Carolyn Kaiser.

finishing many champions, Kathleen finally achieved the ultimate dream of winning Best in Show at Westminster in 1980 with her Ch. Innisfree's Sierra Cinnar (with daughter Trish handling). Cinnar is not only the sire of 114 champions, for which he received the AKC Certificate of Distinction award, but got the Century Club award as well. He is the top-winning Siberian of all time, with 30 Bests in Show and 15 Bests in Specialties.

This win is a magnificent accomplishment for Kathleen, as well as for her daughter Trish, her husband Norbert, and their daughter Sheila. Innisfree has reached the pinnacle of success.

Kathleen must be complimented on her unusual "work learning" program. She takes in, with free room and board, two youngsters dedicated to the breed who learn care, grooming, showing, racing, etc, with hands-on experience.

Innisfree maintains about fifty dogs at the present time; their list of wins and awards is remarkable. They are located in Chateaugay, New York.

Ch. Innisfree's Number One Spy, bred and owned by Sheila Kanzler and handled by sister Trish Kanzler.

Top: Ch. Innisfree's Miska, bred and owned by Kathleen Kanzler. Sire was Ch. Innisfree's Strongbow ex AmCan Ch. Innisfree's Sierra Shawnna. Bergman photo.
Bottom: Like father like son: Ch. Innisfree's Sierra Cinnar, Best of Breed winner (and on to Best in Show!) at the 1980 Westminster KC, and his look-alike son, Ch. Jonathie Cinnar Citka V Sno-Fame, Winners Dog.

Domeyko

The Domeyko Kennels are owned by Peggy and Ed Samerson of Woodland Park, Colorado. Since their beginning in the early 1960s, the Samersons finished numerous champions. They also work their dogs in harness; while they like to think of their dogs as pets first, they are also show and sled dogs as well.

One of their outstanding show and stud dogs is Ch. Darbo Domeyko of Long's Peak. Darbo has taken a Best in Show and picked up ten Group Placings during his ring career. In 1967, 1968, and 1969 he ranked in the top ten list of Siberian Huskies, Phillips System. Darbo's son, Ch. Domeyko's Zadar, has had three Group Placings and also ranked in the Top Ten Siberian Huskies in 1971, Phillips System.

Ed Samerson is a licensed handler for several of the working breeds, but he takes a special joy in showing his own dogs in the show ring.

Almaring

As with so many others, Ingrid Brucato's kennel started with a "pet" Siberian Husky named Marvel. He finished in 1965 however, and his name was Ch. Marvel Black Mask. At this time a bitch from Monadnock was added. Her name was Monadnock's Marina. When bred, she produced two very special puppies named Ch. Almaring's Alai, who was in the Top Ten for 1975 and 1976, and Tatiana, who produced six champions.

When the Almaring Kennels were moved from the East to the West coast in the early 1970s, they added their stud dog, Frosty Aire's Blue Knight.

During the years, Almaring has produced 22 champions. Alai was No. Five Siberian in 1975 and No. Ten in 1976. Their Almaring Elfin was sent to Brazil and is the first Siberian bitch to win the Working Group in that country. They also exported Almaring's Erl King, and he is Brazilian and International champion there. Both are

Sheila Kanzler handled Ch. Innisfree's Silver Harvest to this 1984 Berks County Show win under judge Henry Stoecker.

Top: Ch. Sunset Hill's Blue Arctic Ice winning at the 1977 National Specialty Show. Bred by Anne Brude, Arctic Ice is owned by Nila A. Kelly of Anaheim, CA. The sire was Ch. Weldon's Beau-Tukker ex AmCan Ch. Innisfree's Import, Top Producer in 1978 and one of the Top Producers of all time. *Bottom:* Head study of Ch. Aazar's Tiki taken in December 1983. Owned by Diane Garcia, Tokosh Kennels, Canton, OH.

Ch. Innisfree's Peppermint, owned by Kathleen Kanzler and handled by daughter Sheila Kanzler. The sire was Ch. Innisfree's Red Roadster, CD, ex Ch. Innisfree's Marakesh, a Top-Producing bitch.

Ch. Soka of the Midnight Sun, bred and owned by Janis Church, Of The Midnight Sun Kennels in Nathrop, CO. The sire was Ch. Akkani of the Midnight Sun ex Zela of the Midnight Sun.

owned by Dr. Humberto Rocha.

In 1980, the Brucato s moved to Seattle, Washington, where they live with two of their retired dogs and maintain their interest in the breed.

Of The Midnight Sun

Janis R. Church, owner of the Of The Midnight Sun Kennels in Nathrop, Colorado, began her operation in 1960. She has been active in both showing and obedience, and has also bred some racing Siberians over the years.

Some of her outstanding dogs were Ch. Tonkova of the Midnight Sun, CD, a Group and Specialty winner in the late 1960s and early 1970s. Tonkova was also a racing leader for several years on one of Colorado's top teams. Ch. Kroshka of the Midnight Sun is another Group placer and

Specialty winner. She is also the dam of three champions from her first and only litter, and was a racing leader.

Janis acquired her first Siberian after showing Cocker Spaniels for several years. Until 1980 she seldom bred more than two litters a year and at times, "no litters a year," as Janis puts it. But her record still boasts of approximately fifty title holders to date. Her kennel name was taken from the song "North to Alaska."

Some of her other greats were Ch. Koritza of Kettle Moraine, dam of eight champions; Ch. Kognac of the Midnight Sun, sire of eight champions; Muhfhi of the Midnight Sun, dam of four champions in an only litter; Ch. Akkani of the Midnight Sun, sire of champions; Ch. Zaimar's Scarlet Ribbons, a group and Specialty winner; and Zela of the Midnight Sun, dam of five champions with several others pointed.

There are usually about twenty Siberians at the kennel.

Snoana

Arthur and Mary Ann Piunti of Hobart, Indiana, started their kennel in 1960. Ch. Frosty Aire's Banner Boy, CD, brought fame to their kennel and has sired 29 champions. Banner Boy finished his championship at age ten months; and while he never won higher than Group Second, he placed in the Working Group 18 times, always handled by his owners. His daughter, Ch. Sno-Ana's Kenai Suzee, was Best of Winners at the 1965 Specialty Show.

The Piuntis' Frosty Aire's Norvik is a CDX dog and races, as does Banner Boy. The Piuntis have finished more than half a dozen champions and are more than proud of Banner Boy's record which is as follows: Top Producer for three consecutive years, 1970 through 1972; one of the Top Ten Siberian Huskies, Phillips

The Group- and Specialty-winning Ch. Zaimar's Scarlet Ribbons, owned by Janis Church.

SOUTHERN COLORADO

WORKING

Top: Handled by owner and breeder Gwynn Quirin, AmCan Ch. Scoqui's Amber winning the Brood Bitch Class at a 1983 Specialty Show, with her daughters Scoqui's Firefox of Anjeli, handled by owner Liana Anclam; and Scoqui's Ambrosia, handled by breeder-owner Scott Quirin.

Bottom: Ch. Snocrop's Caribu Lu O'Troika, Best Puppy at the SHC of Greater Kansas City in 1983. Handled by breeder Vearl Jones, Bonner Springs, KS. Sire was Ch. K.C. Jones of Troika; dam, Ch. Ali-Son's Royal Satin O'Troika.

Top: Rosemary Fischer is overcome by the affection of two of her Arahaz puppies. *Bottom:* Phyllis Castelton's CanBda Ch. White Fox's Tatiana Kazankina finishing her championship at this Bermuda KC Show in February 1979.

System, several times; Best of Breed winner at the International Kennel Club show in 1964 and 1968.

Arthur Piunti is an obedience judge and is approved to judge both Siberian Huskies and Alaskan Malamutes in the conformation classes.

Tovarin

Betsy Korbonski of Pacific Palisades, California, chose Tovarin as her kennel prefix in 1960. Out to secure a breed with a sound natural demeanor that would still be able to perform the chores it was created for, Betsy was drawn to the Siberian Husky.

She considers her kennel a small hobby kennel but has done quite well, winning both the 1962 and the 1974 National Specialty shows. Some of her outstanding dogs were Ch. Foxhaunt's Tovarisch, CDX, Ch. Tovarin's Merry Anarchist, and Ch. Tovarin's Feral Faery.

Kaspar

Lula Brattis of Casper, Wyoming, started her Kaspar Kennels in 1961. Lula has been active in the show and obedience rings over the years and some of her winning dogs were Kheta of Caspar; Keno of Kaspar; Kaspar Kheta; Kaspar Keto; and Kaspar Leko. Kheta the Second finished CD for her in just three shows.

The original Kheta of Caspar was the only dog she ever bought; the rest were bred by her and shown for her by Marvin Ross.

"Koona de Beauchien was Ann Sullivan's foundation bitch, and over the years she has bred several champions bearing her Sno-Fame Kennel prefix."

Sno-Fame

In 1962 Ann M. Sullivan of Ewing Township, New Jersey, went out looking for a German Shepherd puppy, but an ad in a local paper brought her to see a litter of Huskies and she was "hooked." All she knew about the breed was what she had observed in the movie, *Call of the Wild*. It was love at first sight, and the breeder let her choose. She took a silver and white male that she started out in obedience, and when everyone told her how beautiful the dog was, she took him to a match show and went Group Second. Her first Specialty was also in 1962 and she came away with a Reserve Dog win from the puppy class.

The next year she joined the parent club and has been interested and active in the breed ever since.

Koona de Beauchien was her foundation bitch, and over the years she has bred several champions bearing her Sno-Fame Kennel prefix.

Whispering Oaks

Susan A. Vosnos of Barrington, Illinois, got her first puppy in 1962 as a birthday present. She had seen her first Siberian Husky in Canada and had been pestering her parents until her birthday gift arrived.

She is working on her first obedience dog, and declares that her sled dogs are for pleasure sledding, not racing.

Her top dogs are Ch. Norstarr's Tara, who has won a

Top: Ch. Sno-Fame Chuka's Solo Odinok, winner of the 1979 SHC of Delaware Valley Specialty Best in Show. Bred and owned by Ann M. Sullivan, Sno-Fame Kennels, Ewing Township, NJ. *Bottom:* Ch. Jonathie's Sequoia of Sno-Fame pictured winning Best of Breed at a 1978 show. Owned and handled by Ann M. Sullivan.

Group Second, 19 Best of Breeds, and 25 Bests of Opposite Sex. Ch. Whispering Oaks Dushinka has eight Bests of Breed and 13 Bests of Opposite during limited showing.

The Whispering Oaks Kennels were "officially" named in 1969 and they maintain five dogs at the present time.

Fortsalong

1963 saw the beginning of Vincent and Phyllis Buoniello's Fortsalong Kennels in Northport, New York. They bought their first Husky from the Baltic Kennels of Mr. and Mrs. John Cline in Commerce City, Colorado. Since that time, they have seen six Huskies of their own breeding finish for their championships, with several more pointed and well on the way. Vincent Buoniello became an AKC judge for Siberians in 1971 and has been very active in the show racing circles.

The Buoniellos point with pride to Ch. Chateauguay's Charlie and the great human interest story behind him. Charlie was given to the Buoniellos when he was seven years old. They felt the dog had something to offer the breed and began showing him. In less than one year, Charlie had become champion and had sired his first litter! Before joining the Buoniellos the dog

Stunning portrait of Whispering Oak's Fred E. Bear and Whispering Oak's Katrina. Bred and owned by Susan Vosnos, Barrington, IL.

had done nothing but work. He raced on some of the better racing teams in New England; he is still enjoying the racing scene, running wheel position on a five-dog team in the New England races for the Buoniellos, and is sharing a family life as well!

The Buoniellos are active in the Mid-Atlantic Sled Dog Club races in New York, New Jersey, Pennsylvania, and Virginia. Charlie's zest for running still continues to delight them, as does his devotion to his family. They are also particularly pleased that Charlie's get are working toward their show ring championships!

Arahaz

Rosemary Fischer, Beaver, Pennsylvania, has always loved dogs and as early as 1956 she had Basenjis. In 1963 she acquired Siberians and, through friends with show dogs, got hooked on showing them.

Rosemary is also a judge of 14 breeds to date. She currently has a champion Basenji at Arahaz and a kennel of about twenty Siberians. Over the years she has finished 28 champions, and there are approximately 31 other Arahaz dogs with points toward their championships. Six others have obedience CD titles, and her Toki and Okalina have been among the top producing Siberians in the breed. There are also Arahaz dogs competing on racing teams.

Rosemary based her foundation line on dogs from Monadnock, Frosty Aire, and Chinook bloodlines. She is a member of the Parent Club; Columbiana County Kennel Club, where she has been an officer for years; the Beaver County Kennel Club; is a past

member of the Husky Club of Greater Pittsburgh, and was a director of the International Siberian Husky Club for two years. She is also a charter member of the South Hills Kennel Club, and has been a member of the Western Pennsylvania Club for nearly 30 years.

Ch. Arahaz Ariane, bred and owned by Rosemary Fischer and co-owned by Dianne Klym. The sire was Ch. Dudley's Varska ex Arahaz Rumyana, CD.

Top: Winner of the Stud Dog Class at the 1978 SHC of Greater Chicago is Clarence Dudley's Ch. Dudley's Varska. Also pictured are his daughter Ch. Arahaz Elizaveta, owned and bred by Rosemary Fischer; and his son Ch. Fireside's Hellbuster, owned by the Rosettas. *Bottom:* Ch. Arahaz Dyengi, handled by Sam Lippincott to this win under judge Phelps at a 1974 dog show. Bred and owned by R. Fischer.

Top: Varskita's Mr. Majik O'Denali, bred and owned by Judi Anderson of Laconia, NH. Co-owner-handled by Sandy Jessop. *Bottom:* Family portrait at Panuck-Denali Kennels, Laconia, NH. Judi Anderson's Shoshanna, Shalom and Andree Bolkonski.

Panuck-Denali

The Panuck-Denali Kennel began in Springfield, Massachusetts, in 1963 with the purchase of a male from Savdajaure Kennels. He was followed by a bitch from the Doonauk Kennels. These two dogs were Panuck and Gidget. The kennel began as a family enterprise, involving Charlotte Anderson, her husband, and her daughter Judi. As their success in the ring continued, the number of dogs they showed also increased, and Panuck-Denali was well established.

When Mr. Anderson retired, the family moved to Laconia, New Hampshire, where the kennel is now, and Judi took up racing the dogs on the NESDC circuit. It turned out that Mr. Anderson was in charge of the kennel and the training, Charlotte went to the dog shows, and Judi went to the races.

Being so close to the border, they began showing the dogs in Canada, and have sold dogs to many countries.

Some of their outstanding dogs have been Ch. Savdajaure's Panuck; Ch. Doonauk's Gidget; Ch. Simba Lion of Denali; Can Ch. Marlytuk Shoshanna of Denali; Can Ch. Shoshanna's Shiren of Kortar; Misty's Andrei Bolkonski; Allerellie's Pappilon; Alakon's Snowbear of Denali; Can Ch. Cheechako's Varskita of Denali; Varskita's Mr. Majik O'Denali; and Varskita's Ms. Sheena Denali.

Mr. and Mrs. Anderson both died in 1983, but Judi carries on with the kennel, giving full credit to her parents' love, support, and family "teamwork" for the 22 years of success at their Panuck-Denali Kennels.

Fireside

Since 1963, there have been

Best in Show Ch. Kirkacha's Suzi Skyhope pictured winning her first points at 6 months of age in 1983, under judge Elsa Marchesan.

AmCan Ch. Fireside's Hellbuster winning the Group at a May 1982 show. There were 800 Working Group dogs competing. Owner, Betty Rosetto of Fireside Kennels, Milford, MI.

many winning champions at Dick and Betty Rosetto's Fireside Kennels in Milford, Michigan. Among their top dogs were American and Canadian Ch. Fireside's Hellbuster and Leading Lady, as well as Ch. Hotshot, Patent Pending, Ladies Man, Cherry Kijafa, and Friendly Fella.

Tops in the obedience department was their Ch. Fireside's Takgamy of Omuyok, UD and OTCH. While they did not always train the dogs themselves, there are many with CD and CDX titles. Gamy is owned, shown, and

was trained by Ginette Scullion of Quebec.

Mr. Rosetto built the kennel himself. The awards they have won over the years attest to the love and care they have for their dogs. They keep approximately seven dogs at any given time.

Lamark

Elsa and Alfred Marchesano of Levittown, New York, are the owners of the Lamark Kennels. The kennel was established in 1963, and by 1970 their Ch. Savdajaure's Eska Lamarchese, CD, was

Top: Sharlene Lawson and her Aurora's Sable Furie; co-owner, Stacey Lance; handler, Mrs. Lawson. *Bottom:* BB Snoopy, 7 years of age at last AKC show. Owner-handled by Vearl Jones.

Top: Ch. Kam-E-Lot's Masterpiece winning Winners Bitch and Best Opposite at the 1980 Livingston KC Show with Beth McClure handling. Co-owner, Richard McClure. *Bottom:* U-CD Cheyenne of the Stalking Moon, AmCan CD titlist shown taking First in the Veterans Obedience Class at the SHC of Greater Detroit Specialty Show in 1984 when he was 9½ years of age. Bred by V. DePriest; owned by R. and B. McClure.

High Country's Movin Molly, winning on the way to her championship at a 1981 show. Owned by Wendy G. Willhauck, Itaska Kennels, Mansfield, MA.

Winners Bitch and Best of Opposite Sex at Westminster. In Eska's first litter of four, three went on to finish for their championship within one year.

The Marchesanos are active in the breed, with Mrs. Marchesano serving as president of the Siberian Husky Club of Greater New York in 1973, and are active in showing, breeding, racing, and more recently, judging.

Itaska

Itaska Kennels was founded in 1964, when Paul Willhauck purchased Doonauks Kiak from Ray and Viola Akers of Doonauk Kennels. Paul quickly caught the dog show bug and soon showed Kiak to his championship. Paul finished his own dog and concentrated on showing other people's dogs as well. In fact, he has finished many Siberians over the years and has put points on hundreds of others. For the last 22 years he has concentrated on Siberians.

Several years ago, Paul married Wendy Wisefield of the Frostfield Alaskan Malamute kennels. They pooled their dogs and their knowledge, and the Itaska

Kennels came into being, concentrating on the Northern breeds and running a breeding and showing kennel.

Valeskamo

Eleanor Grahn, owner of the Valeskamo Kennels in Florissant, Missouri, is now enjoying her "old timers." Having limited space, she is still very interested in the breed and keeps up with the show world while maintaining the old guard, keeping her breeding and showing plans on hold.

Two of her early bitches, which were important to her breeding program, were Annuschka and Marlytuk's Kelly Red. Kelly is the dam and granddam of Canadian, American, and Mexican champions presently being shown and bred. Kelly is still doing very well with her devoted owner.

One of Eleanor's "greats" was Ch. Alakazan's Valeska, CD, and her homebred Valeskamo's Palo holds the spotlight as a Best of Breed winner and proven sire. His sire was Ch. Kotya of the Midnight Sun ex Marlytuk's Kelly Red.

Ch. Alakazan's Valeska, CD, owned by Eleanor Grahm, Valeskamo Siberians, Florissant, MO.

Top: Karnovanda's Troika Kavik winning Best of Winners. Kavik was a racing dog and an obedience dog, but hated the show ring; unfortunately, he died before completing his title.
Bottom: Can Ch. Teeco S Tonee End going Best of Breed from Open Dog Class for a 4-point major under Phyllis Marcmann. Handled by Janet Roberts for owner Margaret Cook. The sire was Ch. Bundas Boston Moonshadow ex Marmik's Toekee of Elektra.

Top: Ch. Fra-Mar's Aja-Tu Diavol, beautiful prize-winning bitch winning points towards her championship. *Bottom:* Ch. Fireside's Leading Lady pictured at a 1979 show. Sire was Ch. Dudley's Vorska. Owned by A. Rosetto.

Tawny Hills

It was love at first sight when Adele M. Gray of Prospect, Connecticut, saw her first blue-eyed Siberian Husky. This was in 1964, when she started her Tawny Hills Kennel. Blue eyes are no longer the *most* important thing for her—a sound working dog is—but there is no denying it was those limpid blue eyes that first attracted her to this breed.

Adele runs dogs for pleasure only, not competition, and concentrates solely on the show ring. Some of her outstanding show dogs are Ch. Tawny Hills Gaibryel, Gamyn Rashima

Taro, and Justin Thyme, all bearing the Tawny Hills prefix and holders of championship titles.

Adele keeps approximately 35 to 40 dogs in her kennel and believes she is trying to raise dogs that follow the standard as closely as possible.

Aurora

Sharlene Lawson and the Siberians at her Aurora Kennels in Phoenix, Arizona, started in 1964 and has concentrated primarily on racing. While Sharlene and her team are very active in racing, she considers her kennel as a

Tawny Hill's Sage N' Thyme winning on the way to the title. Sire was Ch. Tawny Hill's Justin' Thyme ex Ch. Tawny Hill's Gamyn. Bred and owned by Adele M. Gray, Prospect, CT.

hobby; she trains and teaches obedience with a large club in Phoenix. She has finished four CDs and has trained many others as well. Sharlene is a charter member of the Siberian Husky Club of Greater Phoenix and has been treasurer. She is also a member of the parent club, and is a member of and teacher for the Phoenix Field and Obedience Club.

White Fox

Phyllis Castleton's White Fox Kennels are located in Anchorage, Alaska; they started in 1965. Phyllis travels to both Canada and the United States to put championships on her dogs, and she vacations with dog show wins in beautiful Bermuda. Many of her dogs are champions in one or more countries.

One of her top dogs is Canadian obedience dog, Ch. White Fox's Kayakin of Anadyr, CD, and in racing her top dog is AmCanBda Ch. White Fox's Blitzen. When asked for her opinion on whether or not the Siberian is a dog for children, her reply was that she had raised and trained her youngest son with her first Siberian Husky. What could be better proof than that?

Three magnificent silver puppies bred by Aurora Kennels, Phoenix, AZ.

Top: Ch. Bunda's Pisces winning the Breed at the 1983 Progressive Dog Club Show under William Fetner. Bred by Dr. Gabriel Mayer and Susan Wright. Owner-handled by Dick McClure.

Middle: AmCan Ch. Innisfree's Sierra Cinnar as a young dog on the way to his first of 30 Bests in Show. Lorna Demidoff is the judge. Trish Kanzler, handling.

Bottom: AmCan Ch. Innisfree's Return Engagement, one of the top stud dogs of the 1980s at Innisfree. This Best of Breed win was at the Garden State Siberian Specialty Show in 1982.

Top: **Ch. Innisfree's Solid Gold, bred and owned by Kathleen Kanzler; handled by Trish Kanzler. Sire was AmCan Ch. Innisfree's Sierra Cinnar ex Innisfree's Conneameara.** *Bottom:* **AmCanMex Ch. Sekene's Nelmarin Trilogy, owned by the Kanzlers. Jean Edwards photo.**

Tandara

Tandara Kennels in Gio Harbor, Washington, is a mother-daughter team devoted to the breed in the show ring, on the racing track, and in the obedience ring. Starting in 1965, they have truly utilized their dogs in all fields of endeavor open to this breed, along with their quest to breed the perfect Siberian.

Some of their outstanding dogs are Ch. Juneau of Tandara; Ch. Kayak of Martha Lake, CD; AmCan Ch. Tandara's The Kodiak, CD; AmCan Ch. The Bastion's Palacheveyo; and Tandara's Verushka O'Bastion. Obedience winners include Tandara's Zarevna Tatiana, CDX, and Tandara's Black Babushka, CD.

While they agree the Siberian is not the breed for everyone, they do believe that one of the most charming aspects of it is that they do not all look alike. They also love the great versatility of the breed—show, obedience, sledding, racing, pulling, and the ideal pet—few will argue with them on this point.

They were delighted when three of their puppies were featured on the cover of the Christmas issue of *Alaska* magazine. It represented their fourth generation of breeding, namely AmCan Ch. The Bastion's Palacheveyo; his son, AmCan Ch. Tandara's Che Kodiak, CD; followed by his daughter Ch. Tandara's Polynya; and the puppies themselves, her sons Yahoo, Gizmo, and Wahoo.

AmCan Ch. Takkalik's Captain Hook, co-owned by Phyllis Castelton and Jan and Ken Weagle, all of Anchorage, AK. Captain takes Working Group Third for a 5-point major at a Bermuda KC show.

Swany

Swany is not a kennel name; it is the name of Philip Swany of Fremont, California, who since 1965 has amassed a list of awards on his Siberians that few will ever equal or surpass.

Heading the list is Kimsha's Tosca of Kamiakin, CDX, TD, Shutzhund AD, Mexican PCE, PR, Canadian CD, and TD. This must truly be the most titled dog in the breed! Tosca has received two *Dog World* Awards of Canine Distinction; ten ISHC Obedience Awards (an ISHC record); High in Trial, SHCA Specialty Show 1980; high in Trial, Yankee SHC Special Show 1981; All-Breed High in Trial, Northern Interior Kennel Club in Canada (at 11 years of age); SHCA Obedience Award Open 1980; Kodiak's Blitzen Memorial Medal; and is the only Siberian Husky ever to earn Tracking titles in the USA, Mexico, and Canada—all on the first try—and is possibly the only dog of any breed to earn all three on the first try.

Philip Swany's Beriks Shagilluk, CDX, won the ISHC Obedience Award in 1975, and his Tajos Yakima of Iliamna, CD, won it in 1973. His Cinna Moon was ranked No. One Siberian in Novice for 1985 by the *Siberian Quarterly*.

Subahka

The Subahka Kennels (subahka is the Siberian word for dog) are owned by Roger and June Reitano of Tok, Alaska, and were established in 1966. In the subsequent years, nine dogs were finished from their kennel. Not only were the Subahka dogs Bench Show champs, but all were raced in competition in Alaska and elsewhere in the US.

The Reitanos have won many races and broken many records in Alaska. Roger is also a licensed handler for more than 15 breeds, and he judges match shows and teaches obedience. Over the years, many top dogs have been at Subahka, but top

Kimsha's Tosca of Kamiakin, CDX, TD, SchH, AD, Mex PCE, PR, Can CD, TD; owned and trained by Phillip Swany of Fremont, CA. The list of Tosca's awards is astounding — he is among the most titled obedience dogs in the breed.

Yet another of Phillip Swany's winners: son Kyle Swany, photographed with Tosca and Chinna Moon in their Fremont, CA, home.

dog was Ch. Tucker of Chilkat, a Best in Show winner, lead dog for many years, CD, Canadian Best in Show winner in 1972, and winner of the Siberian Husky Club racing trophy for two consecutive years. He also won the parent club's Dual Achievement Award and the bronze

the dogs and racing. Roger still says that they don't make dogs like Tucker anymore, and recalls that he bought Tucker as a reject from a California team when he was one year old in 1966.

Roger laments that Huskies do not have the top speed that is necessary in today's sprint

medallion for Outstanding Siberian Husky in 1971.

The Reitanos' Red Cedar was the 1972 winner of the Alaska State Junior Championship one-dog race.

The kennel houses about 65 dogs, and Roger, now retired from being high school principal, devotes all his time to

racing, especially in Alaska. The best ones have to maintain an 18-20 miles per hour average speed for 16-20 miles, which is no easy feat. Little wonder Tucker is sorely missed.

Totempole
Steve and Nancy Brosque of New Ipswich, New Hampshire,

acquired their first Siberian Husky before their daughter, Tracy, was born. This was in 1966, and until 1970 they were not actively breeding or showing (although by this time they had also acquired Alaskan Malamutes).

competitions. This was followed by the conformation ring and continued until the day she had to decide between Junior Showmanship or professional handling. She decided on handling professionally and that is what

Totempole's Shaun with her young handler, Tracy Brosque, winning a Group Second under Herman Fellton at a 1985 Monticello KC show.

However, Tracy was five or six years of age when she began showing a definite interest in the dogs as did two other Brosque children. It became a family sport, and very soon Tracy began showing in Match shows and then the Junior

she is today—a professional handler! Since then she has handled many breeds, and has finished champions and competed many times in the Group rings.

Tracy campaigned Ch. Marlytuk's Shaun of Totempole

Kiok's Kurtain Kall winning on the way to championship. Bred and owned by Joe and Brenda Kolar, Astoria, OR.

Top: Eight-year-old Zela of the Midnight Sun, dam of 5 champions and a foundation bitch of note at Janis Church's Of The Midnight Sun Kennels. *Bottom:* Ch. Canaan's Rollicking Raven, bred, shown, and owned by Carol Nash.

Tracy Brosque and Shaun winning at the 1985 Greater Lowell KC Show under Dr. Richard Greathouse. Shaun is from Totempole Kennels.

to No. Seven in the nation in 1985. She also owns a Shaun grandson, Totempole's Michael, which she will be campaigning and for which has high hopes. So far, her highest achievement has been a Best in Show for a Malamute Brace under judge Mrs. Clarke. Her goal is to be a handler of multiple Best in Show dogs. She does all her own training and grooming, and she jogs with the dogs as well as trains them.

There are 50 dogs in the Totempole Kennels and Tracy oversees them all, with some kennel help, as she has done to a certain degree since she was five. As a matter of fact, Tracy skipped her own graduation in June 1985 to attend—you guessed it—a dog show!

Aslanlar
1966 was the year B. Sue Adams started her kennel in Aptos, California, and called it Aslanlar. In Turkish, Aslanlar means "lions" and she has used this ever since.

Sue's youngest son had brought home a Siberian mix

when they lived in Montana, and they liked the breed so much that they decided to get a purebred bitch in 1966.

Since then some of their important dogs have been AmCan Ch. Tofchuks Raki and Tofchuks Solor, both carrying the Aslanlar suffix; Ch. K.C. Chaamute, Ch. Fazlett Red of Aslanlar, and Ch. Aslanlar's Nefis Eshek.

All of Sue's dogs have Turkish names, and are bred with the purpose of preserving some of the old line qualities within the newer look in the breed.

Cinnaminson

Sy and Ann Goldberg own the Cinnaminson Kennels in Cream Ridge, New Jersey, which they started in 1967. Sy Goldberg states that his is, at present, the only sled team in America running an all-champion dog team. To his knowledge this has been done only twice before—once in Alaska and once in New Hampshire. So enthusiastic is

Aslanlar's Tesekbur Ederin, dam of many champions, owned by B. Sue Adams, Aslanlar Kennels in Aptos, CA.

Three generations of Siberians win the Team Class at a SHCA Specialty Show. Pictured are Snow Hill's Zorba, Alkas'Iber Steely Dan, Konik's Silver Bullet, and Tokomac's Aivilik Pacesetter. Owners are Cook, Cingel and Serafin.

he about the sport of racing that he managed to win the coveted Siberian Husky Club of America's Racing Trophy for 1971, and he was first runner-up for the same trophy in 1970.

The Goldbergs have done very well in the show and obedience ring. Some of their outstanding show dogs are Ch. Tokco of Bolshoi, Ch. Mischa of Chaya, CD; Ch. Tanya of Cinnaminson; Ch. Koryaks Black Charger; Ch. Chachka of Cinnaminson; and Ch. Cinnaminson's Soaya Fournier.

Teeco

Margaret Cook started her Teeco Kennel in 1967 in Easton, Massachusetts. She is active in several phases of the fancy; she shows her dogs in the conformation rings, and races. Some of her outstanding dogs are Ch. High Country's Hyper Holly, Can Ch. Bakam's Teeco's Taree Night, and Can Ch. Temarko Teeco's Teekeemah, 1982 winner of the Canadian National Specialty show from the Open Class.

In racing circles, her Teeco's

Tweet Rockin Robyn is her lead bitch and Teeco's Mister Tee her lead dog, both running on the six-dog team.

Margaret bought her first Siberian in 1967, a bitch, which she bred; she kept one puppy. Later she bought two showdogs from Martin Bettencourt's

Troika

The Troika Kennels of Vearl and Patty Jones of Bonner Springs, Kansas, was founded in 1968 and based on Monadnock bloodlines. More recently, they have combined the Monadnock with Marlytuk lines to form their Troika lines.

Ch. Dama's Matanuska of Shonko, owned by George and Ann Cook of Ashland, NH. "Mat" runs the wheel on the Cooks' team and finished for his championship with 3-point majors. He is a multi-Group winner too.

Marmik Kennels and got into showing.

Daughter Deena has won several races in the Junior classes, as has son Jason. Their objective is to breed dual purpose Siberians to excel in both show and racing.

They also outcross with the old Frosty Aires and Karnovanda lines.

In 1968, they got off to a bad start with a puppy that died and another with which they had trouble over the papers. But after attending a dog show,

Opposite: Arlington's Fire N Ice, bred and owned by Sylvia Roselli of Arlington Kennels, Staten Island, NY.
Top: Ch. Innisfree's Red Roadster, CD, No. 2 Top-Producing Siberian stud dog in the breed in 1982; 68 champions to his credit. Owned by Sheila Kanzler.
Bottom: Meja's Confederate Gray, bred and owned by James Babb, Jamestown, NC.

Patty was hooked and the rest, as she says, "is history." She was originally involved to keep busy while Vearl was occupied with his archery and golf, but soon Vearl became involved, and now he shows the dogs in the ring right along with Patty.

Patty and Vearl helped to found the Siberian Husky Club of Greater Kansas City and are charter members, and they have served in just about every office, committee, and seminar. Patty was editor for the club newsletter for five years, while Vearl helped get the club sanctioned and able to hold a Specialty. Patty also wrote columns and articles for *Siberian Husky News* and other breed publications. They were given the *Dog World* Outstanding Achievement and Service to Dogs Award.

The list of outstanding dogs and their awards are too numerous to list here. However, the all-time favorite for Vearl was his "Snoopy," otherwise known as Ch. Amarok of the Midnight Sun. Thirteen of their other outstanding dogs are currently

Best Brace at the 1985 CISHC Specialty was Vearl and Patty Jones's Troika's Memorex and Ch. Troika's Sunday Blessing. Vearl Jones handled to this win under judge Betty Moore.

Top: Ch. Cherskiy's K.C. Jones of Troika, owner-handled by V. Jones; at 2 years of age, K.C. wins Best in Specialty at the 1983 SHC of Greater Kansas City. Judge, Bettie Krause.
Bottom: Nostroveya's Laika of Troika, a sled and racing dog by Ch. Snokomo's Commander in Chief ex Missy's Paprika of Troika.

Kossok's Cinndar Fella, bred and owned by Alice J. Watt, Kossok Kennels, Salem, OR. He is winning the Breed under Herman Fellton. The sire was Ch. Sno-Fame Solo's Beau Shandy ex Ch. Kossok's Kiska of Oakcrest.

living with them at Troika. Some of the dogs have been used in advertisements as excellent examples of the breed.

Kossok

Alice J. Watt started her Kossok Kennels in Salem, Oregon, in 1968. Her involvement in the breed began quite by accident. Fresh out of college, she had her first teaching job in a small town on the Oregon coast. Her roommate was sitting for a white dog, and Alice spent a great deal of time with him. She was told it was a Husky, and "Spicey" won her over to the breed (except she learned later that Spicey was a Samoyed!).

Blue-eyed Taji became her first Siberian. In 1976, Alice acquired Kia in a trade with her breeder, and all her stock descends from this bitch, producer of three champions. Her first champion was from her first litter, AmCan Ch. Cassack's Ot-Key Luk of Kossok. Kia is also the dam of several top racing dogs, and is a consistent winner in the weight pulling contests.

Yeti

In the years since 1968, when Robert A. and Joy Graeme Messinger started their Yeti Kennels in Verona, New Jersey, they have finished 28 champions and ten CD dogs—not to mention Bob's racing team and his enthusiasm for the sport.

Top: AmCan Ch. Yeti's Sorrel, a lead racing dog and a winner in the show ring as well. He is the sire of 4 lead racing dogs. Owners, Robert and Joy Messinger, Yeti Kennels, Verona, NJ. His sire was the well-known Rusty Nail; his dam Ch. Barn's Cinnamon. *Bottom:* AmCan Ch. Kossok's Buttercup Bouquet winning the Working Group under William Taylor. The sire was AmCan Ch. Innisfree's Sierra Cinnar ex AmCan Ch. Kohoutek's Kia of Krisland. Owner-bred by Alice J. Watt.

Joy, a native of London, does a great deal of the handling. Bob saw his first Siberian in 1937 while on vacation in Wonancelot and watched Admiral Byrd's dogs being trained for the Antarctic mission. This was at the late Short Seeley's Chinook Kennels, and it obviously left a lasting impression on him.

It seemed only natural then that Bob took over the Coast Guard station's Greenland Huskies in Labrador and was soon driving a seven-dog team there.

Joy, a specialist in folk, blues

Arahaz The Wrath of Khan, 4-year-old male sired by Ch. Arahaz Khan Sin ex Arahaz Vereska. Co-owned by Susanna Rodney and Rosemary Fischer.

Top: AmCanBda Ch. Snowridge's Rusty Nail of Yeti, AmCanBda CD, wins the Veteran Dog Class. His sire was Snoridge's Savda Czar ex Snowridge's Red Devil. Owners, the Messingers. *Bottom:* Let the good times roll! One of Thom and Claudia Ainsworth's Cherskiy Siberians.

VETERAN DOG

Top: Can Ch. Shoshanna's Shiren of Kortar, show dog, racing dog, brood bitch and producer of champions in Canada and Europe. Bred and co-owned by Judi Anderson; Carol Broadhurst co-owner-handler.
Bottom: Can Ch. Temarko Teeco's Teeteemah winning Best of Breed at the Canadian National Specialty Show in 1982 at Quebec, Canada. Judge George Beddard gave this important win to Margaret Cook's 2-year-old dog.

SECOND IN GROUP
LAKE MINNETONKA
JUNE 8, 1980
OLSON PHOTO

Top: AmCan Ch. Fra-Mar's Acco of Innisfree. This multi-Group winner and sire of 3 champions was whelped in 1975. Bred and owned by Marie Wamser. *Bottom:* AmCan Ch. Scoqui's Amber, bred and owned by Scott and Gwynn Quirin, handled by Gwynn. Amber is a multi-Group placer and was top-winning bitch in the USA in 1980, after being shown only 10 times.

Top: Arahaz Kiska Misty Marie, owned by Susanna Windsor Rodney, Kaylee Siberians. *Bottom:* Ch. Czar's Phoenix of Troika with her litter sisters, at the 1985 SHC of Greater Kansas City Specialty. With Phoenix are Troika's Memorex and Ch. Troika's Sunday Blessing. Owners, V. and P. Jones.

Top: Straberre Crush of Troika, Best of Winners at a 1983 show under Maxwell Riddle. The sire was Ch. Poli's J.J. Of Siberkirk; dam was Missy's Paprika of Troika. Owner-breeders, V. and P. Jones. *Bottom:* Vern and Olivia Harvey's Oshvah's Obiwan Kenobi, who is also their lead dog, winning under Thelma Brown.

"The Kaylee braces and teams have won many Bests in Show over the years, but it is still Susanna's wish to have a Siberian that will go Best in Show and Highest in Trial on the same day."

and jazz music, met Bob during a job interview. Bob gave her the job and a marriage proposal. At that time he had a German Shepherd; and when the Shepherd died, they attended a Westminster show and obtained a puppy, from Ch. Savdajaure's Cognac, that had been bred to a Frosty Aire-Monadnock bitch. Her name was Tinya of Taiga, and she was Bob's first lead dog.

A year later their first male was obtained, an experienced lead dog named Sir Lancelot II, purchased from Ray Dworsky. More followed, but it is AmCanBda Ch. Snowridges Rusty Nail of Yeti, AmCanBda CD, that is their pride and joy. He was the first Siberian (and to date the only Siberian) to win both titles in three countries.

Kaylee

Carolyn McDonough Windsor had admired Siberian Huskies for years and loved the stories about how one saved Nome during the epidemic. Carolyn and daughter Susanna were steered to Rosemary and Edward Fischer of Arahaz Kennels and bought an eight-month-old male, future Ch. Arahaz Tengri Khan, CD. Sue showed the dog in both conformation and obedience, up to his last appearance in the Parade of Champions at the 1981 parent club Specialty.

The Kaylee braces and teams have won many Bests in Show over the years, but it is still Susanna's wish to have a

Siberian that will go Best in Show and Highest in Trial on the same day. She says this goal will keep her going forever, if need be.

In my last book, *This is the Siberian Husky*, published in 1973, Susanna was Susanna Windsor; in this publication, something new has been added—she is now Susanna Windsor Rodney.

Cherskiy

1968 was the year Thom and Claudia Ainsworth became interested in the breed and started their Cherskiy Kennels. Currently they maintain about seven dogs, and some of those include winners named Ch. Cherskiy Ankara Likity Split, Ch. Marlytuk's Pride of Cherskiy, and Ch. Cherskiy's Blue Amber.

Sodiax

Sodiax Siberians are owned by Leslie and Daniel C. Haggard of Cocoa, Florida. Sodiax was founded in 1969 with the purchase of a Siberian puppy named Colo's Silverwind of Gonya, who went on to win her CDX degree.

Sodiax breeding is based on dogs from Karnovanda, Fra-Mar, and Monadnock lines.

Fra-Mar's Nikolai Diavol, purchased as a young puppy, was show by Leslie and professional handler, George Heitzman, to International (FCI), American, Canadian, Bermudian, and Mexican championships, with group placings in all countries where

Top:
IntAmBdaCan-Mex Ch. Fra-Mar's Nikolai Diavol, bred by Marie Wamser and owned by Leslie and Dan Haggard of Cocoa, FL. His sire was Ch. Eu Mar's Thuleh of Siber ex Ch. Fra-Mar's Aja Tu Diavol.
Bottom:
Kaylee's Ruffin wins under Carolyn Thomas. Bred, owned and handled by Susanna Windsor Rodney. The sire was Ch. Innisfree's Pegasus ex Kaylee Kittee Katek.

117

Top: AmCan Ch. Sunset Hill's Bella Donna, handled by Chuck McDonald for owners Deanna and Lou Gray. The sire was AmCanMex Ch. Karnovanda's Sasha Groznyi ex Ch. Sunset Hill's Beau-Phunsilady. *Bottom:* Straberre' Crush of Troika going BOS. "Bubbles" is by Ch. Poli's J.J. of Siberkirk ex Missy Paprika of Troika.

Top: Head study of the lovely 6-month-old Eumor's Nakia. *Bottom:* Ch. Indigo's Irma Bombeck, bred and owned by the David Qualls of Jacksonville, FL, making it 3 sisters in a single litter to finish.

119

he was shown. "Nikki" was the first Siberian Husky to obtain all these titles. He was also top winning Siberian in the USA in 1973, all systems.

One of their top dogs of today is Ch. Zodiac's Cherry Bear, who was Best of Opposite Sex at the 1979 National Specialty. Their top producing bitch was Monadnock's Red Bear of Zodiac and Ch. Zodiac's Kara Bear. Their Ch. Aazar's Tiki was Best Opposite at the 1984 American Kennel Club Centennial Show.

Sodiax Siberians can be found throughout the United States as well as in France, Canada, Mexico, Chile, and Colombia, and are excelling at racing, weight-pulling, in the show, and in obedience rings.

Kiok

Joe and Brenda Kolar have had their Kiok Kennels in Astoria, Oregon, since 1969. Their first was Kodiak Koda, which they bred to the famous Ch. Dichoda's Yukon Red in 1972; that was their "real" start

Can Ch. Sodiax Timber Wolf, Can CD, owned by Karen Lang. The sire was Ch. Innisfree's Pegasus ex Ch. Zodiac's Kara Bear.

SECOND IN GROUP
REDWOOD EMPIRE KENNEL CLUB
MAY 1985   FOX & COOK

in the breed. They are interested in both showing and in the obedience ring.

Their first breeding produced Shon-Yak of Kiok, CD, and later introduced some Innisfree breeding into their line.

However, Brenda declares that her main interest in the breed is centered around the study of genetic defects. She recently completed five years researching an inherited trait in the breed, Hair Follicle Dystrophy, often referred to as HFD. The study will be published in the *American Veterinary Medical Association Journal*.

Snoking

When Richard and Janice MacWhade got married in 1976, they decided to keep the Snoking Kennel name that Richard had established in 1969. They wanted to maintain the kennel with around ten dogs or less, since they enjoy competition but want the dogs to have individual attention.

They attribute the success of the Snoking dogs to their excellent brood bitches, namely Karnovanda's Shannon Groznyi and Telemark's Chandelle. Some of their other important dogs are AmCan Ch. Bolshoi's Grey Sinner, a Specialty winner at the largest National Specialty in the history of the breed, and a multi-group placer; AmCan Ch. Innisfree's On The Road Again, a Best in Show and Specialty winner before two years of age, and a Canadian Best in Show out of the classes

Ch. Kiok's Kommand Performance, multi-Group-winning bitch from Kiok Kennels.

Margaret Cook's Teeco's Tweet Rockin Robyn and Teeco's Tzar Tseeka take an afternoon off at their Easton, MA, home, Teeco Kennels.

on the way to his Canadian championship; AmCan Ch. Arcticlights Strawberry Cream, multi-Best Opposite sex winner and multi-group placer; AmCan Ch. Eu-Mor's Copper Warrier, a multi-group placer; and AmCan Ch. Fra-Mar's Arctic Challenger, also a multi-group placer.

The list of champions that both Shannon Groznyi and Chandelle have produced is too long to mention here, but they have truly left their mark on the breed.

The Snoking Kennels are located in Hinckley, Ohio.

Malchuk
May N. (Peggy) Malone of Richfield, Ohio, started her Malchuk Kennel in 1969. She keeps about six dogs at a time, to keep it small and manageable, as she puts it.

Peggy is very involved in the improvement of the breed; she accomplishes this by belonging to several area clubs and holding office in each. She also works full time as a secretary.

Her kennel started with one show quality bitch, purchased to see if she was interested in showing dogs. Needless to say, at the first Match she won Best of Opposite Sex and was "hooked." Ch. Kiska's Frosty Natasha was then owner-handled to her championship.

Since the beginning, Peggy has finished seven dogs and finished two others owned by other people.

Babiche
Edward and Caroline Burke's interest in racing was what got their Babiche Kennel, in Norwell, Massachusetts, started in 1969. Today they are very interested and active in the new SEPP project, and Caroline has written articles on the program for publication.

Their Babiche's Pryde was the 1982 Superior/Excellent dog. Pryde is capable of leading a team at 18 miles per hour over a nine mile stretch. She and their Babiche's Mageik are two very good examples of the Burke's dedication to developing superior racing Siberians.

Both Ed and Caroline are directors of SEPP, and Caroline is both secretary and treasurer of SEPP as well. They are most proud of their undefeated running of a team of four dogs during the 1985 season, with two of the dogs less than ten miles short of the SD degree. They were winners of the 1985 Narragansett Sled Dog Club, the Yankee Siberian Husky Club, and over-all Driver of the Year in 1985. They set a course record in Freetown, Massachusetts, for 2.7 miles in ten minutes and thirteen seconds in 1985, while undefeated in six outings.

Babiche's Grey Wolf and Babiche's Solitaire are also members of their undefeated four-dog team.

AmCan Ch. Snoking's Gold Rush, owned by Richard and Jan MacWhade of Hinckley, OH. Gold Rush wins Best of Breed at a 1984 show.

123

Top: Ch. Zodiac's Sir Ikabod of Indigo, bred by Dan and Leslie Haggard. He was shown by his breeder, Leslie Haggard, for owners Dr. and Mrs. David K. Qualls. The sire was Ch. Fra-Mar's Nikolai Diavol ex Monadnock's Red Bear of Zodiac. *Bottom:* Can Ch. Cheechako's Varskita O'Denali, bred by Charlotte Anderson.

Top: Monadnock's Artvic Akela, one of the Top Ten Siberians for many years during the 1970s. Akela is a Dichoda's Flare litter brother. *Bottom:* Ch. Arbo's Foxy Lady winning a major under Neal Koonts at a Louisville, KY, show. Bred and owned by Arbo's Siberians of Decatur, IL. Handled by Patti Causey.

125

Roy-A-Lin

Roy, Linda, and Margie Arnett's Roy-A-Lin Kennels began in 1969 in Southern California. They are now located in Estacada, Oregon (the facilities in Oregon were superior to those in California for breeding, which is what they wanted to do). At one time they had 27 dogs, with their interests running more to the

Ch. Toko's Twenty Four Karat Gold, CD, winning a Veteran Bitch Class at 10 years of age. As always, breeder-owner-handled by Jean Fournier, Simsbury, CT. Karat was the No. 5 Siberian for 1976–78. She was also winner of the SHCDV Specialty Show under Eva "Short" Seeley. The sire was Marlytuk's Red Sun of Kiska ex Ch. Fournier's Tiffany of Toko.

working Siberian than to show dogs.

However, their AmCan Ch. Roy-A-Lin's Valentikko O'Snoshu, CD, was the first dual champion Siberian of piebald coloration. He was also the first Siberian of this coloration to be a competitive racing dog in addition to

holding an AKC Obedience Degree.

After almost two decades of involvement in the breed, they are now limiting their activities in the breed, with their primary interest still centering around the racing dog.

For many years, Linda Arnett has been editor of the *International Siberian Husky Club News*, a most worthy publication (with ten area directors feeding all the pertinent information to her) for the benefit of the breed.

Toko

Jean Fournier of Simsbury, Connecticut, started her kennel in 1968, when she was given a Siberian as a birthday present.

It turned out to be a fine dog, later Ch. Dovercrest Aletha Pesna, CD, and after their first Match show, she was hooked—not only on the breed, but on showing.

Some of Jean's dogs have had remarkable show careers. Perhaps the best known is her Ch. Toko's Mr. Chip of Yago, CD. He is the *only* Best in Show Siberian to ever win the Five Siberian for 1976, 1977, and 1978. Her latest is Ch. Toko's Four-Leaf Clover. Jean personally won the Siberian Husky Club of America's Working/Showing Trophy in 1972.

While Jean no longer actively breeds or exhibits on a regular basis, she intends to pursue the judging of dogs, starting with the Working Group. Her

Winner of the Brood Bitch Class at the 1984 SHC of Greater Cleveland Specialty was Telemark's Chandelle, with Snoking's Streak of Silver and Ch. Snoking's Cotton Candy.

Top Obedience Novice Award, presented by the Siberian Husky Club of America, and his Best in Show at the age of eight, in 1983. He was also No. Two Siberian in the US in 1980 and 1981.

Another top winner was Jean's Ch. Toko's Twenty-Four Karat Gold, CD, who was No.

assignments take her all over the country. One of her most prestigious assignments has been to judge the breed at the 1986 Westminster Kennel Club Show.

THE 1970s and 1980s
By 1970, a little more than half a century after the first

Siberian Husky reached Alaska, the breed had flourished and had reached the very heights of popularity. The great sport of sled dog racing mushroomed all over the United States, and entries at the dog shows and obedience trials increased at an amazing rate.

1963 was a record-breaking year for Siberian Husky registration with the American Kennel Club. For the first time, they went over the one thousand mark. By 1969 registrations were just under 5000.

Entries at the dog shows equal interest in the breed. An early 1970 Specialty Show drew over 150 entries, and many of the larger dog shows pulled entries in the three figure category.

Dud's

Clarence and Gladys Dudley, of North Syracuse, New York, while only getting into the breed in 1970, have found almost phenomenal success! Their AmCan Ch. Dudley's Tavar of Innisfree was winner of Best in Show at the Ramapo Kennel Club in New Jersey in November 1972. Clipper's show ring successes have been impressive. He finished his American Championship from the puppy classes at just 11

Ch. Innisfree's Turfire, winner of Group, placing from the classes and sister to the IntMex Best in Show winner Castor Spirit of Innisfree. Bred by Kathleen Kanzler; handled by Sheila Kanzler.

Toko-Rock's Timber Woof winning on his way to championship in 1986. Timber is owned by Jean Fournier and Angele Porpora, shown handling him, with judge Dr. Sheldon Rennert.

BEST OF WINNERS
DELAWARE COUNTY
KENNEL CLUB
1986

months of age, all under different judges, and he finished his Canadian championship at 19 months.

Grawyn

Lou and Deanna Gray are the owners of Grawyn Kennels located in Woodstock, Illinois. They have owned Siberians since 1970. Their first two dogs were strictly pets, but Deanna did put a CD title on one of them in three consecutive shows.

It wasn't until 1978 that their interest in the conformation classes came about and they purchased their first show bitch. During the next year, they bought a male puppy who was to become their first champion. This was the Best in Show and Specialty winner, AmCan Ch. Gilpak's Kris Kringl of Grawyn. He was No. Five Siberian in 1982, and has over 65 Bests of Breed and many group placements.

That first show bitch died in 1981, so they purchased a gray and white bitch, AmCan Ch. Sunset Hill's Bella Donna, bred by Anne Bruder. She finished for these titles in 1981 (the Canadian title, in one weekend) the other in 1984.

There are approximately 18

Top: "Critter," top lead dog owned by Bob and Roberta McDonald. *Bottom:* A lovely portrait of Arahaz Lizzie Bullet, bred by Rosemary Fischer. Olan Mills photo.

Top: Bo-Gerick's Hey Hey Mr. J.J., owned by Dick and Gerry Dalakian of Flemington, NJ. Hey Hey's sire was Ch. Sunset Hill's Jo Jo Starbuck ex AmCan Ch. Innisfree's Ms. Cinnar. *Bottom:* Itaska's Goodtime Charlie, bred and owned by Paul and Wendy Willhauck and owned by Paul and Debi Allen. Debi Allen handled to this 1985 win under Donald Booxbaum.

Top: Ch. Kadyak's Ms. Kiswin, Best in Show winner under judge Betty Krause at a 1984 show. Al Lee handled to this win for owners Ardene Eaton and Dr. B. Edwards.

Bottom: AmCan Ch. Gilpak's Kris Kingl of Grawyn winning the 1982 First Annual Specialty of the SHC of Greater Chicago. The sire was Ch. Danasha's Irish Kaper ex Sunset Hill's Midnite Magic. Handler was Phil Norris.

to 20 Siberians at Grawyn on the seven beautiful acres they maintain for their Grawyn Kennels. The Grays are members of the Siberian Husky Club of Greater Chicago and of the parent club.

Kadyak

Ardene Eaton's Kadyak Kennel is located in Anchorage, Alaska. Established in 1974, she keeps around a dozen Siberians for show and her dog teams.

Her original Siberian was purchased to show, but she soon realized that it would be great fun to exercise the dogs in front of a sled. Ardene's husband was born in Kodiak, Alaska, and from the Russian name for Kodiak—*Kadyak*—she took her kennel name.

In 1984, her Ch. Kadyak's Ms. Kiswin was the No. One Husky in Alaska and also top winning bitch in the breed history. She was winner of the National Specialty Show for the parent club that year as well. Top show dogs, in addition to Ms. Kishwin, are Arctic Raider and Akelana of Synordik, both

Tawny Hill Brenna Brea winning at a 1985 show on the way to championship. The sire was Ch. Tawny Hill's Justin Thyme ex Tawny Hill's Pippatu. Bred and owned by Adele M. Gray.

Top-winning Siberian on the 1983 Oklahoma circuit, Ch. K.C. Jones of Troika, owned and handled by Vearl Jones, winning the Working Group under Tom Stevenson.

Top: Scoqui Sakonnet's Cante Ista owned by Leroy Simons. *Bottom:* AmCan Ch. Boshoi's Canadiana Ne Gerick. Owned and shown by Dick and Gerry Dalakian of Flemington, NJ.

bearing the Kadyak prefix. Two outstanding racing dogs at her kennel are Ch. Kadyak's Arctic Raider and Kopper Kyan.

Trivalent

It was in 1970 that Richard and Mutsuko (Mickie) Punnett bought their first Siberian Husky. This male puppy started out as a pet, but it wasn't long before the puppy had them involved in obedience work. Soon after this, they found themselves in the ring.

The Punnetts maintain a small kennel of five to seven dogs so that they can train and show them all. Their most outstanding dog is AmCan Ch. Trivalent's Ivanova Ruffian, AmCan CD. In 1983, at eight years of age, he returned to the ring four times as a Special and took three Bests of Breed, a Group Third, and a Group First, always owner-handled by Mickie.

Shalimar

Karl and Jo Geletich of Escalon, California, had Samoyeds before they got into Siberians. After admiring Ch. Dichoda's Yukon Red in the group ring, they decided in 1970 to get into Siberians and acquired a puppy that later became their first champion and foundation stud dog at their kennel. His name was Ch. Shalimar's Velika Noga.

They now keep a total of 20 dogs, of both breeds, and their Ch. Kia's Miss Tanya of Shalimar won Best of Opposite Sex at a National Specialty show. Another champion is Ch. Blue Dashka. There are several others that belong to other owners.

Umiat

Marcia Hoyt of Walnut Creek, California, got into Siberian Huskies in 1970 and has covered a lot of territory ever since. She currently has 35

Kari Skogun loading up her dogs for the trip home from Nome after the 1984 Iditarod Race.

Top: AmCan Ch. Trivalent's Ivanova Ruffian, CD. Owner is Mutsuko Punnett of Tonawanda, NY.
Bottom: Ch. Beorthwulf Boreas R. Rehymen, CDX, at the 1983 SHCA Specialty in California. He is here competing in the Veterans Class.

Top: Ch. Troika's Sunday Blessing taking Best of Breed honors at a 1985 show at 2 years of age. Vearl Jones, handler. *Bottom:* Big day for the Fireside Kennels of Betty Rosetto. Judge Robert Wills gives Best of Breed to AmCan Ch. Fireside's Hellbuster; Best of Opposite to his daughter, Ch. Big Trails Kia Karina; and Best of Winners to Fireside's Yukan Red.

Top: Ch. Fireside's Hotshot with owner Betty Rosetto of Milford, MI. *Middle:* Ch. Arahaz Xanadukhan Obet, bred by Rosemary Fischer and owned by Bill Gregg. Gilbert photo. *Bottom:* Kaylee's Tengri Nor owned by Susanna Windsor Rodney, under Peggy Grant.

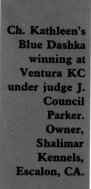

Ch. Kathleen's Blue Dashka winning at Ventura KC under judge J. Council Parker. Owner, Shalimar Kennels, Escalon, CA.

Siberians; but without a doubt her Ch. Beorthwolf Boreas Re Tymen, CDX, and Ch. Dichoda's Ullar of Umiat are her top dogs. Ullar is the foundation for her running dogs.

Boreas finished her CDX with scores in the 190s, and Ullar was the first dual purpose dog.

Umiat's Trailblazer, SD, has been another strong lead on her six-dog team for six years and shows no signs of slowing down. Blazer was one of the first Siberians to receive the Sled Dog degree from the Siberian Husky Club of America, as was Snoshu's White Lightning. Umiat's Dallas of Nicholai earned her sled dog degree in one season.

Marcia attributes much of the success of her eight-dog team to the fact that she was able to purchase many of Linda Trinkaus's dogs when she got out of racing.

When Marcia purchased her first Siberian, she was interested strictly in racing and obedience. When she moved from Colorado she began to show, and she now indulges in all three. And while she races mostly an eight-dog team she has been known to run in all classes! She has been both a first and second vice president in the parent club as well as recording secretary and directory. In addition to many other positions, she is a former vice president of the Iditarod Trail Committee, ISDRA, and the SEPP International Siberian Husky Club, and has taught obedience.

Talocon

John and Gail O'Connell, Talocon Kennels, began in 1970 when they purchased a blue-eyed, black and white son of Ch. Koryak's the Red Baron and Ch. Carmalin's Fresca of Snoridge. He became Can Ch. Tala of Carmalin. In 1975 they had their first litter out of Monadnock lines. This first litter produced Talocon's Crimson Casanova, but "Nova" died tragically at a young age and never reached his full potential. However, he did sire a litter which produced another foundation bitch for Talocon Sno Tow's Erica. Their Ch. Talocon's Arctic Flash, a major stud in their kennels, is also their first champion.

Some of their other top dogs are Ch. Talocon Nova's

Double header for John and Gail O'Connell's brace at this 1982 show. Ch. Talocon's Arctic Flash and Ch. Talocon's Arctic Echo, a father-son combination, not only are a Top-Winning Brace in the breed but have 17 Bests in Show in all-breed competition. They were undefeated in the Working Group.

Top: Ch. Almaring's Alai, winning a Group Third at a 1975 Land O' Lakes KC show. *Bottom:* Travis and Lora Henderson's Chilly Willy of Troika shows us how to make the most of a hot summer afternoon.

THIRD IN GROUP
LAND O' LAKES K.C.
JUNE 8, 1975
OLSON PHOTO

Top: Kaylee's Lady in Red winning at a match show under Joyce Reynaud. Bred, owned, and handled by Susanna Rodney. *Bottom:* Arahaz V.O. Dudley, bred and co-owned by R. Fischer.

Top: Ch. Tai Wind's Xanadu, a Specialty Show winner and multi-Best of Breed winner. She has also placed in the Group for owner Gail O'Connell. *Bottom:* Ch. Marlytuk's Kelo O'High Country finishing for his championship at age 8 years. He is co-owned by Carol Nash and Peggy Grant.

Calypso; Ch. Talocon Nova's Taneha; Ch. Tai Wind's Xanadu; Ch. Talocon's Arctic Echo, Eleta, Polaris and Aurora, CD.

Talocon is located in Hauppauge, New York, and the dogs are handled by Gail to their prestigious wins.

Synordik

The Synordik Kennel of Richard T. Nist, MD, and Cynthia R. Nist, PhD, had its beginnings in 1970 in a one-bedroom apartment in the graduate students' residence at Rockefeller University in New York City. The Nists raised three puppy bitches and went to shows, and as they put it, "sat at the feet of the masters" for three years while they studied dogs.

In June 1972, they moved to California, where they now have eight dogs selected from Monadnock, Marlytuk, and Savdajaure breeding.

Their Tara's Rhory has had several Bests of Breed over Specials while finishing, and their first litter, sired by Rhory ex Ch. Koritea of Kettle

Best Brace at the 1983 Delaware Valley SHC Specialty. Outside is Canaan's Brendon; inside is Canaan's P.T. Barnum next to breeder-owner-handler Carol Nash of Plaistow, NH.

Moraine, was productive.

Cynthia Nist is a cell biologist and molecular geneticist; Richard Nist is in pediatrics and was a resident in obstetrics and gynecology at the University of Seattle during the early part of his career.

Canaan

Carol A. Nash of Plaistow, New Hampshire, got started in the fancy as Peg Grant's kennel girl while still in high school. In 1971 she got a Sunny daughter from Peggy Grant while in Denver, and moved to Canaan, New Hampshire, taking the name of the town as her kennel name. In 1976, she bought "Sachem," Ch. Marlytuks Sachem of Canaan, one of her most outstanding dogs to date.

Some of the others are Ch. Marlytuk Elektra; Marlytuk Kiska-Trey; Canaans Go Diva; Canaans P.T. Barnum; Canaan's Resurrected MacInri; and Canaans Calamity Jane; the latter of these dogs were for her racing team.

Carol enjoys showing braces at the shows, which she believes are excellent examples of consistency in breeding.

Her dogs have all enjoyed top wins during their show ring careers, and were usually owner handled.

Des Mar

The Des Mar Kennels in Manteca, California, belong to Desmond and Mary Cole. Formerly, Desmond's kennel name was Desha and Mary's

AmMex Ch. Deshas Prince Jascha with his 5-week-old daughter Desha's Anya. Owners, Desmond and Mary Cole.

Ch. Kontoki's Minute Made, dam of champions and Best of Winners and Best Opposite at the 1980 Central Indiana Specialty Show. She is also the dam of Ch. Kontoki's Made in the Shade. Owner, Tom Oelschlager and Marlene DePalma of Finleyville, PA.

was Maridel. El Cid was Mary's first home-bred champion and was a top winner in the breed ring. Des and Mary are very interested in racing now, yet continue to show. Their top racing dogs are Des Mar's Phoenix and Des Mar's Susitna.

Des met Mary when he sold her one of his Jascha puppies, later MexCanInt Ch. Maridel's Nicholai of Desha. He had purchased his Desha's Prince Jascha who was later No. Four Siberian in the country. The Coles keep approximately 12 adults, and they have an occasional litter.

Kontoki

Thomas L. Oelschlager and Marlene A. DePalma are partners in the Kontoki Kennels in Finleyville, Pennsylvania, which began in 1971.

Tom's first Siberian came after a pet chicken and a Collie became friendly with a Siberian that lived next door. The Siberian "hunted" Tom's chicken and Tom was given the dog as a peace offering. The Husky's name was Dovercrests Tonya of Trotwood, bred by Audrey Kent.

The kennel now houses about 25 dogs, including the

Top: Ch. Arahaz Vershina, bred and owned by Rosemary Fischer. By Ch. Dudley's Varska ex Arahaz Okolina. *Bottom:* Ch. Grawyn's Sinful Simon Glacier, bred by Deanna and Lou Gray and owned by Lois and Laurel Olmem and Deanna Gray, winning at a 1985 dog show. "Hardy" was sired by Ch. Innisfree's Pagan Sinner ex Grawyn's Ravin' Beauty.

Top: Future Ch. Sunset Hill's Wild Belle Star, bred and owned by Anne Bruder of Taos, NM. The sire was Ch. Sunset Hill's Wild Beau-Canyon ex Gerick's Stardust of Sno-Sky.

Middle: Kossok's Flights of Fancy pictured at 7 months of age. Sire was Ch. Innisfree's Aazar Bit-A-Thor ex Ch. Kossok's Good As Gold. Bred and owned by Alice Watt.

Bottom: Judith Russell's 8-month-old Ch. Karnovanda's Deputy Dawg at the 1982 SHC of Greater Cleveland Show. Sire was Ch. Jonathie's Keystone Copper ex Karnovanda's Zinka Raven.

outstanding Ch. Kontoki's Natural Sinner, many times Best in Show winner, and sire of 22 champions to date; as well as Ch. Kontoki's One Mo'Time, Ch. Kontoki's Minute Made, Ch. Kontoki's Opposum's Holler, Ch. Savdajaure's Cass Raina, and Happy to be Innisfree.

Sunset Hills

Anne Bruder of Taos, New Mexico, started Sunset Hills Kennels in 1971. Her first dog was bought as a pet, but was spotted by someone who thought he was a good dog and should be shown. Ch. Czar Nicoli of Togo subsequently finished for his championship and Anne was hooked on Siberians—and showing them!

Since the beginning, Anne has been interested in all phases of the sport—show, racing, and obedience. Some of her outstanding show dogs are AmCan Ch. Weldon's Beau-Phunsi; and AmCanMex Ch. Karnovanda's Shasha Groznyi, her original foundation bitch. In the obedience department is her AmCan Ch. Innisfree's O'Dwyer, who is also an American and Canadian CD titlist and Best in Show. O'Dwyer and Sunset Hills M's Molli, CD, have both won several High in Trial awards.

Anne didn't start breeding her dogs for six years after becoming involved. She practiced first on pedigreed rabbits until she was convinced she knew what she was doing. Since then, she has bred three

"Anne Bruder didn't start breeding her dogs for six years after becoming involved. She practiced first on pedigreed rabbits until she was convinced she knew what she was doing."

top producing bitches and has top stud dogs which are producing top producers and winners themselves.

To date, she has finished nine champions and put CDs on two others, with more to come.

Kirkachas

Mickey Zinger, of Arlington, Texas, started her Kirkachas Kennel in 1972 on the old Cichoda, Monadnock, and Anadyr lines. Later, she added Innisfree, Karnovanda, and Fireside to her breeding program, and these are the dogs she is still showing, though her breeding program is quite limited.

Her most outstanding dog is the bitch, Ch. Kirkacha's Suzi Skyhope. "Suzi" is out of Best in Show Ch. Innisfree's Pagan Sinner from Ch. Sunset Hill's Morning Glory. Bred by Skyhope Kennels, Suzi is third generation Best in Show.

Suzi, as well as all the other Specials at Kirkachas, is always owner-handled and has won many group placements.

Another outstanding dog at this kennel is Ch. Achruni's Tsu Du-Wak, who was shown in the early 1970s and was a multi-breed winner and group placer. She was also the dam of some outstanding racing dogs.

Ch. Kirkacha's Twinkle of Stargat is now semi-retired, but was also owner-handled to multi-breed and group placement wins.

Indigo

The Indigo Kennels in

Top: AmCan Ch. Sunset Hill's Lochness Bobbi, owned by Anne Bruder. The sire was Ch. Weldon's Beau-Tukker ex AmCan Innisfree's Import. *Bottom:* Ch. Kirkacha's Twinkle of Stargate finishing for championship under Larry Bane. Handled by Mickey Zinger. Sire was Ch. Fireside's Hellbuster ex Ch. Fireside's Black Star.

151

Top: Ch. Highpoint's Black Eyed Susie, owned and shown by H. Levell Leahy of Archer, FL. *Bottom:* Ch. Indigo's Intity at the 1986 *Kennel Review Magazine* Tournament of Champions, where he was ranked Ninth Show Dog of the Year. Bred and owned by Dr. and Mrs. David K. Qualls. The sire was Ch. Innisfree's Trademark ex Ch. Innisfree's Newscent's Niavar.

Ch. Snowfire's Tovarish winning a 4-point major at the 1983 Yankee SHC Specialty Show on the way to his championship. Owner-handled by Sandra Porter, Skrimshaw Siberians, Rexford, NY.

Jacksonville, Florida, began in 1972, when David K. Qualls and his wife acquired David's Prince Igor, CD. To date, they have been directly responsible for 22 Siberian champions that they either own, have bred, or co-own with other Siberian fanciers.

David, a veterinarian, handles the dogs himself a great deal, and the kennel houses approximately 25 dogs, which Mrs. Qualls delights in showing and living with.

Skrimshaw

Sandra L. Porter started her Skrimshaw Siberians in 1972 in Rexford, New York. She is interested in both showing and obedience, and keeps her operation on a rather small scale, with only two dogs at this time.

Some of her important dogs were Ch. Snowfires Tovarisch, and Ch. Keraseva's

Harlequinade, CD, her top notch obedience dog.

Sandra teaches obedience classes and used "Raska" in her classes. She also has a grooming and training business in Latham, New York, which means she has to hold off her breeding plans until the future.

Apparition

Though only starting their Apparition Kennels in 1972, Larry and Susan Govedich of Port Matilda, Pennsylvania, have accomplished quite a record in the obedience rings. Their Yama Av Karnik earned his UD title, their Can Ch. Apparitions Genghis Khan his CDX title, and Tazza Sious Av Karnik also has a CDX title.

The Govedichs purchased their first Siberian in 1972 as a pet. Needless to say, they were off to obedience classes to help keep the dog under control and they were hooked, taking the

UD-titled dog Yama Av Karnik, owned by Larry and Susan Govedich, winning in Obedience at the 1977 SHC of Greater Cleveland Specialty Show.

dog all the way to his Utility Dog title. And, as Larry says, "Now who knows where it will end"! Two other CDX dogs have followed to prove his point.

They have also excelled in the show ring. Their Ch. Aazar's Sure Hit is a Best in Show winner and is the first back-to-back Specialty Best of Breed winner, and the youngest to ever win a Best in Show, which she did at just one-and-a-half years of age. In the winter of 1984-85 she was rated No. Five Siberian Husky, and owner-handled all the way.

Veleah

Ms. L. Levell Leahy, better known as Vel, started her

kennel in 1972 as Velterr. In 1980 it was changed to Veleah, and is located in Archer, Florida.

Vel keeps an average of ten dogs at Veleah, and her Best in Show Ch. Veleah's Silver Patriot is believed to be the youngest owner-breeder-handled Best in Show Siberian in the history of the breed. He was just one year and seven months of age at that time.

Her Ch. Highpoint's Black Eyed Susie was ranged nationally in 1983-84. Vel's Veleah's Scarlet Fever was Best of Winners at Westminster in 1986 under breeder-judge Jean Fournier and was handled for her by Suzanne Brand.

Oshvah

Oshvah began in 1972 in Atlanta, Georgia, by Vern and Olivia Harvey. The third member of Oshvah is daughter Calico, who has been running Siberians and winning since she was seven years of age!

Presently operating at Tucson, Arizona, Oshvah has been mentioned in several publications including *TVS PM* magazine regarding their participation in the sport of dogs. Some of their more important dogs are Ch. Misha of Snow's End, Ch. Innisfree's Beau Kara, Ch. Sierra's Centorian of Tioga, Ch.

Oshvah's Miss Piggy, and their lead dog, Oshvah's Obiwan Kenobi.

Their first breeding produced Oshvahs Ivashko of Tova, CDX, and Oshvah's Prince Beta of Tara. All are trained in obedience and Vashka was top winning obedience Siberian in the southeast for several years. Beta ran on their team until ten years of age and excelled in weightpulling, his top pull 1020 pounds.

Kolyma's Racing Siberians

Stu and Sherry Galka began in the show ring with their first

Olivia Harvey showing Ch. Oshvah's Miss Piggy. The Harvey's Oshvah Kennels are in Tucson, AZ.

Top: Ch. Kia's Miss Tanya of Shalimar winning under Dolly Ward. "Misty" went on to win Best of Opposite Sex at the 1980 National Specialty Show in Washington with an entry of over 400 Siberian Huskies. Bred by C. Jones, she is owned by Shalimar Kennels, Escalon, CA. *Bottom:* Ch. Toko's Misty Dawn of Northsea finishing her championship at this 1986 show by winning the Working Group. Pictured here with judge Mrs. Estelle Booxbaum Cohen; shown by Jean Fournier for co-owner Janet Linnehan. The sire was Ch. Toko's Mr. Chip of Yago, CD, ex Ch. Innisfree's Sierra Sassafras.

Top: **Ch. Arahaz Kelieti, bred and owned by Rosemary Fischer, Beaver, PA.** *Bottom:* **Gone fishin'! Robert Causey and his pal Jonah off on a fishing trip near their Arbo Kennels in Decatur, IL.**

Siberian, Ch. Kolyma's Red Tannu of Mayhill, CDX, back in 1972. Once Tannu was a champion, their interests changed to racing the dogs and they have excelled at this ever since. They maintain a kennel of about 17 dogs which they race in winter and train in obedience during the summer.

Stu and Sherry have both been obedience instructors, since 1973, with the Sierra-Tuolumne Club and teach two to four classes a year. In addition, they belong to the ISDA, the Racing Awards committee of the parent club, several other racing clubs, and the Tuolumne County Humane Society. The awards the dogs have won are too numerous to mention as all have excelled in

their endeavors. Stu and Sherry state that they both enjoy the dogs and the rides over the snow-covered mountains, which they find are one of the most peaceful places on earth. Stu says that to him, half of the thrill of running the dogs is the quiet run, when they are alone with nature.

The Galkas' Siberians have grown up with their children and now their grandchildren. Their children, Don and Lori, were involved in racing when they were teenagers, and now the grandchildren are competing in the Pee Wee Races at Truckee, California, where, for two years in a row, Ryan took first place and Scott second place. Needless to say, they feel the Siberians are

The Pee Wee Races at the 1984 Truckee, CA, event; Kolyma's Sierra Silver Tomari, CD, comes in first with a "friend."

family dogs.

Ma-Ri-An Wind Siberians

Mrs. Rosalind M. McEnroe and her American, Canadian, Mexican, International and World Champion broke all the records in the early 1980s when "Stormy" became the youngest dog ever to achieve world status as an international champion, at just one year of age. Together they made history.

Rosalind, whose kennel name was taken from the words of the song from *Paint Your Wagon*, is the exclusive handler of the dogs, and has already put an American and Mexican championship on her Ch. Black Velvet Snow. Her Princess Kira Karalott has the three highest

Top: Calico Harvey showing her dog "Osh." *Bottom:* Stu and Sherry Galka's Ch. Red Tannu of Mayhill, CDX, shown taking a 5-point major, owner-handled, for a championship title at the 1973 San Joaquin KC Show.

159

Top: Ch. Niavar's Spirit of the Wind, CD, bred by M. Ravain and owned by M. Ravain, Laura Hirsch and David Qualls, DVM. Spirit is pictured winning on the way to championship, and is a Group winner with multiple placements.
Bottom: Ch. Karnovanda's Freya Groznyi winning the Breed from the classes at a 1979 show. This win represented the 63rd Karnovanda champion for Judith Russell.

Top: Kczar's Red Baron, sired by Ch. Marlytuk's Red Noho ex Noatuks Molyna Kczar, CD.
Bottom: Stu and Sherry Galka's Best in Match winner, Kolyma's Flashy Koni Mayhill, CD.

Top: Off to a good start. Majula's Thundershadow at just 6 months, 9 days old, winning the class over 12 other puppies. This win was at the 1980 Yankee Specialty Show under Roxanne Mahan. Owner-bred, handled by Phylis Secrist. *Bottom:* Ch. Veleah's Honeysuckle Rose at 7 months of age. "Rosie" finished her championship with 3 majors. Owned by Vel Leahy of Archer, FL.

obedience titles in the US and topped the Canadian utility trial with a high in trial win.

Rosalind's husband, Tim, builds the hurdles and other equipment necessary for the obedience title training; and the children, William and Christopher, enjoy the dogs and the activity they provide as well as the roomful of ribbons and trophies they have won. "Patience and a sense of humor" is Rosalind's theory for training her dogs successfully— and who can deny that it works! The McEnroes' home base is in Oshkosh, Wisconsin.

Majula

Phylis Secrist of Knoxville, Tennessee, established her Majula Kennels in 1973, and today she houses four adult dogs. Cosey Majula is her CD dog, and Ch. Majula's Russlan and Mujula's Thundershadow are two of the others.

In 1972, Phylis began her search for a Northern breed dog to keep as a pet. It was at this time that she found a bitch puppy, Cosey Mujula, CD, who became her steady companion and housedog until her death in 1985. Soon after buying Cosey, Phylis became interested in dog shows (she still enjoys them).

In 1976, Phylis's search for a good foundation bitch ended with her purchase of Marlytuks Natasha of Sunny. Her first litter produced Ch. Majula's Russlan and Majula's Melody. Majula's Smokey, also from this litter, is the dam of Majula's Thundershadow. Russlan was breeder-owner-handled to his championship in 1980.

Phylis maintains that her kennels are a hobby, with never more than ten dogs at a time so that each can get individual attention. During the winter she enjoys the dogs in harness and the rest of the year these dogs go to the shows.

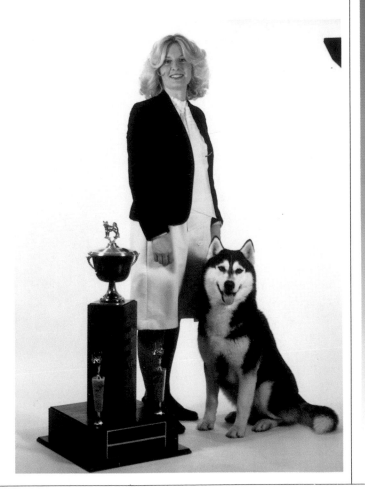

Proud owner-handler Rosalind McEnroe with the famous IntAmCanMex World Champion Storm Prince. "Stormy" is one of the Top-Winning dogs in Siberian show-dog history.

Top: Arahaz Kuva Khan, CD, co-owned by breeder Rosemary Fischer and Barbara Hoard, winning under Anthony Hodges. The sire was Ch. Toki of Rockrimmon ex Arahaz Anika. *Bottom:* Tokomac's Makushkin Nunatak, foundation bitch of the Alkas'Iber Kennels of George and Ann Cook in Ashland, NH.

Top: Winner of the Brood Bitch Class is Arahaz Bersues Nefertiti with her get, Ch. Arahaz Shali and Arahaz Tovari. Breeder, Rosemary Fischer. Gilbert photo. *Bottom:* Ch. Arahaz Khan Sin finished with 5 Bests of Breed wins over Specials for his championship.

Arbo

The Arbo Kennels of Robert and Arline Causey in Decatur, Illinois, came into being in 1973. Many of their dogs, over the years, attained their CD titles and performed well in obedience circles. The Causeys like to think that they give newcomers to the breed encouragement and help when necessary, which is probably why their daughter Patti has been involved in showing their dogs all along.

At the present time the kennel consists of seven dogs. Their two most outstanding dogs over the years have been Ch. Arbo's Big Red Snowbear and Ch. Arbo's Foxy Lady. Tessa, their original Siberian is now thirteen years old and has obtained her obedience title. All of the dogs are owner-handled, mostly by daughter Patti. Most all of the dogs have been used extensively in 4-H programs, and their Arbo's Meliska finished eighth in the state 4-H obedience competition in 1981.

Ch. Arbo's Big Red Snowbear pictured finishing for his championship with a major win at a 1984 show. Bred and owned by Robert, Arlene and Patti Causey, Arbo Siberians, Decatur, IL; and handled by Patti.

GROUP
PLACING
CHENANGO VALLEY
KENNEL CLUB
1980
ASHBEY

Ch. Sunset Hills Jo Jo Starbuck, owned by Dick and Gerry Dalakian of Flemington, NJ. Jo Jo's sire was Ch. Innisfree's O'Dwyer, CD, ex Ch. Sunset Hill's Beau-Phunsilady.

Gerick

Gerick Siberians came into being in 1973, the property and kennel operation of Dick and Gerry Dalakian of Flemington, New Jersey. The Dalakians decided to get into dogs, and they had to decide which categories they wished to pursue. At that time they could not both race and show, so they decided on showing with a little obedience work thrown in as well.

Dick is president of the Working Dog Education Fund that drafted and lobbied for New Jersey's Bill A1509, which legalized dog racing and other activities that had been outlawed in the state. He is also president of the Garden State Siberian Husky Club and is on the finance committee of the parent club. Gerry is also on the Board of the Delaware Water Gap Kennel Club. She and Dick also judge at match shows.

They have finished 12 champions, some of which they have bred or co-bred with more on the way. Some of the most important dogs are AmCan Ch.

Innisfree's Ms. Cinnar, Boshoi's Canadiana Ne Gerick, Gerick's Gypsy Fantasy, and Bo-Gerick's Top of the Line; Am Ch. Twindolphs' Gypsy of Gerick, Dudley's Sir Vartan of Gerick, Sunset Hills Jo Jo

Black Oaks

Don Young started his Black Oak Huskies operation in 1974 at Dayton, Tennessee. Like so many others, he started out with a Husky as a pet. But after working with Max Parris, a

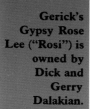

Gerick's Gypsy Rose Lee ("Rosi") is owned by Dick and Gerry Dalakian.

Starbuck, Gerick's Candi's Dandy, and Gypsy in Daskys. There are also Can Ch. Anikitas Kymetta of Gerick, Boshoi's Josi Ne Vartan and Boshoi's Limited Edition. Gerick's Taurajack, CD, is moving up.

successful animal trainer, it was soon apparent that obedience work was not for his dog. Max suggested that the show ring and a trip to see handler Houston Clark would be in order.

Don then began breeding on a limited basis, and it took about five years to obtain the type of animal that Don felt was a good representation of the breed Standard.

Ch. Black Oak's Beau Jacque was Don's first homebred champion and Group winner.

Beau Bree, and Winter Breeze, CDX.

Shihoka

The Shihoka Kennels started in 1974 in Colorado, and later moved to Ogden, Utah, after sojourns in Missouri, Nevada, and Texas! Like so many others, Rich and Jan Walker

AmCan Ch. Black Oak's Crescendo, AmCan CD, was bred by Black Oaks and is co-owned by S. Ward and D. and B. Young, Dayton, TN. He is winning the Working Group at a 1984 show under Marie Moore.

Jacque has now produced several champions.

Another of Don's outstanding dogs is Ch. Black Oak's Crescendo, AmCan Ch.; he is a Group winner and a multi-group placer as well. Some of the racing and/or obedience dogs are Ch. Black Oak's Winter Stormwatch,

bought their first Siberian as a pet. But when their "pet" developed some promising show qualities, they ventured into the show and obedience rings.

This first Siberian was their Ch. King of the Rockies, who is a multiple working Group winner and a sire of champions.

Ch. King of the Rockies, a multi-Group winner, is owned by Rich and Jan Walker of Shihoka Siberians, Ogden, UT.

He was followed by Ch. Rockies Rhett Butler, CD, and Ch. Shihoka's Ozark Singer.

Their kennel consists of five dogs, all of which have been owner-handled to their championship. The Walkers are members of the Siberian Club of America.

Sakonnet

In 1974, Leroy and Leslie Simons started their Sakonnet Kennels with a Siberian of questionable ancestry. However, he qualified for an ILP number and was trained in obedience (through some Utility, but only received his CD). C-Lee's Chimosa Scoundrel, CD, is now more than 12½ years old.

As Leslie wrote in her letter to me, "obedience school and your book came soon after" the arrival of Scoundrel in 1974, and Sakonnet was established. They were encouraged, as she puts it, by my book and certain members of the Siberian Husky Club of Greater Oklahoma, of which they became members. They also belong to the Metropolitan Dallas club. Soon after Scoundrel's arrival, the search for the "perfect" Siberian began. Marie Wamser's AmCanBda Ch. Fra-Mar's Soan Diavol was the dog they fell in love with, and by

1976 they were led to the Eumor Kennels in Long Island by Eumor's Nakia.

In 1978, the move was made from Texas to their present Iowa location, and in early 1982, three more Sibs entered their lives: Scoqui Sakonnet's Osota, Woniya, and Cante Ista. In 1985, their Sno-mate Sakonnet's Tecihila arrived.

Sakonnet is an Indian word meaning "a place to get away from it all," and all the dogs have Indian names. The Simonses are members of local clubs, the parent club, and the International SHC.

Luna del Norte

Dave and Penny Schultz of Espanola, New Mexico, started their Luna del Norte Kennel in 1974 with one dog. But shortly afterward they were introduced to the racing scene and it changed the program right away. They have been hooked ever since!

Their Luna del Norte's Pine Cone and Foxhaunt's Smokie Sipapu, CDX, have both sired ten racing dogs each, and two out of each of these litters have their SDX already.

Some of their other outstanding racing dogs are

Ch. Alkas'Iber Tokomac Tycho, bred by George and Ann Cook and owned by Stephen Serafin. He is winning at a 1983 show.

TJS Easy Nites, SDX, and Song to Orion, SDX, both with the Luna del Norte prefix. Coming along are Orphan Annie, Pow Wow, Spirit of Togo, Tekila Sunrise, and J. Lone Wolf.

During their racing careers, the dogs have won the sled dog class at the 1980 National Specialty in Olympia, Washington and at the Rocky Mountain Specialty in Denver, to name just a few. The dogs live outdoors at Luna del Norte so, as the Schultzes say, "they can run around, dig holes, chew on trees, and just be Siberians."

Kayak

Kayak is the name Richard and Elizabeth McClure of Milford, Michigan, chose as their kennel prefix in 1974. Actually it didn't *start* as a kennel—Dick received a Siberian Husky in exchange for his services as a lawyer when he drew up a will for a client. He was then encouraged to take the puppy to a match show and from there, they were hooked on both obedience and showing.

In the years that followed, there have been a succession of dogs including Ch. Kam-E-Lots Masterpiece, Ch. Bundas

Eumor's Nakia, owned by Leroy and Leslie Simons, Sakonnet Kennels in Leighton, IA. The sire was Eumor's Tuktu ex Ch. Eumor's Nootka.

Top: U-CD Kayak's Magic Man, AmCan CD title holder, shown taking first in Novice A in Canada at the Centennial Dog Obedience Club under Peter Kirk. Breeder-owners, Richard and Elizabeth McClure, Kayak Kennels, Milford, MI. Dick handling. "Zeke" scored consistently in the 1980s and qualified for the Detroit/Windsor Dog Obedience Club "World Series" Tournament. *Bottom:* Kayak's Good Mornin' Starshine winning at a 1984 show. Dick and Beth McClure, owners; Beth handling.

*Opposite:
Silver
Shadow of
Valleynorth,
CD,
Haclund,
Amaroq
Kennels,
Moorhead,
MN. Steve
Breyer photo.*

Pisces, U-CD Cheyenne of the Stalking Moon, AmCan CD, U-CD Kayak's Magic Man, AmCan CD, Ch. Snoking's Snowdrift, and Kayak's Good Mornin' Starshine.

Both Dick and Beth McClure are active in showing the dogs, and they consider the breed versatile and excellent with children. Their four-and-a-half-year-old son will attest to that. Few Husky owners will deny that the breed is among the most reliable with children.

Amaroq

Amaroq, which means the Spirit of the Wolf, is the kennel name of Roger and Margaret Haglund of Moorhead, Minnesota. They started in 1974 and since then, Siberians have become a way of life for their family. Margaret does some showing, assists with race training, and in general enjoys the dogs. Their main interests are sledding and obedience, though two of their dogs have earned points in the conformation classes. Son David started racing a three-dog team in 1984, when he was just 12 years old. In 1985, he won the North Star Sled Dog Club Season Point Championship in the three-dog amateur class.

The Haglund's first dog was a puppy acquired from Frosty Aire Kennels named Wind Chill. Most of their dogs over the years have been acquired from other breeders involved in racing competition (such as the Norrises, the Brockmans, and Al and Ann Stead). While their Silver Shadow of Valleynorth has his American and Canadian CD titles, they are also very proud of their homebred Amaroq's Snow Speeder, a CD and SD dog. He has won awards in racing, weight pulling, and obedience; in his first year at weight pulling, he was ISDRA Region seven champion in the under-50-pound class. In 1984 he got his CD and in 1985 he became one of the first Siberians in the country to earn the new SD or Sled Dog degree from the Siberian Husky Club of America.

The Haglunds have received the Chilkoot Trophy for a best all-Siberian team in Minnesota and, in 1985, Shadow earned the Combination Award for racing and obedience from the International Siberian Kennel Club.

Arlington

Since 1974, when Sylvia Roselli started her Arlington Kennels in Staten Island, New York, she has bred every two or three years. She considers it a small kennel, with four of her ten dogs show quality. They are Ch. Arlington's Amber Ice, Arlington's Always On My Mind, Ch. Dejay Nugget of Arlington, and Chanooka's of Arlington, CD. Chanooka is Sylvia's only obedience dog; her husband enjoys racing dogs while she prefers conformation and obedience.

The Roselli's foundation stems from Ft. Salonga

Sylvia Roselli's "Tonka" winning at a 1984 show.

breeding and is based on Baltic lines. It is Sylvia's ultimate desire to breed only the best dogs which excel at obedience and are structurally correct according to breed standards.

Princess Pines

Jerry and Arden LeVasseur started the Princess Pines Kennel of racing dogs in 1975 in Madison, Connecticut, when Jerry purchased a male Siberian and his neighbor bought a female. They added their own female when they joined the Connecticut Valley Siberian Husky Club and watched their first race. They ran in the next race and have been winning locally ever since!

Over the succeeding years the LeVasseurs have had a top six-dog team, winning at the Saranac races in 1985 and 1986, the New England Sled Dog Club six-dog championship in 1986, and Top Siberian Team. While their love is really racing, their dogs have also been active in obedience.

Some of their outstanding dogs are Igloo Pak's Snow Bandit; their lead dog, Igloo

Paks Urich; Princess Pines Nadia, also a lead dog; Princess Pines Hooker; Tzgahns Dan; and Krislands Black Pepper. All but Hooker have been SEPP evaluated, with Bandit and Nadia being two of the best.

The Princess Pines Kennels maintains about 16 dogs, from which Jerry says he would love to have a top all-Siberian racing team to further the purposes of SEPP.

Scoqui

Scott Quirin had owned Siberians since the late 1960s. When he married Gwynn they decided to establish the Scoqui Kennels in Duluth, Minnesota. This was in 1975.

They purchased the best possible dogs they could find.

Their bitches were from the Fra-Mar and EuMor lines and it is with outcrosses to Innisfree that they base their breeding program.

To date, their most outstanding dog is their bitch, AmCan Ch. Scoqui's Amber, a multiple Group placer and Top Winning Bitch in the nation in 1980 although shown only ten times during that year.

Scott and Gwynn consider Scoqui a small hobby kennel and enjoy showing the dogs themselves. Since the inauguration of their kennel, they have bred only eight litters, and to date have not gone in for racing or obedience.

Turick/Winslow

Carol Kaiser of the Turick Kennels and Leonard Bain of

Jerry LeVasseur's Igloo Pak's Snow Bandit, rated superior/excellent in a SEPP trial. Jerry's Princess Pines Kennel is located in Madison, CT.

Top: Ch. Talocon's Arctic Timbre, Group-placing son of Ch. Talocon's Arctic Echo, owner-handled and bred by John and Gail O'Connell. *Bottom:* Ch. Sodiax Chonya, owned by Carolyn and Eli Pietrack of Florida. Bred by the Sodiax Kennels.

Top: AmCan Ch. Arcticlight's Silver Shadrin, AmCan CD, bred and owned by Eric and Nancy Van Loo of Ontario, Canada. This multi-Best in Show winner was Top Siberian Husky in Canada in 1982 and No. 6 in the Working Group. He is a sire of champions in Canada, USA, Europe and Australia. To date, this is the only Siberian Husky to win the Ward Young Award for combined show, obedience, and racing accomplishments. *Bottom:* Ch. Talocon's Arctic Flash, winning a 3-point major in 1977 as Best of Winners at the Putnam KC. Owners, John and Gail O'Connell of Hauppauge, NY. The sire was Ch. Corrak of Tawny Hill ex Weydigs Angelique.

BEST OF WINNERS

Top: "Keachi" owned by Verla McFayden of Westminster, CA, photographed in 1979 at Verla's NeeChee Kennels. *Bottom:* Fra-Mar's Cree of Scoqui, one of the last daughters of AmCanBda Ch. Fra-Mar's Soan Daivol, and foundation bitch of Scott and Gwynn Quirin's Scoqui Kennels in Duluth, MN. She is also a producer of champions.

the Winslow prefix joined forces and now maintain a kennel facility for their racing and show dogs in Acworth, New Hampshire. The kennel now consists of thirty Siberian Huskies which are winning in the rings and excelling in racing competitions. They have won many Team trophies with their dogs.

Nee Chee

Verla McFayden's Nee Chee Kennels are located in Westminster, California. She considers her operation a small and very slow growing kennel. Her chief desire is to breed and exhibit sound dogs. Only now is she beginning to show her "bred-bys." Their sire is her undefeated, for eight years straight, weight-pulling dog (in under 65 pounds). Her chief dog now is Nee Chee's Wind Walker of Poli, a grandson of one of the Top Ten Siberians during the 1970s.

Meja

Melanie and Jim Babb live in Jamestown, North Carolina, where they maintain the Meja

Ch. Sunset Hill's Indiana Jones finished for championship at 18 months of age with a 5-point and a 4-point major. The sire was Ch. Karnovanda's Sasha Grozyni ex Gerick's Stardust of Sno-Sky. Owned and handled by James Babb, Jamestown, NC.

Kennels with six of their own dogs plus those of Jim's clients. Jim is a professional handler of several breeds, and there is no doubt that his personal choice for his own line is the Siberian Husky. The Babbs have been in dogs since 1976; they have run their own dogs in some big races and have taken some of their dogs through obedience training.

Some of their top dogs are Ch. Sunset Hills Indiana Jones,

showing, they do state their respect for those who put in the hard work to make the Siberian Husky an all-around working dog.

Kahmikhan
Relatively new to the breed (1977) Raymond and Irma Marshall are off to a good start with some excellent dogs that they show and train in obedience.

Some of their outstanding

Kimlan's Erica of Turick, handled by owner Carolyn Kaiser of Acworth, NH, winning Sled Dog Bitch Class under judge Estelle Cohen.

finished for his championship at 18 months of age; Ch. Innisfree's Standing Ovation, who has placed in the Group; and Ch. Indigo's Saroja Cinsation, a producer of champions. Their current activity is showing their homebred, Meja's Confederate Gray.

Although their priority is in

dogs are Ch. Blue Shadow Marshall, CD, Shadows Tara of Takupak, CD, Ch. Innisfree's Brandy O'Kahmikhan, and Kahmikhan's Lady in Red.

The Marshalls purchased their first Siberian in 1976, a gray and white with blue eyes. Thanks to the Chesapeake Siberian Husky Club members, they learned a lot and made their puppy a champion.

They also became involved in the local Canine Training Association, near their home in Crownsville, Maryland, and the Siberian Husky Club of America. Since then, they have served as newsletter editor, recording secretary, board member, Specialty chairman, and other positions, and have found their experiences very rewarding. Needless to say, they are devoted to the breed.

No Kita

The main objective at the No Kita Kennels of Bob and Pam Thomas in Glen Ellyn, Illinois, is to breed a "four-dimensional dog." That is to say, a dog that is a family pet, a superb running dog, a competitive obedience dog, and typey enough to win a championship in today's show ring.

The Thomases have owned Siberians since around 1977, and maintain a rather small

Kamikhan's Lady in Red, shown winning a 3-point major on the way to her championship. The sire was Ch. Takupak's Son of a Sinner ex Shadow's Tara of Takupak, CD. Owned by Raymond and Irma Marshall of the Kamikhan Kennels in Crownsville, MD. Lady is a granddaughter of Best in Show winner, AmCan Ch. Innisfree's Sierra Cinnar and Ch. Winsum's Yermak.

Innisfree's King Tut winning the Breed under Dr. Richard Greathouse. Owner-handled to this win by William Miranda, MD, Camelot Siberians.

kennel housing only six dogs. Misha's Earnest of Satan is co-owned by them with Dr. Rob and Susan Tucker of Massachusetts. He ran on their eight-dog team for years until the younger dogs took over. The Thomases consider him one of the best lead dogs they have ever seen. Now that he is in retirement, Bob intends to put a CD title on him, in addition to the Sled Dog Excellent title he has earned.

Kamchatka's Netske, CDX, is also a Canadian CD title holder and has Schutzhund AD as well. She is currently working on a UD and won the parent club High Scoring Open Dog title in 1984.

The Thomases also have a female and male who are sled dogs. Kuma, the male, finished for championship with three majors and has four Group placings; Nikko has a CD and championship title. "Echo," or Shiroi Kiba No Kita, is their first homebred, and he runs lead with his dad, Earnest, and has a leg on his CD.

Nezumi Shinju No Kita is promising, and great things are expected in Pearl's future.

Ikon-Tu

Marilyn Hayward of Santa Ana, California, gives credit for her success in racing to "Wolf," her lead dog, and to her husband Tom who lent his support, but still believes anyone who gets on a sled has to be a little crazy. In fact, he vowed years ago never to do it himself and that still holds true.

Since the Haywards formed their Ikon-Tu Kennels in 1977,

Marilyn has not only raced successfully, but has been active in many clubs and has held many positions in the fancy, from editor of the newsletter to president of the Siberian Husky Club of Southern California. She is also a member of the parent club, and is proud of her massive collection of Siberian memorabilia, which includes a copy of Togo's *Fireside Reflections,* autographed by none other than Leonhard Seppala.

Marilyn states that during her initial "time" between breed racing and starting to show she poured all her time and money into building her collection of books on the breed, which she claims might be equalled but not surpassed by anyone else's. She has over 2500 postcards alone.

Top: Ch. Sikisha's Kuma No Kita, CDX, winning under judge J. Robert Page. Owner-handler, Pam Thomas of Glen Ellyn, IL. *Bottom:* Camelot's Carbon Copy going Best of Winners at the 1984 Chaparral KC Show with owner William Miranda, MD, handling.

Top: Arahaz Bersue Nefertiti pictured winning on the way to championship under the late Winifred Heckmann. Bred by Rosemary Fischer, Beaver, PA. *Middle:* Ch. Zodiac's Cherry Bear, bred and owned by Leslie and Dan Haggard, Sodiax Kennels, Cocoa, FL. The sire was IntAmBdaCanMex Ch. Fra-Mar's Nikolai Diavol ex Monadnock's Red Bear of Zodiac. Cherry Bear is winning Best Opposite Sex at a SHCA Specialty Show. *Bottom:* Ch. Savdajare's Cass Raina, winning Bitch Class under Henry Stoecker at the Detroit KC. This was the first major for Tom Oelschlager, Kontoki Kennels, Finleyville, PA.

Top: Ch. Rockies Rhett Butler, CD, multi-Best of Breed winner and finished for his CD title at just 9 months of age. Owned by Rich and Jan Walker.
Bottom: FrostyAire's Wind Chill, winning a 3-point major under Larry Downey. Windy is being handled by his owner, Margaret Haglund, Amaroq Kennels, Moorhead, MN.

WINNERS MALE

FT. GARRY K.C. 76

"The doctor and Tut enjoyed a very successful show career, and Dr. Miranda began to look for the perfect mate for him. It took four years—until he found Innisfree's Dreamboat Annie."

Marilyn says that Zharkov's Little-Wolf of Japego, or Wolf, was her first Siberian and one of her dearest friends as well as a fantastic lead dog. Currently her blue-eyed black and white dog, Polrbays Ebony and Eyce and her multiple Best in Show and Specialty winner Ch. Kontokis Natural Sinner and Tokosh's West Coast Debut are taking her time and interest in the breed, at their Santa Ana home.

Camelot

Camelot Siberians in El Paso, Texas, had been a dream of William Miranda MD since 1978, when he received Innisfree's King Tut from Kathleen Kanzler. The doctor and Tut enjoyed a very successful show career, and Dr. Miranda began to look for the perfect mate for him. It took four years—until he found Innisfree's Dreamboat Annie. Two years after that he had his first litter.

By this time he had decided to name his kennel Camelot, because he envisioned a world full of kings and queens and things of beauty. As Dr. Miranda will tell you, nothing could be more beautiful to him than those puppies of his. So with the establishment of Camelot came his own reign of knights and ladies in the dog fancy. Most all of his dogs have points toward championship in both the US and Mexico.

In addition to Tut and Annie, some of his show dogs include Snowplow, Carbon Cop, and Lil Red Corvette, all bearing his Camelot prefix.

Tokosh

Diane M. Garcia of Canton, Ohio, started her Tokosh Kennels in 1978. She maintains about four dogs. When Diane found a stray Siberian in 1978, she also found the owners, so the dog had to be returned. But the experience was enough to make her go out immediately and get a Siberian of her own.

This was a female puppy not of show quality, and Diane was disappointed that it wasn't a winner. After reading everything she could about the breed Diane bought another, this one a bitch named Ch. Kontoki's Happy Go Lucky. She is Diane's pride and joy, and her kennel grew from there.

"Cybil" was followed by Ch. Aazar's Tiki and Ch. Innisfree's On the Road Again. But Diane's top thrill in the show ring was when she handled Cybil to her Best Opposite Sex win at the 1982 National Specialty Show. This was followed by Tiki's completion of her championship at the 1984 American Kennel Club Centennial Show.

Ch. On the Road Again as a puppy won four Best in Sweepstakes and finished his championship at 14 months of age. Diane then sold him to Richard and Jan MacWhade of Snoking, where he went on to win many Breeds, Groups, Specialties, and three Bests in Show.

Alka's Iber

Alka'sIber Kennels began in 1978 with George and Ann Mariah Cook, in Ashland, New Hampshire. They are both dedicated to the dual-purpose Siberian and race as well as show. They also have put obedience titles on a few dogs, their top two being Alka'sIber's Kid Kreko and Alka'sIber's Steely Dan who are primarily for racing.

The Cooks have run in spring races for over five years but in the last three years have taken up mid-distance racing, with courses of 60 to 100 miles in length. With their friend Pete Johnson, who drives

another team, they have run dogs that qualified for Sled Dog Classes at the Specialties.

Their top dogs are Alkas'Iber's Dig It Deeper, CD, who had a High in Trial at the Yankee Siberian Husky Specialty in 1984 and was twice high scorer at all-breed shows; Alka'Iber's Oh Canada, CD, Steely Dan; Kid Kreko, who was best of the sled dogs at the 1985 Greater New York Specialty; Tokoma's Aivilik Pacesetter, best sled dog (same show) 1984; Ch. Nordic's Ikkuma of Alkas'Iber; and Ch. Dama's Matanusko of Shonko. This is just a partial list of their team. They have won

Ch. Nordic's Ikkuma of Alkas'Iber. Bred by Bettie Woodson and owned by George and Ann Cook, Ashland, NH.

numerous awards for these dogs' accomplishments wherever they have competed.

Konik

Gary and Janet Cingel of East Hampton, Connecticut, started their Konik Kennels in 1978. They got their first Siberian as a pet in 1974. Shortly thereafter, they learned that dogs could be worked in harness at clinics in their area; this led to their getting a second dog, then a third, and they were soon "off and running" and have been active ever since.

They began to exhibit in the show ring in 1980 and have come up with remarkable Best in Show and Best in Group wins with both their brace and their teams, with Janet handling.

When their Sep of Temakiva retired from racing at the age of 12, they switched to mid-distance racing, and this is currently where they are concentrating.

Skyhope

While Ann Dussetschleger has been handling dogs for other people since 1975, it was

Alkas'Iber Steely Dan, bred and owned by George and Ann Cook. The sire was Can Ch. Channikkos Nordic Digger, Am CD, Can CDX, Can TD, ex Makushkin Nanatuk.

BEST OF OPPOSITE
NORTHWESTERN CONNECTICUT
1984 DAVE ASHBEY

Koniks Silver Belle, bred and owned by Janet and Gary Cingel of the Konik Kennels in East Hampton, CT.

in 1979 that she started her Skyhope Kennels with Bryant Dussetschleger in Spring, Texas.

Anne does enjoy showing though she says she doesn't have the patience for obedience; she feels it is too hot in Texas for racing the dogs. Some of their important dogs were Ch. Lobo's Misty Morn of Phunse, Skyhope's Black and Gold, Ch. Sunset Hills Morning Slory, Ch. Skyhope's Stardust Memory, and Ch. Kirkackas Susyn Skyhope, a Best in Show winner.

Kryska

James and Maureen Kent of Bow, New Hampshire, started their Kryska Kennels in 1979 and are active in racing and obedience with some conformation classes as well. Some of their outstanding racing and obedience dogs were from the Shjegge Mann line and with their own breeding as well. Shjegge Flame and Shjegge Sparks were early dogs and their Khipokate, Knoah, CD, and Kalypso, CD and SD, are some others; not to mention their Krystal Kluane of Denali,

CD, and Kamelot. More recently, they have been doing well with Kortar's Kranberry Captain, CD, and they credit the Andersons for their Krystal Kluane of Denali, CD. The Kents' hopes are also pinned on a dog they co-own with Judy Anderson, Varskitas Ms. Sheena Denali.

The Kents usually breed one litter a year but occasionally more in their effort to breed the ultimate in perfection for the racing and obedience field.

The Kents have a young man helping them in their kennel who has had Siberians all his life. His name is Brian Kenney and his Siberian is named Marco, Prince of Denali. Brian got this dog from Judi

Anderson and races him with his Alaskan Malamute and another Siberian Husky that he borrows from the Kents. Brian expects a female named Manooka from Kaptain breeding, and will eventually breed her to "Marco P."

Timberon

It wasn't until 1981 that Walter and Nancy Belknap of Alamogordo, New Mexico, purchased their first two Siberian Huskies. They had actually fallen in love with the breed when they saw a picture of newscaster Jessica Savitch and her black and white dog, but two years elapsed before they did something about acquiring one.

Then in 1981 they purchased Ch. Cinnaminson Copper Prestige and a black and white bitch, Revelry's Titania. Their first litter came in 1983 and produced Ch. Zatmieniya Tyene, a gray and white bitch who finished her championship with a Group First at the 1984 Lewis-Clark show. Tyene is owned by Marsha Folks.

The Belknaps recently had stationery made from a composite of three drawings of their dogs.

THE 1990s

Those kennels with their illustrious beginnings and accomplishments in the fancy can in no way be considered as a complete list of everyone who played a part. We can however say that, as we find ourselves in the start of the 1990s and look to the 21st century, we can only see continued progress in our breed.

Built on such a good foundation, we have managed to sustain the true purpose of the breed, have enhanced its good health with progress made in the field of nutrition, have brought it to even greater beauty with better grooming, and have managed to enjoy its sharing our lives without destroying the true purpose of its being.

It is the dedicated breeders of today who must carry on the propagation of this remarkable working dog, and it is our obligation to help others to learn and do right by the breed. With this in mind, we can face yet another century of greatness and achievement in our breed as we get closer to the turn of a new century. May the 21st century bring as much greatness to the breed as this one has!

Skyhope's Black Gold taking his first major under judge Elsa Marchesano. Bred and owned by Bryant and Anne Dussetschleger, Skyhope Siberians, Spring, TX.

Top: Ch. Black Oaks Beau-Jacque, Group-winning Husky bred and owned by Don Young, Dayton, TN; and handled by Don to this Breed win at a 1983 show under judge Lubin. *Bottom:* Ch. Talocon Nova's Taneha, finished with a Best of Breed from the classes over a Best in Show winner. Bred and handled by Gail O'Connell.

Top: Ch. Tawny Hill's Justin Thyme. Sire was Ch. Tawny Hill's Rashima Taro ex Tawny Hill's Jholi. Bred and owned by Adele M. Gray.
Bottom: AmCan Ch. Karnovanda's Gryphon, bred and owned by Judith Russell.

SOME BREED GREATS

Opposite: Best Worker at the eighth annual dog show of the North Shore KC held in Hamilton, MA, August 23, 1941. This is Wonalancet's Baldy of Alyeska. Owner-handler, Mrs. Milton J. Seeley of Chinook Kennels. This is the first time in history that a Siberian Husky won a Group!

In the world of sports there are always heroes who stand head and shoulders above the crowd and go down in history as great leaders in their field. While everyone who has owned a Siberian Husky can claim, to some degree, a part in bringing the breed to public attention, special praise is due to a few exceptional people who pioneered in the breed and were instrumental in the Siberian Husky's taking its rightful place in the world of dogs.

Here, then, are the success stories of some of the pinnacles in the breed, people who, with their devoted dogs, went all the way to fame and greatness in making their memorable contributions.

LEONHARD SEPPALA

Leonhard Seppala, born in Skyjaevoy, Norway, had the great pleasure of becoming a legend in his own time. He, perhaps more than any other single person, established the Siberian Husky breed in the minds of dog lovers and sled dog enthusiasts. More than a half century later, one of his heroic feats—his part in the Great Serum Run—lives on as a highlight in the history of the breed.

In 1914, Seppala emigrated to Alaska and got involved in sled dog racing. A ski champion in his native country, he had some experience driving freight teams in the gold fields of Alaska and transporting supplies to and from the railroads of Nome. His first Siberians, which he had acquired less than a year before he came to Alaska, presented a challenge to him. Seppala decided to race the dogs and to pit his skill against the racing heroes of the day.

These dogs were given to

Best Brace in Show at the 1960 Westminster KC Show was Mrs. Nicholas Demidoff's Ch. Monadnock's King and Ch. Monadnock's Pando. They are winning under judge W. Ross Proctor, Mrs. William Wood Prince presenting the trophy, with Mrs. Demidoff handling. William Brown photograph.

Seppala by his friend Jafet Lindeberg. Lindeberg had intended to hand them over to Roald Amundsen for his expedition to Alaska, and Seppala was training them for the trip. World War I cancelled plans for the expedition, and Seppala used the dogs to enter the 1914 Sweepstakes.

This first exposure was a complete disappointment to Seppala. He had to withdraw from the race after a series of mishaps, which included sore feet on several of the dogs, frostbite, blizzard conditions and an almost fatal accident along the trail. But in actuality, this bad start only served to fire his determination to return and

to succeed—and the following year he did! Victory was doubly sweet—his future wife, Constance, was Queen of the All-Alaska Sweepstakes. They were married and later had one child, a daughter, Sigrid.

Seppala went on to win the race again in 1916 and 1917, and he claimed that his chief reward was his pride in proving the stamina of the Siberian Huskies when he brought them across the finish line in such magnificent condition.

The All-Alaska Sweepstake victories were followed by the Borden Handicap, Borden Marathon, Ruby Derby, and the Yukon Dog Derby, to name a few. Breeding his own team dogs while he was winning was also a source of great pride to him. During this period of intensive breeding came Seppala's most famous dog, and one of the most famous dogs in the breed, Togo. With Togo in the lead, Seppala and his team of Huskies won races and did rescue work in the mine fields and logging camps, making a wonderful reputation for themselves.

But Seppala's chief service to his fellow man came about in 1925, during what has since been referred to as the Great Serum Run. A diphtheria epidemic broke out in Alaska and wiped out whites and Eskimos alike along its path.

Many drivers participated in that 655-mile relay run between Nenana and Nome, but it was Leonhard Seppala who had the longest and most arduous stretch of it, proving his strength, stamina, and driving ability.

Seppala was honored for this contribution by Senator Dill, who introduced the account of the Serum Run into the Congressional Record. Sportsman Lowell Thomas paid additional tribute to Seppala at the Alaskan Press Club Banquet in Anchorage in 1961 by saying, "...but justice was never done, as the eyes of the world were focused...the man who made the final dash

The 1957 parent club Specialty winners were Ch. Monadnock's Pando shown by breeder-owner Lorna Demidoff and Best Opposite win to Mrs. B.D. Hulen's Monadnock's Belka.

into Nome and had driven his dogs only a few miles...[while] none but Seppala mushed more than 55 miles."

A certificate was awarded by Governor Bone to Seppala for his heroic service in the Nome Diphtheria Crisis. It read: "In the Name of The Territory of Alaska, Grateful Recognition and Appreciative Acknowledgment are Hereby Given to the Self-sacrificing Service Rendered by Leonhard Seppala in response to humanity's call in speeding relief by dog team to the diphtheria sufferers at Nome during the epidemic in January-February, 1925. His prompt performance of duty under severe climatic conditions and hardships stamped him as a true Alaskan and will ever be remembered by his fellow-countrymen. Given under my hand and the Seal of the Territory of Alaska, in Juneau, the Capital, this Fourth day of March, in the year of Our Lord one thousand nine hundred twenty five. Scott C. Bone, Governor."

In 1927, Seppala was invited to compete in the sled dog races in New Hampshire. He not only competed but broke all records in the New Hampshire

Right: Ch. Innisfree's El Ferro, important stud dog in the early 1960s at Kathleen Kanzler's kennels. *Opposite:* Ch. Doonauk Ivanova's Tzarina winning the breed at a Valley Forge KC show in the 1960s under judge Ackland. Ken Golden handled for owner Mrs. MacVetterlein.

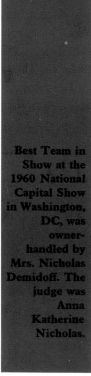

Best Team in Show at the 1960 National Capital Show in Washington, DC, was owner-handled by Mrs. Nicholas Demidoff. The judge was Anna Katherine Nicholas.

and Canada events while doing it! Seppala did much in those early days to endear the Siberian Husky breed to all, and he helped Huskies gain future recognition with the American Kennel Club. Important pedigrees still bear traces of the names of the dogs brought to the New England scene in the late 1920s.

Seppala retired to Seattle, Washington, in 1948, and lived there until his death from a cerebral hemmorhage on January 28, 1967. The true character of this great man can best be captured in his own words. When asked what he considered to be his greatest achievement, he did not recall the prize money he won or the speed records he had set or even the deeds he had done; he replied simply that his greatest satisfaction was in the good influence he had had toward the better treatment of sled dogs in Alaska!

Small wonder his name has become synonymous with greatness and the breed!

TOGO—MOST REMARKABLE DOG

There are many memorable and remarkable stories to be told about man's uncanny relationships with dogs. If you are interested in the Northern breeds, and Siberian Huskies in particular, the story of Togo is

Foxhaunt's Tovarisch, CD, winning the Breed at the 1962 Specialty Show held by the SHCA on December 1 of that year in Philadelphia. John W. Cross, Jr., was the judge, owner-handler Mrs. A. Korbonski. Shafer photographed this early dual-purpose dog who was a credit to the breed.

one that must be told—the story of Togo and the remarkable Leonhard Seppala.

Togo's parents came to Seppala's kennel from Siberia. His dam, Dolly, though gentle, was an independent bitch which took a special delight in Suggen, the lead dog on Seppala's team. Both dogs had come from the Kolyma River region of Siberia. It was Suggen who saved Seppala's life on the 400-mile grueling trail in the 1914 All-Alaska Sweepstakes race. There was a raging blizzard and they strayed off the path and came within twenty feet of a precipice which dropped down 200 feet. Seppala just managed to stop the team in time, and it was Suggen who, sensing the danger, obeyed his commands and successfully pivoted the team around to a reverse position and headed back up the mountain once again.

From this skilled, intelligent sire and gentle dam came Togo. Born in Little Creek, Alaska, he was originally the property of Victor Anderson, though bred and raised by Seppala and his wife. An Englishman named Fox Ramsey had first imported Siberians to Alaska, and these dogs represented the early beginning of the breed there. Togo was an "only child" and

A 1966 double header for Kathleen Kanzler and her Innisfree Kennels at the Ladies' Dog Club Show. Ch. Innisfree's Oomachuk winning a 5-point major, and Ch. Innisfree's Barbarossa Best of Winners for a 5-point major under Dr. A.A. Mitten.

was spoiled because of it. He was small and not very attractive; only Constance Seppala could handle him. When he was six months old Anderson gave him to Mrs. Seppala for her trouble. Like other arbitrary adolescents, Togo ran away from home a few times, only to be brought back again by the Seppalas, before he finally made up his mind to stay with them. He teased the other dogs by snapping at their heels and biting their ears and, in general, was a nuisance to Seppala.

But the day was to come when it was more important to Togo to impress than to distress Leonhard Seppala. It happened one November day when Leonhard headed off with a friend and a team for Dime Creek. Togo wanted to go along and had to jump a seven-foot fence to do it. His foot was badly injured when it caught in the fence; a kennel man had to cut him free, but he took out across the snow to follow Seppala in spite of it.

After running all night to catch up with Seppala and his group, he spotted them the next morning. At first the two men thought it was a fox bearing down on them, but as Togo came up to the team and bit the ear of the lead dog, Seppala knew it was Togo! Seppala was impressed with the fortitude of the dog from that moment on, and a close relationship which was to last a lifetime was spawned. Togo ran free with the team for a while before Seppala took out an extra harness and started him out close to the wheel.

Togo's spirit made for a quick promotion; he was soon up near the lead dog, and when they reached their destination at the

"Like other arbitrary adolescents, Togo ran away from home a few times, only to be brought back again by the Seppalas, before he finally made up his mind to stay with them."

"Seppala and Togo were to share many exciting times together, both racing and with their miraculous rescue work against amazing odds."

end of the day's run, he was in the lead with old Russky. Seppala realized that Togo, like his father before him, was a born lead dog. From then on he was Seppala's favorite. How could he be denied, an eight-month-old puppy running 75 miles his first day in harness and pulling in ahead of the team! Togo's respect for his master earned him the reputation of being a "one-man dog."

In the year that followed, Seppala had Togo out on the trails training. All during the winter of 1919 they crossed the peninsula a total of six times. Togo was stubborn at times, with a mind of his own, but Seppala realized he possessed all the attributes of the perfect lead dog—a lead dog he had been trying to breed for a long time.

Seppala was out on the trail when the scheduled April Borden Race was to be run, and he had very much wanted to run against Fred Ayer's team. He thought they would miss competing, but the people of Nome demanded that the Kennel Club invite Seppala to run once he returned. Seppala accepted with great pleasure, and over Fred Ayer's objections.

The race was run in May, when it was warm, which put Seppala's dogs at a disadvantage. But they ploughed ahead and even passed Fort Davis, where they were missed by the people, and who therefore thought they had lost the race. But they crossed the finish line in Nome, breaking the speed record by 55 seconds. Seppala's time was 26 miles in one hour, 50 minutes, 25 seconds, a record which stood for many years in Alaska, Canada, and the United States. It also proved Seppala's firm belief that Siberian Huskies could run equally as fast as any other dog (Siberians at that time were mostly believed to be at their best only on long, steady hauls).

Seppala and Togo were to share many exciting times together, both racing and with their miraculous rescue work against amazing odds. In 1921, Major John Gotwals, Chief Engineer of the Alaska Road Commission, hired Seppala to proceed from Nome to Nenana. Many exciting experiences occurred during this 400-mile adventure, including Togo's participation in a relay race to save the life of a banker. By the end of that year Seppala and Togo had logged nearly 8000 miles. This feat helped Togo earn another of his many deserved titles—the most traveled dog in the world!

In 1923, Togo and Seppala won the Borden Race again, beating the nearest competitor by 12 minutes, and made several trips over the Seward Peninsula with Seppala's friend, Roald Amundsen. In 1924 they traveled to Nenana once again, which kept them in good training condition for the most important event in their lifetime—the 1925 Great Serum

Run.

Seppala was chosen to carry the serum for the terrible epidemic in the area. He got off with a rousing send-off with his lead dogs, Togo and Scotty, and 18 other Siberian Huskies, on one of the most heroic and difficult missions in Alaskan history. Along the trail he would leave some of the dogs behind to be cared for by the villagers and readied for the return trip.

Originally, Seppala had been asked to run the whole distance with the serum, but the epidemic was spreading so rapidly that it called for a relay race, and when Seppala reached Golofnin he learned his job was done. They had covered about 96 miles all told, more distance than any other team, and returned home tired but with the satisfaction of a job well done.

This event marked Togo's last long run. He was used only sparingly thereafter, and in 1927 he was presented to Elizabeth Ricker (Nansen) to spend his last years at her home in Poland Springs, Maine. In a letter to Mrs. Ricker dated February 15, 1927, from Frank Dufresne of Fairbanks, Alaska, this event is commemorated as follows:

"...I wonder if you realize what a beautiful gift you have received. Up here in Alaska

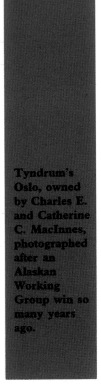

Tyndrum's Oslo, owned by Charles E. and Catherine C. MacInnes, photographed after an Alaskan Working Group win so many years ago.

Ch. Monadnock's King, a Best in Show-winning Siberian Husky from the kennels of Lorna Demidoff in Fitzwilliam, NH. This win under Mrs. Edward Renner.

where sentiment gives way to cold reality we think superlatively of Seppala and his wonder dog. They have been unseparably linked for the past ten years, and one does not speak of one without mention of the other."

"We in Alaska envy you the gift of this dog, 'Togo,' but find consolation in knowing the appreciation he will receive in your hands, and of the very high esteem in which Leonhard must have held you to part with his gritty little pal of the trails. I congratulate you on your wonderful gift of the greatest little racing leader in the history of Alaskan

Sweepstakes."

This is just a brief revelation of the wonderful life of Togo and his feats of bravery. More about him appears in a delightful book titled *Togo's Fireside Reflections*, by Elizabeth M. Ricker, published in 1928. But most of Togo's life is recorded on the pages of the history books on the great state of Alaska!

ARTHUR TREADWELL WALDEN AND CHINOOK

Arthur Treadwell Walden left his home in New Hampshire and headed for the Alaskan gold fields in 1896. He was not as caught up in the idea of striking it rich as he was with the idea of what could be accomplished by using the native dogs and sleds for freighting purposes. His endeavors along these lines won him renown of one of Alaska's best-known dogpunchers.

In later years he was to gain additional fame with a book he wrote entitled *A Dog Puncher on the Yukon*, the story of the freight dogs and their uses in Alaska. Later still, he handled the training and the conditioning of the dogs for Admiral Byrd's expeditions; the training was carried on at his Chinook Kennels in Wonalancet, New Hampshire. Walden firmly believed that a dog team could go farther "on its own food" than any other team in the world and did much to prove his belief.

Walden's most famous dog was Chinook, after whom he named his famous kennel; it still carries that name today. Walden said of his dog, "One of the best dogs I ever owned was Chinook, a large, half-bred MacKenzie River Husky. I got him in Dawson in 1898. The man who owned him had used him as a one-man's dog. He wouldn't sell him for money, but I traded him for three sacks of flour, worth sixty dollars a

A repeat win for both the Best of Breed and Best of Opposite from the 1957 parent club Specialty were Mrs. Demidoff's Ch. Monadnock's Pando and Mrs. B. Hulen's Ch. Monadnock Belka.

SHEBOYGAN
KENNEL CLUB
APR. 29,1962
BEST
WORKING
JUDGE: MR. FRANK FOSTER
DAVIS

sack, and two sacks of rolled oats, making two hundred dollars in all. He claimed that Chinook could start a heavier load than any other dog in the Yukon. He cried when he left, carrying his food." Walden rejoiced at his good fortune!

MILTON AND EVA "SHORT" SEELEY

Short Seeley deserves her title of Matriarch of the Breed. The Seeleys eventually purchased the Chinook Kennels from Arthur Walden and established the great interest in sled dogs and sled dog racing which thrives today. For this, Siberian Husky devotees shall be eternally grateful.

Eva Brunell Seeley, known today as Short Seeley, was born and brought up in Worcester, Massachusetts, and prepared herself for a teaching career. In 1922 she was Director of Sports at the Bancroft School in Worcester. At Bancroft she met Milton Seeley, also on the school staff and a brilliant chemist, and they were married in May 1924. It was while on their honeymoon, mountain climbing in New England, that they first met Arthur Walden and his dog team. They ordered a son of Chinook before their visit had ended and they knew they were hooked on the breed.

Opposite: Ch. Little Joe of North Wind, owned by Doris Knorr, North Wind Kennels, winning at the 1962 Sheboygan KC under Frank Foster Davis. *Bottom:* From the early 1950s: Louis Hall, judge, over Ch. Otchi of Monadnock, CD and Aleka's Czarina.

Opposite: A notable Best Working Brace from the 1950s. These are Carol and Andrew Maxfield's Huskies winning at the International KC in Chicago under famous dog man Alva Rosenberg.

For reasons relating to Mr. Seeley's health, in 1928 they moved to Wonalancet, where there was great activity going on at the Chinook Kennels. Intensive training was underway for dogs which were to accompany Admiral Byrd's expedition.

Milton Seeley instantly saw the need for a substantial diet for dogs which would be expected to endure the hardships of the frozen North, and he brought all his knowledge of chemistry to bear in order to perfect such a diet for them. While his formula was never patented, it was undeniably the basis for some of our best commercial dog foods today.

Arthur Walden, an instrumental breeder and trainer of dogs for the polar expeditions, went along with Byrd on one of the expeditions and took his famous husky, Chinook, with him. Unfortunately, Chinook did not return. Short and Milton went into partnership with Walden before he left and kept the inn and the kennel running while he was in Antarctica. It was during their first winter at the Chinook Kennels that Short learned to drive a team, and her interest in racing and sled dogs became firmly established in her heart.

When the Seeleys first arrived at Chinook, a Siberian Husky bitch named Toto caught their attention. They leased Toto, a daughter of Leonhard Seppala's lead dog, Togo, which had been left with Walter Channing, and they bred her to Moseley Taylor's blue-eyed black and white lead dog, Tuck. Toto had one lone female puppy, which the Seeleys named Tanta of Alyeska. They also managed to get her accepted as a trial bitch by the American Kennel Club. At her first dog show in Manchester, New Hampshire, she won Best of Breed over the nine males competing!

When Arthur Walden returned from the Byrd expedition, he sold his share of the kennel to the Seeleys. They built new kennels on the site and in 1932 moved into what was intended to be the museum and trophy building when their house burned down.

Tanta was bred to a male named Duke which had come from Seppala's bloodlines in Alaska; one of the litter, Togo of Alyeska, was purchased along with six others by Moseley Taylor to be driven as a team by his wife, Lorna. Lorna Demidoff, driver and trainer, is another of the great people in the breed, and she drove her pleasure teams well into the 1980s.

At least three more expeditions were made by Admiral Byrd, with the dogs all being trained at Chinook Kennels, and it was during this time that the friendship between Admiral Byrd and the Seeleys developed. Also during this time the Seeleys' interest broadened to include the Alaskan Malamute, and it was largely through their efforts that this breed became recognized and registered by the American Kennel Club. In 1932 Short drove a team of Malamutes in the Olympics at Lake Placid, New York, and brought additional fame to the breed. A second Chinook team was driven by Norman Vaughan and included their Tanta of Alyeska as a member of that top team.

With World War II raging in 1942, army dogs were being assembled at the kennel. Dogs for search and rescue units used in the war were trained at Chinook. Many dogs were offered by members of the New England Sled Dog Club drivers, and several went off to Camp Rimini in Montana for training.

Milton and Short were very active with the New England Sled Dog Club; Short served the club as secretary for many years, while Milton served as president and as a member of the executive committee. Eventually, both were made life-long honorary members.

During their time as active officers and racing participants with the group, their interest extended to include the children of the members of the club, and they were successful in establishing a Junior Sled Dog Club. This juvenile extension of the parent club is still most active today, with as many as 60 teams competing at their events.

In 1937, Short started to organize a breed club and to set the standard for the breed. She asked Dean Jackson to help her set up an organizational meeting to be held on April 19, 1938, in Cambridge, Massachusetts, to do just that.

Winner at the 1958 Catonsville, MD, KC Show was Rear Admiral and Mrs. Robert J. Foley's dog, photographed by William Brown.

At this meeting, where a constitution and by-laws were laid down, as was a Standard, the list of those present included Lorna Demidoff, Richard Moulton, Millie Remick, Dean Jackson (officiating), and, of course, Short Seeley. Short served the club in just about every capacity and in 1963 was given a life membership.

Milton Seeley died in 1944, but Short never had any doubt in her mind about maintaining the kennel herself; she continued to do so with help from the young people in the area who helped make the Chinook Kennels a popular tourist attraction for dog lovers from all over the world.

Short Seeley's interests extended beyond the dog world. For many years she was an active worker for the Republican Party on all levels, and she included congressmen, senators, governors and presidents among her personal friends.

In October, 1971, in the city of Philadelphia, a testimonial dinner was given in Short Seeley's honor to commemorate her 80th birthday and to pay tribute to her many accomplishments in the fancy. Some of the accomplishments mentioned in a "This Is Your Life, Short Seeley" pageant were: her initiation of the Siberian Husky and Alaskan Malamute Clubs, her formation of the New England Sled Dog Club, being a breeder-owner of the first Siberian Husky bitch to become a champion, being the only woman to be given a military award by President Eisenhower, and receiving the award from Admiral Richard Byrd as Chief Consultant for the Sledge Dog Division of Operation Deep Freeze.

An acknowledgment of this testimonial dinner and a list of these accomplishments were read into the Congressional Record on October 29, 1972, by the Honorable Norris Cotton of New Hampshire.

In December, 1985, Short Seeley passed away at the age of 94 at McKerley Health Care Center in Laconia, near her home in Wonalancet Village. Her obituary headline stated that she was a noted Republican and dog trainer. For years she was president of the Tamworth Republican Club, and upon her death former Republican Governor Meldrin Thomson said, "Not only the Party but the state as well has lost a great, constructive citizen."

The obituary also mentioned that Short co-authored *The Complete Alaskan Malamute* with Maxwell Riddle. Short will be missed, and will always remain a legend in the history of the Siberian Husky.

LORNA B. DEMIDOFF

Training her dogs to harness and driving her team were for many years the late Lorna Demidoff's greatest pleasure. Lorna was just 16 when her parents moved to Fitzwilliam, New Hampshire,

"In October, 1971, in the city of Philadelphia, a testimonial dinner was given in Short Seeley's honor to commemorate her 80th birthday and to pay tribute to her many accomplishments in the fancy."

On the left, the late, great Short Seeley at age 91 making a final appearance before her death in Concord, NH, in September 1981. On the right, Jean Fournier, SHCA president, doing a video tape interview with Short for the Specialty program.

and it was there that she had her first ride behind a team; she decided then and there that someday she would have her very own team.

Lorna married Moseley Taylor, publisher of the *Boston Globe,* a sportsman in his own right who had imported several racing Siberian Huskies from Alaska. Early in their marriage they lived in Massachusetts while the dogs were kept in Fitzwilliam. Lorna's kennel was established in 1931, and she took its name from the Monadnock Mountains. It was primarily a racing kennel for about 25 years, with Lorna racing in top competition. Roger Haines became their kennel manager and helped train the teams for racing; he drove the team in the 1932 Olympics Exhibition Race.

Lorna began showing in the conformation classes in the 1930s to have something to do with the dogs during the summer months, and she finished her first champion, Togo of Alyeska, in 1939. Togo was purchased from the Chinook Kennels and was a fine lead dog in the racing competition and racked up many victories at several of the New England Sled Dog Club races. Lorna's first homebred champion was Panda of Monadnock, finished in 1941. Other top racing and show dogs were Ch. Belka of Monadnock, Ch. Otchki of Monadnock, CD, all racing leaders, and Ch. Monadnock Norina, Ch. Monadnock Penelope and Ch. Monadnocks Zita, leaders of her pleasure teams.

In 1941, Lorna married Prince Nikolai Alexandrovitch Lopouchine-Demidoff, a

Russian nobleman who emigrated to the United States during the revolution in his country. Many champions and racing greats followed, since Lorna wanted them to excel in both fields, but just how many champions with the Monadnock name there were Lorna did not know, since she did not keep score. But it is safe to say she has won all the big important shows a couple of times over and has the silverware and ribbons to prove it!

She was also active as a judge of Siberian Huskies and several other breeds.

To commemorate her years of contribution to this breed for over 30 years, on the night of Friday, August 17, 1979 Lorna Demidoff was honored at a dinner following the Cheshire Kennel Club dog show where

Mrs. Lou Richardson's Best Brace in Show at a California show several years ago. Mr. Ferguson presenting the trophy in this Joan Ludwig photograph.

she had been invited to judge the Best in Show award. The event was held at the Winding Brook Lodge in Keene, New Hampshire, and was sponsored by the Yankee Siberian Husky Club, the first area Specialty Club to be formed in the breed in the United States.

More than 120 fanciers gathered for a tribute to this great lady, which included a commendation from Governor Hugh Gallen.

Those attending represented other greats in the breed over the years and included Phyllis Brayton, the president of the parent club; Bob Page, a past president; Carol Deeks; Short Seeley, Peggy Grant, a past Yankee club president and chairman of this event and moderator for the evening. Anna Mae Forsberg was a primary speaker, and Mrs. Ragnar Forsberg, founder of the Savdajaure Kennels and founding member of the Yankee Club, were also among the prominent guests. Others included John Holad, Stewart Cochrane, Millie Turner, Mrs. Nancy Riley, Rosemary Fischer, and the Dudleys, to name a few, with Judith

Two outstanding representatives of 2 of the top kennels in the USA during the 1950s and before. Bluie of Chinook and Mina of Monadnock. Photo by the famous dog photographer, Percy T. Jones.

Anderson handling the publicity. Also honored was Prince Nikolai Alexandrovitch Bouchine-Demidoff, a top sled dog driver in his own right, and co-founder of Lorna's Monadnock Kennels. The honor to Lorna was handled in a "This Is Your Life" format, with Peggy Grant narrating a tale of Lorna's 30-year contribution.

DR. ROLAND LOMBARD

The highly respected Dr. Roland Lombard is a veterinarian from Wayland, Massachusetts; he is also the world's leading sled dog driver of all time. He is a past founder of the Siberian Husky Club of America and his kennel name is Igloo-Pak, which means "House of the White Man" in Eskimo language.

Dr. Lombard was 14 years old when his interest in sled dog racing manifested itself. It was in Poland Springs, Maine, and the 1927 race featuring winning teams and drivers like Leonhard Seppala and Arthur Walden from New Hampshire who did so much to spur interest in the sport with teams from his famous Chinook

"The highly respected Dr. Roland Lombard is a veterinarian from Wayland, Massachusetts; he is also the world's leading sled dog driver of all time."

Kennels.

It was his tremendous interest in the sport that led Seppala and Mrs. Ricker to give him his first Siberian Huskies, named Paddy, Frosty and Arctic. This led to a five-dog team. His winning of a handicap race in Laconia, New Hampshire in the early 1930s produced a $1000 prize which started his education in veterinary medicine.

Dr. Lombard won trophies representing wins at Quebec City, Maniwaki, Ste. Agathe, Ottawa, and La Pas, to name a few, and he raced in competition with other great racing drivers, including Emile St. Goddard, Emile Martel, Charles Belford, Earle Brydges, Keith Bryar, Seppala, and others.

Dr. Lombard was an eight-time winner of the Rondy Races, having won this event in 1963, 1964, 1965, 1967, 1969, 1970, 1971 and 1974!

There is no denying that Dr. Lombard is the idol in the racing circles and set the pace for the sport. He is the "one to beat," the driver to watch, to emulate, to admire for both his driving skill and demeanor and for his remarkable workmanship on his sleds, which he made himself.

Louise Lombard is also greatly admired by the fancy for her quiet support and devotion to both the good doctor and the dogs. In 1973 she distinguished herself by winning second in the Women's Championship race, missing first place position by only 15 seconds. For many years she was active in the Alaskan Malamute Club.

The Story of Nellie

Nellie was Dr. Roland Lombard's remarkable lead dog, and she well deserves her place of honor in the Sled Dog Hall of Fame in Alaska.

Dr. Lombard purchased Nellie from George Attla in Alaska. The price was a record-breaker for the time: one thousand dollars! But as time was to prove, Nellie was worth every penny of it both on and off the racing trail. So highly did the Lombards value Nellie that the phrase "her gift is devotion" was often quoted when speaking of this dog.

Nellie lived over a dozen years, every one in devotion to her equally devoted owners. Her admirers extend far and wide, and when at the 1969 Anchorage races Nellie caught the flu and was pulled, "get well" cards found their way to the Lombard's lodgings at Orville Lakes, Alaska, addressed simply to "Nellie" at that address. At the last race at Tok that year, Dr. Lombard's lead dog tired and quit. She sat down at the starting line and refused to move. After valuable minutes of the race were lost, Dr. Lombard immediately substituted the recovered Nellie at the lead. Although nearly twelve years old at the time, Nellie knew what the doctor wanted and they took off down the trail!

"So highly did the Lombards value Nellie that the phrase 'her gift is devotion' was often quoted when speaking of this dog."

The famous Eva "Short" Seeley embracing a future brace at her Chinook Kennels in Wonalancet, NH, photographed by Judy Rosemarin.

SIBERIAN HUSKIES AROUND THE WORLD

"From the early 1930s until 1963 Don McFaul of Maniwaki, Quebec, was active in the breed."

EARLY CANADIAN KENNELS

By the 1930s Siberian Huskies had reached Canada. Harry Wheeler bought some of the original Alaskan Seppala dogs in 1932 and established his Gatineau Kennels in St. Jovite, Quebec. The kennel remained in operation until 1948. Shortly thereafter he sold out.

From the early 1930s until 1963 Don McFaul of Maniwaki, Quebec, was active in the breed. He bought some of the original Seppala stock which Seppala had been racing in New England in the late 1920s, and used Seppala as his kennel name. In the winter of 1963 he sold out the kennel; the dogs returned to Alaska with Earl and Natalie Norris, who bought them from him.

Based on the McFaul and Seppala breeding, the Malamak Kennels arrived on the scene in the 1940s. J. Malcolm McDougall's kennel was located at Ste. Agathe, Quebec. The kennel was still in existence in the early 1970s.

It was during the 1940s that Bunty Dunlop Goodreau, Elizabeth Ricker Nansen's daughter, established her Snow Ridge Kennels in Chelmsford, Ontario. Based on the early Seppala stock from three of his original kennels, her kennel remained active for many years.

Tony Landru began in the late 1940s with the White Water Lake Kennel in Ontario, and continued breeding until 1968. This kennel was formed on the McFaul, Seppala, and Gatineau lines. Also around this time were Eva Havlicek and her Shady Lane Kennels of Ontario.

Arcticlight
This kennel was founded in

1976 by Eric and Nancy Van Loo in Tottenham, Ontario; the first dogs were purchased from the Snowmist Kennels in the USA. One of these was the sire of the Top Siberian in Canada in 1982, and his name was AmCan Ch. Arcticlight's Silver Shadrin, who later earned his American and Canadian CD titles as well. To date, he is the only Siberian who was No. One dog in the country and also won the Ward Young Award, given each year for being top Siberian in the show ring, the obedience ring, and in sled dog racing.

Their foundation bitch was Ch. Rix's Gypsy of the Bastion, producer of many good working dogs and show dogs when combined with the Yeso Pac and Calivali bloodlines.

Their Arcticlight's Quincy is an International, Canadian, and Belgian Champion plus the 1985 Vice World Champion, and is owned by Mr. and Mrs. F. Lizin of Belgium. He was top Siberian in Belgium for 1985 as well. Arcticlight's Gypsy Sinner was best female in Belgium the same year.

Arcticlight Siberians are winning all over the world. A son of Shadrin in Australia won a Best in Show over 7000 dogs in 1985.

Nancy Van Loo was top woman driver in Ontario one year, but lack of time means the Van Loos only race for fun now. They have the only kennel

An impressive line-up of Canadian Siberian Huskies: Can Ch. Rix's Gypsy of the Bastion, foundation bitch of Arcticlight Kennels, with 2 of her daughters, AmCan Ch. Arcticlight's Snowmist Magic, owned by Snowmist Kennels and producer of over 7 champions; and CanBelDut Ch. Arcticlight's Gypsy Sinner, owned by F. Lizin in Belgium, where she was acclaimed Best Female in 1985. Rix's Gypsy is owned by Eric and Nancy Van Loo, Tottenham, Ontario, Canada.

SIBERIAN HUSKY CLUB GR. CLEVE. APRIL 19, 1980

POOLE

Mrs. Anderson believes the temperament of the Siberian Husky is of prime importance when considering a breeding program, and she breeds for quality, not quantity, at Racecrest."

in Canada to have bred five American champions that have their Canadian championships as well. They are, in addition to Shadrin, Sharina, Strawberry Cream, Snowmist Magic, and Snoking Stardust, all bearing the Arcticlight prefix.

Racecrest

Mrs. J.W. Anderson established her Racecrest Kennels in Ontario, in 1958. Her Ch. Racecrest's Bandit was her top stud dog and was active at the Canadian Kennel Club shows. Mrs. Anderson enjoys showing her dogs in Obedience; her bitch Shady Lane's Kolyma Princess has earned her Companion Dog title.

Mrs. Anderson believes the temperament of the Siberian Husky is of prime importance when considering a breeding program, and she breeds for quality, not quantity, at Racecrest.

Whelped in March, 1961, Bandit finished his Canadian Championship at 15 months of age, undefeated in the classes. He has three Group Placings as well. He was also Breed Leader in all-breed competition in Canada in 1962, and was handled for his owner by Lorna Jackson.

Other Canadian Kennels

Other Canadian Siberian Husky owners in Canada include the Jeffrey Braggs, Mr. Ian McDonald, Mrs. Robert Auslitz, Mr. J.M. McDougall, Mr. Robert Murray, and Mrs. Clare A. Vipond. All of these

people are members of the Siberian Husky Club of America, thereby helping to keep their interest in the breed alive in both their country and the United States. By the 1980s Brent and Kathy Thomas were active in Manitoba, as was Eric Van Loo in Ontario.

THE BREED IN ENGLAND

Through the combined efforts of Lt. Commander William Cracknell and Mr. Derrick C. Iverton, the Registrar of the Kennel Club in England, the Siberian Husky is now recognized as a breed in Great Britain. Early in 1969, when LCDR Cracknell was assigned as a naval liaison officer with the Ministry of Defense in England, his Siberian Husky, Yeso Pack's Tasha, won great admiration. She survived a lengthy quarantine (lengthy because of the rabies scare in Britain), but was released in July, 1968. The Kennel Club was initially going to register Tasha in the Husky category, but Cracknell and Mr. Iverton managed to establish the Siberian Husky as an individual breed, and Tasha became the first Siberian Husky registered in England.

Upon her release from quarantine, the Cracknells imported a mate for her. They imported Savdajaure's Samovar from the Forsberg's Kennels in the United States. While they showed only sparingly while in England, they entered many times and won many prizes.

AmCan Ch. Arcticlight's Strawberry Cream. Owned by R. and J. MacWhade of Ohio, she was bred by Eric and Nancy Van Loo. The sire was AmCan Ch. Boshoi's Grey Sinner ex AmCanBda Ch. Karnovanda's Sparklin' Delite.

They returned to the United States in the early 1970s with their original pair, but left in England the puppies from two litters from these dogs.

When the rabies scare abated in England and the quarantine was reduced to the usual six months, additional Siberian Huskies were imported into England. Peter Proffitt of Lancashire purchased two from Helge and Benedict Ingstad's kennels in Norway. They were named Togli and Killik of Brattali.

Don and Liz Leich returned to England from America in 1971 with their Doushka of Northwood and Ilya of Northwood. That same year they established their Forstal Kennels in Kent. The Leichs were the first English people to register a Siberian Husky kennel in the United Kingdom, and consider themselves "pioneers" in the breed there. They have won numerous awards and Best of Breed with Ilya in a rare breed class as well as awards in variety classes. Their puppy, Nanuska, is the only red and white Siberian Husky in England.

The Leichs attend obedience classes also, but in England "the retrieve" is included even in the beginners' classes, and so far they have gotten only one of their dogs to do this consistently. The Leichs also have a training cart for the dogs; like all other Siberian

Ch. and Gr. Ch. Karnovanda's Boris Groznyi sent to Brazil by breeder Judith Russell and pictured winning at a national show in 1983. Judge was José Machline, handler was Flavio Werneck for owner Oscar de Souza.

Husky enthusiasts in England, they are hoping that the law forbidding the working of a dog in harness will be repealed.

Part of the growing interest in the breed in England is due to the efforts of Mrs. Stella-Colling Mudge, president of the Husky Club of Great Britain, who has championed the breed for many years.

Mrs. Leich informs us that there are approximately 30 Siberian Huskies in England. They've come a long way since the first import in 1969 and the first registered litter of seven (three males, four females) born on May 30, 1971. Liz Leich is one of the leading proponents

of the breed at Forstal in Norfolk and is a member of the Siberian Husky Club of America.

In 1986, Siberians left the AV class and have breed classes of their own.

SIBERIAN HUSKIES IN FINLAND

The Siberian Husky first appeared in Finland in 1965, where Mrs. Kerttu Alm imported a puppy from Switzerland. Mrs. Alm's Lumimaan Kennel was established this same year with her Fin Ch. Anya-Alaska, the bitch she imported from Switzerland. Anya was the first

Top: IntMex Ch. Castor Spirit of Innisfree, owned by Adriana Vasquez. Spirit was No. 1 Working Dog in Mexico in 1985 and had 7 Bests in Show. Bred by Kathleen Kanzler. *Bottom:* Brz Ch. Almaring's Elfin winning the Working Group at the KC de Campos in Brazil under American judge Charles Harendeen. The breeder was Ingrid Brucato, the owner is Dr. Humberto Rocha of Rio de Janeiro.

Top: Alice Watt's bitch, Kossok's Wechunuk, winning Best of Opposite at a 1985 Canadian show. The sire was Ch. Jlahka's Chotovotka Black Jac ex Ch. Kossok's Kiska of Oakcrest. *Middle:* Ch. Kontoki's Made in the Shade winning over 2 Best in Show dogs on the way to her championship for a 3-point major at the Delaware Specialty Show in 1985 from the Bred by Exhibitor Class. Judge Ingram presiding; owner, Tom Oelschlager handling. *Bottom:* Ch. Norstarr's Tara, handled by Brian Meyer for owner Susan Vosnos of the Whispering Oaks Kennels in Barrington, IL.

Top: Ch. Tandara's Nakina Polynya, sired by AmCan Ch. Tandara's Che Kodiak, CD, and bred and owned by Lynn Patterson. *Bottom:* Kaylee's Rikki Tikki Tavi wins under respected judge Winnifred Heckmann. The sire was Ch. Savdajaure's Happiness Is ex Arahaz Kaylee Keenu. Breeder-owner-handled by Susanna Windsor Rodney.

Ch. The Gambler of the Midnight Sun, now living with his owner in Belgium. The breeder was Janis Church.

Siberian Husky in Finland and has whelped five litters. Her sire was the Int Ch. Savdajaure's Pavo, imported to Switzerland from the United States, and her dam was Maya v. Nordpol.

Another of Mrs. Alm's outstanding Huskies is a son of Anya, Lumimaan Tojon. Mrs. Alm also exported four Siberian Huskies, Nor Ch. Lumimaan Alasuq and Lumimaan Salka, both bitches; and two males, Lumimaan Talvi to Switzerland and Lumimaan Ukko-Pekka to Norway. Mrs. Alm was somewhat concerned about the appearance of monorchidism in the breed during the past, a condition we hope has changed in the 1980s. She was also concerned about faulty bites, improper coats, overweight, and too much curve to the tails. We can only hope these conditions have improved.

Also in Finland, and active since 1966, was Stina Blomquist of Nickby. All of her dogs are shown in conformation rings and are used as sled dogs and are raced. Stina was winner of the Ladies Championship Race in 1971, 1972, and 1973. The few litters she had were used for breeding and produced stock for both showing and racing.

Her kennel features Fin Ch. Ahtojaan Pikoo (Ch. Monadnock's Konyak of Kaza–Kanakanaks Kishka), Green Berets Snowy Angara and Green Beret's Snowy Anusjka. Pikoo is an American import, and Angara and Anusjka were imported from Holland. Their ancestry goes back to the Alaskan Kennels in the USA. Pikoo was also the winner in 1968 of the Ladies Championship Race with his mistress and was rated one of the Top Ten in Finand.

SIBERIANS IN SWITZERLAND

The Siberian Husky appeared first on the European continent in the early 1950s, and the first of record were exported to Switzerland in 1955 from America. They were named Grey Cloud of Little Tanana and Winemuca of Little Tanana. They were followed by Manitoba of Little Tanana. Grey Cloud was the first Siberian Husky to become an International champion, and unfortunately, died in 1959.

Varskimo II, owned by Peter Graf of Switzerland, who purchased the dog from the Panuck-Denali Kennels in Laconia, NH. Mr. Graf, owner of a Swiss ski resort, purchased Varskimo II in 1977.

It was only after 1963, when the Swiss Club for Northern Dogs was established, that crossbreeds were frowned upon and Husky owners began once again to have interest in promoting the *purebred* Siberian Husky.

More importing from the United States began at this time when Winnie of Whalom arrived in Switzerland; she was followed in 1964 by Savdajaure's Paavo, and Arctica of Baltic, which went to Switzerland with Mr. Thomas Althaus, who fell in love with the breed while he was an exchange student at Colorado College. Today's Swiss Siberian Huskies are of such quality that they are being exported to establish and improve bloodlines in Italy, Holland, Germany, and Finland.

Before this breakthrough in 1963, the Alaskan Malamute, the Samoyed, the Greenland Dog, the Norwegian Elkhound, the Karelian Bear Hound, and the Akita Inu, as well as our Siberian Husky, came under the protection of the Swiss Club for Northern Dogs. This organization maintained a firm hold on the breed, much more so than any breed club in this country.

Annually or semi-annually, the official breed clubs hold a meeting for a selection of dogs worthy of breeding. No dog received papers unless his parents have also passed this breeding selection and abilities test. First of all, they maintained that the dog must be one year of age or older, must be X-rayed and declared by a veterinarian to be free of hip dysplasia. The dog is weighed, measured, and examined thoroughly by a judge and the president of the breeding committee for any breed disorders or major faults. Even character defects are duly noted on the record for their registry.

The club has a record of every dog and bitch in the country, to record which are and which are not eligible to be bred, thereby giving them complete control of any breeding programs. They further declare that no dog under 18 months of age is eligible to be bred and only six or fewer puppies per litter are allowed. Furthermore, breeders must put their dogs through this judging every three years, and even non-members of the Swiss Club for Northern Dogs must have the club approval of their dogs if they wish to breed.

These are rather stringent methods of control, to be sure, but they have held quality high in Europe and eliminated further crossbreeding of the Northern breeds, and established beyond doubt quality in the individual breeds, which is, after all, what we are striving for all over the world.

In Switzerland today, Mr. Thomas F. Althaus is active in the breed and is a member of the Siberian Husky Club of America.

Sneginka Kennel's bitch Chukchii Nanooska at 7 months. Victoria, Australia, is Chukchii's home.

Top: Michele Thie and her Almaring's Grand Finale, pictured winning on the way to her title. *Bottom:* An early start for Ch. Medvezhi's Indigo Islander, bred by Dr. and Mrs. David Qualls and owned by Richard and Gayle Atkinson. Islander went on to become one of the Top Ten Siberians for 1983–85.

Top: Ch. Czar Nicoli of Togo, first champion at Anne Bruder's Sunset Hills Kennels in the early 1970s. *Bottom:* Ch. Kossoks Patch of Bleu, bred and owned by Alice J. Watt, winning at a 1985 show. The sire was Ch. Kaila's Beau Bleu of Rusojhn ex AmCan Ch. Kossok's Buttercup Bouquet.

THE BREED IN NORWAY

In 1958, Molinka of Bowlake made her appearance in Norway and was bred to a Siberian Husky which had been exported to that country some time before. The Siberian seemed to have caught on in Norway, much to the credit of Benedicte Ingstad, who established the breed and was active for many years. Other exports to Norway followed Molinka, and about the time of her appearance there, three other Bowlake Siberians were exported to France.

THE BREED IN FRANCE

A French airline pilot imported three Bowlake Siberian Huskies; but in

Aus Ch. Chukchii Yukon Lad in harness and ready for the race. Owned and trained by Ev Baker, Sneginka Kennels, Victoria, Australia.

France, as in Switzerland, the crossbreeding with France's recognized Greenland dog destroyed the purebred Siberian Husky lines, and the breed did not flourish or even get a foot hold to any degree.

THE BREED IN BELGIUM

In the 1980s Dr. Ronald and Mrs. Casey are interested in the breed sufficiently to be members of our Siberian Husky Club of America. They reside in Brussels.

THE BREED IN HOLLAND

In 1965, a puppy exchange was made between the United States and the Netherlands, where a Miss Elizabeth M.R. Urlus had been promoting the breed for several years. She imported Kayak's Thunder Taku and Vaskresenya's Tanana Taku, the first Siberian Huskies to appear in Holland. Other Dutch Siberian Husky enthusiasts are Mrs. L.J.H. Van Leeuwen, Mr. Bareld Van Der Meer, Ernst Muller-Tuoff, and Mr. Josef Felder.

HUSKIES IN AUSTRALIA

Kolyma

Rex and Edna Harper own the Kolyma Kennels in Victoria. Their first Siberian Husky became Aust Ch. Myvore Layka, (the first Australian born sire) and was purchased from Mr. D. George, who imported the first dog and two bitches to Australia from England in the late 1970s.

In 1981, the Harpers acquired their first brood bitch, Aust Ch. Frostypines Anya.

Sharon Baker trying to convince Nanooska that the bathtub is big enough for her. The Bakers' Sneginka Kennels are in Victoria, Australia.

BEST IN SHOW
PENSACOLA
DOG FANCIERS ASSOC.
FALL 1985
PHOTO BY
L. SOSA

PENSACOLA DFA

BEST IN SHOW

Anya was bred from Huenvos Tushin, a dog imported from New Zealand and a bitch bred from Mr. George's original stock.

Anya was best Siberian Bitch at the 1983 Royal Melbourne, defeating 13 other bitches, the largest number to be shown in Australia to date. Her daughter, the Harper's homebred Koyma Czarina Tasha, was second place at the same show at seven months of age. The judge was Mrs. V. Segerstrom from Sweden.

The Harpers imported Rossfort Nijinski from England in December, 1983. His sire, Arcticlight's Silver Shadrin, was Canadian Champion dog in show in 1980 and his dam was imported to England in whelp, so the Harpers were fortunate in obtaining the first purebred Canadian dog to arrive in Australia.

The Harpers currently have three bitches and two stud dogs. Unfortunately, they tell us, sledding with Huskies as a sport has not yet arrived, to any extent, in Australia, but they expect to be into it as soon as possible! Their kennel stationery explains their

Top: Jean Fournier and her Ch. Toko's Mr. Chip of Yago, CD, the 25th Siberian Husky to win a Best in Show in breed history. This win was in 1981 at the Wheaton KC Show at the SHCA supported entry. Chip was also No. 2 Husky during his show career, and obtained his CD degree at age 8.
Bottom: Best Brace in Show winners Veleah's Love Potion and Veleah's Scarlet Fever with owner Vel Leahy.

Kaylee Kitkit Kayikay winning the Veterans Class at the 1981 Chesapeake Specialty Show under Virginia Hampton. Bred, owned and handled by Susanna Windsor Rodney of Baltimore, MD.

feelings on the breed—it states, "Hug a Husky."

Sneginka

Ev and Keith Baker have their Sneginka Kennels in Victoria. While they live only 20 miles from a snow resort, they find that they are doing most of their race training on cement to be prepared for the snow once it arrives.

The Bakers have just two Siberian Huskies, namely their Aust Ch. Chukchii Yukon Lad and a bitch Chukchii Nanooska, who is slightly younger. Yukon's sire was a British import, Aust Ch. Forstals Tomac out of Danlee Karelia, also a United Kingdom import. Nanooska was also sired by Tomac but out of Aust Ch. Skimarque Duska, an import.

Yukon became an Australia champion at just 11 months of age, often having defeated dogs that were much older. He has won numerous Age Classes in Group and Age Classes in Show, and was a reserve challenge winner at the 1982 Royal Melbourne show.

The Bakers have obtained a sled and are starting their sled training. Yukon has also done a slight bit of obedience work, but obviously prefers the sled and the snows. The Baker children, Wayne and Sharon, are also involved with the dogs, making it a real family affair.

Top: Ch. Dichoda's Ullar of Umiat completing his championship at a San Joaquin KC show.
Bottom: Ch. Konik's Silver Bullet wins a 4-point major under judge J. Robert Page at this 1985 show. Owned and handled by Janet L. Cingel of Konik Kennels.

DESCRIPTION AND CHARACTERISTICS

STANDARD FOR THE SIBERIAN HUSKY

In 1990, the A.K.C. and the Siberian Husky Club of America approved a new standard for the breed. The language in the new standard is essentially the same as in the standard presented here, only the format is different.

General Appearance—The Siberian Husky is a medium-sized working dog, quick and light on his feet, and free and graceful in action. His moderately compact and well-furred body, erect ears and brush tail suggest his Northern heritage. His characteristic gait is smooth and seemingly effortless. He performs his original function in harness most capably, carrying a light load at moderate speed over great distances. His body proportions and form reflect this basic balance of power, speed and endurance. The males of the Siberian Husky breed are masculine but never coarse; the bitches are feminine but without weakness of structure. In proper condition, with muscle firm and well-developed, the Siberian Husky does not carry excess weight.

HEAD

Skull—Of medium size and in proportion to the body; slightly rounded on top and tapering gradually from the widest point to the eyes. Faults—Head clumsy or heavy; head too finely chiseled.

Muzzle—Of medium length; that is, the distance from the tip of the nose to the stop is equal to the distance from the stop to the occiput. The stop is well-defined and the bridge of the nose is straight from the stop to the tip. The muzzle is of medium width, tapering gradually to the nose, with the tip neither pointed nor square. The lips are well-pigmented and close fitting; teeth closing in a scissors bite. Faults—Muzzle either too snipy or too coarse; muzzle too short or too

"He performs his original function in harness most capably, carrying a light load at moderate speed over great distances."

long; insufficient stop; any bite other than scissors.

Ears—Of medium size, triangular in shape, close fitting and set high on the head. They are thick, well-furred, slightly arched at the back, and strongly erect, with slightly rounded tips pointing straight up. Faults—Ears too large in proportion to the head; too wide-set; not strongly erect.

Eyes—Almond shaped, moderately spaced and set a trifle obliquely. The expression is keen, but friendly; interested and even mischievous. Eyes may be brown or blue in color; one of each or parti-colored are acceptable. Faults—Eyes set too obliquely; set too close together.

Nose—Black in gray, tan or black dogs; liver in copper dogs; may be flesh-colored in pure white dogs. The pink-streaked "snow nose" is acceptable.

BODY

Neck—Medium in length, arched and carried proudly erect when dog is standing. When moving at a trot, the neck is extended so that the head is carried slightly forward. Faults—Neck too short and thick; neck too long.

Shoulders—The shoulder blade is well laid back at an approximate angle of 45 degrees to the ground. The upper arm

Susanna Windsor Rodney's Best in Show Brace pictured winning under Joe Gregory at a 1980 Carroll KC show. Kaylee Kitkit Kayikay and Kaylee's Ruffin are the beautifully matched brace, owner-breeder-handled.

BEST IN SHOW
CARROLL
KENNEL CLUB
1980

angles slightly backward from point of shoulder to elbow, and is never perpendicular to the ground. The muscles and ligaments holding the shoulder to the rib cage are firm and well-developed. Faults—Straight shoulders; loose shoulders.

Chest—Deep and strong, but not too broad, with the deepest point being just behind and level with the elbows. The ribs are well-sprung from the spine but flattened on the sides to allow for freedom of action. Faults—Chest too broad; "barrel ribs"; ribs too flat or weak.

Back—The back is straight and strong, with a level topline from withers to croup. It is of medium length, neither cobby nor slack from excessive length. The loin is taut and lean, narrower than the rib cage, and with a slight tuck-up. The croup slopes away from the spine at an angle, but never so steeply as to restrict the rearward thrust of the hind legs. In profile, the length of the body from the point of the shoulder to the rear point of the croup is slightly longer than the height of the body from the ground to the top of the withers. Faults—Weak or slack back; roached back; sloping topline.

LEGS AND FEET

Forelegs—When standing and viewed from the front, the legs are moderately spaced, parallel and straight, with elbows close

Best in Show win for Ch. Kontoki's Natural Sinner at the 1982 Old Dominion KC over 3200 dogs. The judge was Gwen Bradley from England. Tom Oelschlager handling, co-owner with Marlene DePalma of the Kontoki Kennels in Finleyville, PA. Sinner has won 9 all-breed Bests and 15 American Specialty Breed wins. He was the No. 1 Siberian from 1980–82, and No. 6 in the Working Dogs in 1982. He is the sire of some 22 champions.

A pastel portrait rendered by D.L. Redding of Kaylee's Tengri Nor, bred and owned by S.W. Rodney.

Top: Kaylee's Ruffin, 11-week-old male, gets his show career off to a good start. Bred, owned and handled by S.W. Rodney. The sire was Ch. Innisfree's Pegasus ex Kaylee Kittee Katek. *Bottom:* Talocon Taneha's Tumai, major-pointed at 12 months of age, and winning at a 1985 show. Owner-bred and handled by Gail O'Connell.

Top: Susan Vosnos' homebred Whispering Oaks Cayenne, handled for her to this Best of Breed win by Richard Orseno. Whispering Oaks Kennels are located in Barrington, IL.
Middle: Ch. Arahaz Omela, sired by Ch. Dudley's Varska ex Arahaz Okolina, takes Best in Show. Bred and owned by Rosemary Fischer.
Bottom: Ch. Arahaz Elizaveta, owned by L. Lippincott and co-owned by breeder R. Fischer.

to the body and turned neither in nor out. Viewed from the side, pasterns are slightly slanted, with pastern joint strong, but flexible. Bone is substantial but never heavy. Length of the leg from elbow to ground is slightly more than the distance from the elbow to the top of withers. Dewclaws on forelegs may be removed.

ground. Dewclaws, if any, are to be removed. Faults— Straight stifles, cowhocks, too narrow or too wide in the rear. **Feet**—Oval in shape, but not long. The paws are medium size, compact and well-furred between the toes and pads. The pads are tough and thickly cushioned. The paws neither turn in nor out when dog is in

Faults—Weak pasterns; too heavy bone; too narrow or too wide in the front; out at the elbows.
Hindquarters—When standing and viewed from the rear, the hind legs are moderately spaced and parallel. The upper thighs are well-muscled and powerful, the stifles well-bent, the hock joint well-defined and set low to the

natural stance. Faults—Soft or splayed toes; paws too large and clumsy; paws too small and delicate; toeing in or out.
Tail—The well-furred tail of the fox-brush shape is set on just below the level of the topline, and is usually carried over the back in a graceful sickle curve when the dog is at attention. When carried up, the tail does not curl to either side

of the body, nor does it snap flat against the back. A trailing tail is normal for the dog when working or in repose. Hair on the tail is of medium length and approximately the same length on top, sides and bottom,

seemingly effortless. He is quick and light on his feet, and when in the show ring should be gaited on a loose lead at a moderately fast trot, exhibiting good reach in the forequarters and good drive in the

Ch. Kokoda of the Midnight Sun, sired by Ch. Akkani of the Midnight Son ex Zela of the Midnight Sun. Owner-breeder, Janis Church, Nathrop, CO.

giving the appearance of a round brush. Faults—A snapped or tightly curled tail; highly plumed tail; tail set too low or high.
Gait—The Siberian Husky's characteristic gait is smooth and

hindquarters. When viewed from the front to rear, while moving at a walk the Siberian Husky does not single-track, but as the speed increases the legs gradually angle inward until the pads are falling on a

Kadyak's Salute to Innisfree, bred by Kathleen Kanzler and owned by Ardene Eaton and Annella Cooper, Anchorage, AK.

line directly under the longitudinal center of the body. As the pad marks converge, the forelegs and hind legs are carried straight forward, with neither elbows nor stifles turned in or out. Each hind leg moves in the path of the foreleg on the same side. While the dog is gaiting, the topline remains firm and level. Faults—Short, prancing or choppy gait, lumbering or rolling gait; crossing; crabbing.

Coat—The coat of the Siberian Husky is double and medium in length, giving a well-furred appearance, but is never so long as to obscure the clean-cut outline of the dog. The undercoat is soft and dense and of sufficient length to support the outer coat. The guard hairs of the outer coat are straight and somewhat smooth-lying; never harsh nor standing straight off the body. It should be noted that the absence of the undercoat during the shedding season is normal. Trimming of the whiskers and fur between the toes and around the feet to present a neater appearance is permissible. Trimming of the fur on any other part of the dog is not to be condoned and should be severely penalized. Faults—Long, rough or shaggy coat; texture too harsh or too silky; trimming of the coat, except as permitted above. **Color**—All colors from black to pure white are allowed. A variety of markings on the head is common, including many striking patterns not found in other breeds.

Temperament—The

Siesta for Ch. Talocon Nova's Taneha.

characteristic temperament of the Siberian Husky is friendly and gentle, but also alert and outgoing. He does not display the possessive qualities of the guard dog, nor is he overly suspicious of strangers or aggressive with other dogs. Some measure of reserve and dignity may be expected in the mature dog. His intelligence, tractability, and eager disposition make him an agreeable companion.

SIZE

Height—Dogs, 21 to 23½ inches at the withers. Bitches, 20 to 22 inches at the withers. **Weight**—Dogs, 46 to 60 pounds. Bitches, 35 to 50 pounds. Weight is in proportion to height. The measurements mentioned above represent the extreme height

and weight limits, with no preference given to either extreme.

Disqualification—Dogs over 23½ inches and bitches over 22 inches.

Summary—The most important breed characteristics of the Siberian Husky are medium size, moderate bone, well-balanced proportions, ease and freedom of movement, proper coat, pleasing head and ears, correct tail, and good disposition. Any appearance of excessive bone or weight, constricted or clumsy gait, or long, rough coat should be penalized. The Siberian Husky never appears so heavy or coarse as to suggest a frightening animal; nor is he so light and fragile as to suggest a sprint-racing animal. In both sexes the Siberian Husky gives

Ch. Indigo's Saroja Cin-sation, co-owned by Sharon Wilson, Sandy James and Melanie Babb.

Krisland's Blackie, interesting racing dog bred by Chris Landers.

the appearance of being capable of great endurance. In addition to the faults already noted, obvious structural faults common to all breeds are as undesirable in the Siberian Husky as in any other breed, even though they are not specifically mentioned herein.

FIRST SIBERIAN HUSKY IN THE AKC STUD BOOK

The first appearance of a Siberian Husky in the *American Kennel Club Stud Book* was in the December 1930 issue, Vol. 47. Fairbanks Princess Chena, a bitch was number 758529 and owned by Mrs. Elsie K. Reeser.

Top: Snokomo's Ricochet of Troika winning a 4-point major under judge Mrs. Robert Ward at a 1981 show. *Bottom:* Ch. Sno-Fame Rum Runner owned by Mr. and Mrs. Minard Crane and Ann M. Sullivan.

Top: Kadyak's Cavalier of Starfire winning 4 points under judge R.Stephen Shaw. Owned by Lynne Nale, bred by Ardene Eaton, Cavalier finished title at 1 year of age. *Bottom:* Ch. Talocon Taneha's Kamiah, a winning bitch bred and owned by John and Gail O'Connell.

"Huskies do shed, they do love to dig, and they do get stubborn once in a while; but you will find yourself forgiving them anything because they are so beautiful, loyal, and companionable."

The breeder was Julian A. Hurley of Fairbanks, Alaska. The bitch was whelped September 16, 1927. The lineage was recorded as follows: "Ch. by Bingo II out of Alaska Princess by Jack Frost out of Snowflake. Jack Frost by Scotty out of Vasta. Bingo II out of Topsy."

The very next issue of the *Stud Book*, January 1931, Vol. 48, was quite another story. There were 21 entries, every one bearing the Northern Light kennel prefix; eight of the 21 were bitches. Until 1952 the count went as follows:

Year	Number of Entries
1930	1
1931	69
1932	11
1933	4
1934	2
1935	17
1936	25
1937	10
1938	2
1939	38
1940	49
1941	55
1942	15
1943	16
1944	12
1945	14
1946	21
1947	72
1948	105
1949	84
1950	124
1951	80

After June 1952, the stud book was not published again until December 1952. With that December issue, the stud book listed only dogs which had been bred.

TEMPERAMENT AND CHARACTERISTICS

Once you've made up your mind that this breed is for you, and you've read all you could find on its exotic and heroic background, you will want to learn more about what you can expect of it as a house dog, especially if you do not intend to show, race, or train it in obedience. Huskies are wonderful pets and companions, and while they prefer the outdoors more than the indoors and a cold rather than a hot climate, it doesn't mean that they can't survive happily and comfortably in both. But it is up to you to make sure that their living conditions are suitable.

Otherwise, the temperament, personality, and size of the dog make it an ideal house pet. Huskies do shed, they do love to dig, and they do get stubborn once in a while; but you will find yourself forgiving them *anything* because they are so beautiful, loyal, and companionable. I have received 100% agreement as to the breed's strongest selling point—personality. However, while you can live with a Husky everywhere, let us not forget that it was bred to excel in outdoor activities, and we must preserve this ability at all costs.

COLOR AND MARKINGS

One of the keenest delights with the Siberian Husky breed is that any and all colors and markings are acceptable. Their very colors and markings make them so unique and exotic! Each dog seems to have its very own individual patterns that set it apart from every other.

Many admirers prefer the Siberian Husky when it is marked in the pattern and color of the wolf! Most Husky enthusiasts, however, love them in any color or with any pattern, and every litter is a complete and wonderful

surprise. The black markings around the eyes, up the forehead, and around the nose and ears are intriguing and lean toward an expression which can be described by saying that the dog seems to be looking far off across endless miles of snow to the North Pole.

These unique markings accent the Husky's beautiful eyes. The blue eyes which are most frequently associated with this breed are truly magnificent—the deeper the blue the better! While brown eyes are also acceptable, they never seem to draw the excited

Igloo Pak's Lobo of Kolyma as a puppy, pictured with owner Sherry Galka at their home in Sonora, CA. The sire was Ch. Kolyma's Red Tannu of Mayhill, CDX, ex Igloo Pak's Midget.

comments that the lovely blue eyes evoke from the crowds and from those seeing the breed for the first time.

Many Siberian Huskies possess one blue eye and one brown eye, and this odd-eyed combination is also completely acceptable. The eye rims should have black pigmentation, the exception being flesh-colored rims on the all-white Siberian Husky, though, here again, the black pigmentation on a pure white dog is highly desirable. Red Siberian Huskies also have flesh-colored pigmentation around the eyes and nose; such coloration is within the standard for the breed.

Since both color eyes and a combination of both are permissible in the breed, eye color should never be more than a final consideration in your selection of a dog for the show ring, the obedience ring, or for racing. The true devotee of the breed would consider the whole dog rather than any one individual characteristic, no matter how beautiful the shade of blue eyes, which are almost guaranteed to make your dog a crowd-pleaser!

Turkick's Overdrive winning Best in Bred by Exhibitor Class under Victor Clemente at just 1 year of age. Handled by breeder-owner Carolyn Kaiser, Rurick Kennels, Acworth, NH. Sire was Ecohils Richochet; dam was Turkick's Chulitna.

Top: Carol Nash and her Ch. Marlytuk's Sachem of Canaan winning in 1980 under Sam Pizzino. The same day, this dog's daughter, Ch. Marlytuk's Sachem of Kiska-Too, was Best of Winners and his mother, Kiska-Trey, was Best of Opposite Sex. *Bottom:* Ch. Indigo's Islamorada, a second-generation champion from Indigo Kennels of Dr. and Mrs. Qualls. Sire was Ch. Innisfree's Trademark ex Ch. Innisfree's Newscent's Niavar. Breeders co-own with Christopher T. Neal.

Rosemary and Edward Fischer's Ch. Arahaz Red Rocket, sired by Ch. Innisfree's Barbarossa ex Arahaz Karenina.

THE SIBERIAN HUSKY COAT

There are two major types of coat in the breed: the medium-to-long and the short coat. Some long coats are allowed—and even get by—in the show ring! But the wooly, or "brillo-y," coat is not to be desired, especially in the show ring. While the undercoat is soft, it should very definitely be in contrast to the outer thick coat.

When the dog is in its natural state, the coat should present a definite, clear, smooth outline of the body structure. The diet is also important to maintaining a good coat. A properly-fed dog will have a good coat with a high gloss to it without needing the application of commercial sprays, etc. Heredity also plays a major part. Good breeding stock will produce a head start toward a good coat, and the Siberian Husky is easy to care for when in proper coat.

Changing Coat Colors

One occurrence for which you must be prepared is the gradual change in your dog's coat color. Not every Husky changes color; but not only do many of them change from dark to light or light to dark, but a few may change from dark to red or copper. This is another fascinating idiosyncrasy of the breed! Most puppies (in any breed) are usually born black or dark with a blackish cast to them, unless they are always to be pure white!

Piebald Siberian Huskies

Spotted puppies occasionally appear in a litter. These puppies are sometimes referred to as pintos, but more correctly they should be called piebalds. More often than not, breeders are inclined to put them down

generally sheds twice a year, and it is usually exactly when he feels like it! There has been no positive proof that a full shedding has to do with whether or not they race, with extreme heat or cold weather conditions, with diet, or the part of the world in which they live! Generally speaking they shed twice a year—spring and fall.

Ch. Indigo's By Invitation Only, sired by Ch. Innisfree's Sierra Cinna ex Indigo's Optical Illusion. Breeders, Dr. and Mrs. David K. Qualls; owners, Drexel and Bobbie Matthews.

at birth, considering them as mis-marks or as "unsaleable." A few rare breeders will sell them as pets.

Shedding

All dogs shed—yet the question of just how much is always asked by anyone thinking seriously about buying a dog, especially if it is a new breed to them.

The Siberian Husky

Some Huskies shed completely and all at once. One day they are magnificent in the show ring, the next day they are naked! Others shed in clumps, and still others just lose varying amounts of loose hair. Many Siberians go through no more than a sort of thinning process and merely lose hair evenly all over.

For those who exhibit their Huskies in the show ring, this

Opposite:
Timber and Honcho enjoying the Connecticut winter snow. Both of these young Toko puppies were bred by Jean Fournier and Robin Mott.

occasional going-over with a rubber-based wire brush will be sufficient to keep your dog in well-groomed condition and will present him in his natural beauty.

If you have a few important shows coming up and you have already sent in your entries, there are a few things to remember that might help your chances of winning in spite of the loss of hair. One is *not* to give a hot bath if shedding has started. There are dry shampoos to use on legs, face, and tail, or other places where dirt has gathered so that a regular brushing dry will not take out most of the coat. There are also sprays that can be used to give a little extra gloss to the coat without having to wet down the dog or submerge it entirely in water.

Lack of undercoat during the shedding season is normal, and most judges will allow for it. But trimming the dog to make it look more even is not allowable! Trimming toes and whiskers is one thing— scissoring a dog to even it out, or trimming guard hairs to level off a body line, is not permissible. And if you use chalk, cornstarch, or powder of any kind on the white areas, we caution you to be sure to get it all out before entering the show ring!

GROOMING THE SIBERIAN HUSKY

We have mentioned the shedding process in this breed, now for additional tips on keeping your dog "looking good." The dogs in the show ring usually have their whiskers trimmed off and the excess hair trimmed from between the toes on the bottom of the feet. Nails are cut, of course, as are hairs over or around the eyes and on the cheeks if there are any. Eyes should be clean and clear as should the ears.

Ordinarily, a stiff bristle brush and/or a slicker will do for the two or three brushings a week. An occasional spray with a lanolin coat conditioner enhances the coat; and around shedding time, a pin brush for getting out all the dead hair is a help.

Be sure to brush the lanolin conditioner into the coat so that it doesn't rub off on the furniture. Brush the topline back toward the tail, and brush the rest of the coat outwards before brushing it into place; give a light final wipe-off with a cloth after the conditioner if you feel it is necessary.

The best possible way for you to plan a grooming process is to observe professional groomers at a shop or, preferably, at a dog show. They know all the tricks and can save you a lot of mistakes. A veterinarian is the best to teach you how to cut the nails; ask him how when you take your dog for a checkup or shots. Also ask him to recommend an ear powder to make sure the ears are clean at all times.

Bathing is optional unless absolutely necessary. You will learn when to bathe as you go

along. Consult the person from whom you bought the dog, or a grooming professional for the best way to tell when your dog needs a bath.

STAKING OUT

One of the best ways to keep a Siberian Husky that you intend to use as a working or racing dog, if you do not have a yard or run for it, is to stake it outside rather than to keep it indoors. Here again, the workings of the Husky mind can better tolerate the thoughts and conditions of a stake, because Huskies do prefer outdoor living.

A soft, secure harness with a chain approximately ten feet long will give the dog a sufficiently large area to move in. Shelter should be provided in some form, perhaps a simply constructed lean-to or doghouse made from half-inch thick plywood with a flat roof slightly tilted to let the rain run off and yet allow the dog a resting place off the ground. Some prefer to feed the dog up on the roof in order to protect it from ground insects and other small animals.

If you intend to show your dog, some protection from the sun must also be provided to prevent the coat from burning or changing color and texture in constant sunlight.

Care must be taken to make certain that the dog does not get tangled in the chain or rope and that it can defend itself at all times.

LIVING OUT

You must determine at the beginning whether your Siberian Husky is to be an indoor or outdoor dog. Depending on the severity of the climate in the region where you live, your dog may be more

King of the mountain. One of Sylvia Roselli's Arlington Siberians on guard at her Staten Island home.

comfortable living outdoors all year round. In the great snows which occur in the North, the Husky is able to take care of himself under most conditions. He sleeps in a hole he digs for himself in the snow, curled in a semi-circle with his furry tail as a cover for his face; this helps to prevent the frigid air from blasting into his face.

It is not in the dog's best interests to suddenly take pity on him during a blizzard and bring him inside to warm up. Once the ice and snow melt and wet the coat, it must be *completely* dry before the dog is put outside again, or the wet hair will freeze and either give the dog pneumonia or cause it to freeze to death.

A dog which lives outdoors must be given enough chain to be able to walk about and keep its circulation going or it will freeze. The chain must be long enough for it to move out of the way of the drifting snow so that it does not get buried and suffocate beneath the snow. The dog must be able to move about and shake off the snow.

LIVING IN

Aside from the shedding problem, the Husky makes an ideal indoor dog. He is not clumsy in the house, nor is he particularly given to jumping on the furniture, being content to remain on the floor. It is almost useless, however, to try to designate a special bed for the dog. You will find that he will much prefer to sleep near a favorite member of the family.

Siberian Huskies are unusually clean eaters. They eat their food promptly and all at once, and they aren't known to play in the water dishes the way

They have no typical doggy odor the way some of the other breeds have, except occasionally when they are soaking wet or have been exposed to special circumstances that might cause odors to cling to their coats. Occasional brushings will keep them clean and odor-free under

Kristi and Ciara, Arahaz Siberians owned by William Creamer.

certain other breeds do, at least not after they have grown up!

The Siberian Husky is a particularly clean dog in other respects, too. At times they lick themselves clean in somewhat the same manner as a cat. This cleanliness most likely goes back to the North, where they could always keep themselves clean by rolling in the snow.

normal circumstances.

For the dog that will be living in and will get its exercise in the form of walks each day, make sure that the dog is handled by a capable person. It is not considered cute to see a tiny child being pulled along by a dog that has just caught scent of a bitch in heat down the street, or suddenly gets the urge to chase some children flashing by on bicycles. If the dog has to defend itself in a fight, the child could end up in the middle of a canine scrap. Also, since the exotic appearance of the Siberian Husky sometimes inspires fear in those who don't understand its docile temperament, such persons often doubt the ability of the child to handle it when it is in their vicinity.

A dog that lives in must be exercised several times a day, and this should be done by an adult with sufficient strength to restrain the dog under any circumstances and sufficient walking speed to let the dog exercise at its normal gait. More and more people are seen in the roads and in the parks jogging with their dogs. Signs of the times!

THE CALL OF THE WILD

All of us who love dogs and remember Clark Gable in the movie *Call of the Wild* will remember the distant howl of the Arctic wolves!

Siberian Huskies are given more to howling than to barking. In the dead of the night they are likely to lift their voices in "song," and there it

Magnificent setting for Chilly Willy of Troika, backpacking in the Rockies at Vail, CO, with owners Lora and Travis Henderson of Oklahoma City. Willy also loves to go camping with his owners.

Carol Nash's Canaan's Grey Sun of North Star at 10 months of age.

remains at fever pitch for long periods of time and carrying over great distances—just like in the movies, baying at a full moon.

The voices of these dogs have been described in earlier written records by men in the North as "long, melancholy howls of a wolf-like [animal]." Early commentators have remarked to the effect that you never hear these dogs bark—they are like wolves and only howl—except maybe when revving up for a race! This is perhaps a slight exaggeration. Any dog, except perhaps the Basenji, can bark simply by instinct. However, anyone who has owned a Siberian Husky will attest that they seldom bark *unnecessarily*.

Down through the centuries, as man needed his dog to serve as a guard for him, it was trained to give voice and bark on certain occasions. However, Huskies' inclination not to bark is one reason why they do not make superior watch dogs—the other is that they *love everybody!*

A watchdog the Siberian Husky is not—not unless his facial markings give him a wild expression, or if someone truly obnoxious intrudes on his family or domain. The Siberian does not bark unnecessarily, so if he barks, listen and investigate. But remember, a real watch dog he is not; if you need or want a watch dog, *don't* get a Siberian Husky.

THE ALL-AROUND WORKING DOG

We have lauded this breed for its all-around working abilities as a sled, racing and weight-pulling dog, and companion on so many expeditions to the poles. Mention must also be made that Huskies served well in the Army's Arctic Search and Rescue Unit of the Air Transport Command during World War II.

THE SIBERIAN HUSKY AND ITS RELATIONSHIPS WITH OTHER ANIMALS

The legends of the hunting instincts and keen nose of the Siberian Husky are many! Drivers from the earliest times could recall countless stories of

Ch. Fra-Mar's Rayle Diavol and friend. Rayle has been Best in Show many times during his career. Owned and bred by Marie Wamser.

lead dogs finding the way home when the driver became hopelessly lost, and of teams suddenly veering off course when they caught the scent of bear, moose, or reindeer, leaving the driver hanging on desperately until he could manage to stop them and get back on course again. Huskies were hunting with their owners long before they were pulling sleds.

Their hunting instinct, however, caused one of the major problems in trying to get Huskies used to domestic animals. With this strong, inherent hunting instinct, they could not discern which animals belonged to the family and which they were meant to pursue and bring down. Everything from chickens to calves and foals were within their territory, and cats were favorite victims. All were chased, caught by the throat, and with a swiftness that almost could not be observed, finished off! Waldemar Jochelson wrote in 1908 that on occasions when he had tried to domesticate dogs he had brought back from the wilds, he found that they never lost this instinct to hunt, and did all sorts of damage to local game and domestic animals while showing no hostility to strangers or their owners.

But Huskies are no longer the aggressive hunters they were during the days they were first kept as pets, as opposed to being strictly work animals. Perhaps it is because they are no longer half-starved and always hungry; also it has been a long time since they lived in the wilds, where game was plentiful and where they were expected to make a kill. Domestication has made stalking prey an exception rather than a rule of life. (This also depends on the owner, and on the individual dog.) The

Arahaz Kaylee Keenu, one of the foundation bitches at Susanna Windsor Rodney's Kaylee Kennels, winning under the late Kitty Drury at a 1974 show. The sire was Ch. Arahaz Tengri Khan, CD, ex Arahaz Ilka.

Kryska's Krying Wolf with Baggage the cat. All of James and Maureen Kent's dogs love cats.

instinct to capture anything that moves is inherent in many animals—especially in the cat family. It is up to the owner to prevent "the law of the jungle" from causing a tragedy within the household if he is to harbor animals in addition to the Siberian Husky.

THE L'IL ABNER DOG TEAM

This story comes from Leonhard Seppala via Irving Reed, who says that Seppala told him of an incident which occurred during a dog team race in New England. The course ran along a road by which stood a house in which a woman was frying pork chops. The doors to the house were open, and when the dogs picked up the scent of the meat there was no stopping them. The woman fled the house, screaming at what she believed to be a wild pack of wolves coming in her front door. The team hardly broke stride, but went through the house and on out the back door, picking up the pork chops on the way. Seppala was just along for the ride, and holding on for dear life!

Opposite: The obedience team at the 1983 SHCA Specialty Show and Trial in California. Judge Sharon Fulkerson and C.T. Fulkerson preside over the winning performance of Ch. Beorthwulf Boreas Re Tymen, CDX, owned by Marcia Hoyt; Berkeley's Major Nuisance, CD, owned by Judy Loos; Shepmar Shyak's Russkaya, CD, owned by Sue Munson; and Kimsha's Tosca of Kamiakin, CDX, owned by Philip Swany.

SIBERIAN HUSKY CLUBS

While the Siberian Husky was recognized in 1930 by the American Kennel Club, it was not until 1938 that the Siberian Husky Club of America was founded. The purposes of the club are to support specialty shows, promote the use of this working dog in racing competition and–what is even more important—to encourage members to breed true to the Standard approved by the American Kennel Club, toward a standard of excellence which brings out the true qualities for which the breed originated.

The increased popularity of the breed—which is almost alarming in numbers of registrations—has made the role of the parent club even more important than ever before, in working toward control and strict breeding principles within the membership and the education of those who are not members. In accordance with this, the club recommends and actively promotes the purchase of purebred Siberian Huskies from amongst their membership and the education of the public to the importance of buying good stock from reputable breeders. The Club also counsels and advises, and distributes a newsletter which contains the latest information pertinent to the breed.

The first National Specialty Show to be held independently by the Siberian Husky Club of America was staged on June 2, 1972 in Wellesley, Massachusetts. The judges for this event were Mrs. Norbert Kanzler, dogs, and Mrs. Lou Richardson, bitches; Mrs.

Augustus Riggs, III, officiated in the Inter-Sex and Non-Regular classes.

SPECIAL PRIZES AND TROPHIES

Based on an idea proposed by Lorna Demidoff in 1959, each trophy is a reproduction of an antique Georgian sterling silver punch bowl and is a most cherished prize.

In 1973, the name was changed to the Showing-Working Trophy, with the idea that the "all around" Siberian

year since 1960 the Siberian Husky Club of America has awarded a special trophy to the team of Siberians whose performance in both the show ring and on the trail best exemplifies the valued dual capabilities of the breed. The Husky should be honored. The point system is based on wins in the show ring, wins in sled dog racing, and obedience degrees, and no more than two-thirds of the applicant's total points can come from either racing or showing.

Top: An informal shot at the 1980 Westminster KC Best in Show judging with Trish Kanzler and AmCan Ch. Innisfree's Sierra Cinnar. Owned and bred by Kathleen Kanzler, Innisfree Kennels, Chateaugay, NY. *Bottom:* Ch. Kiok's Kancelled Chex, CDX, bred and owned by Joe and Brenda Kolar, Astoria, OR.

REGIONAL SIBERIAN HUSKY CLUBS

Over the years, in addition to the parent club, fanciers saw the possibilities of local clubs, where information and support could be given to newcomers and old timers alike. The parent club oversees four district areas in which breed clubs are functioning.

AREA 1:

Connecticut Valley Siberian Husky Club
Garden State Siberian Husky Club
Mohawk Valley Siberian Husky Club
Seneca Siberian Husky Club
Siberian Husky Club of Greater New York
Siberian Husky Club of the Jersey Shore
Siberian Husky Club of the Niagara Frontier
Yankee Siberian Husky Club

AREA 2:

Central Indiana Siberian Husky Club
Central North Carolina Siberian Husky Club
Chesapeake Siberian Husky Club
Greater Washington Siberian Husky Club
Hampton Roads Siberian Husky Association
Siberian Husky Club of Central Florida
Siberian Husky Club of Central Ohio
Siberian Husky Club of Delaware Valley
Siberian Husky Club of Greater Atlanta
Siberian Husky Club of Greater Canton
Siberian Husky Club of Greater Cincinnati
Siberian Husky Club of Greater Cleveland
Siberian Husky Club of Greater Detroit
Siberian Husky Club of Greater

Top: Ch. Skyhope's Sitka of Battle, owned by Jan Neville and handled by Mickey Zinger. *Bottom:* Ch. Troika's Memorex winning on the way to championship under Don Duerksen. Bred, owned and handled by Patty Jones.

Top: Talocon's Arctic Polaris winning at the 1986 Mohawk Valley KC Show. Bred and owned by John and Gail O'Connell and shown by Gail.

Bottom: Ch. Talocon's Arctic Aleta, a Best of Breed winning female and a Specialty winner, winning under judge Robert Forsythe at a 1982 show. Bred and owned by John and Gail O'Connell of Hauppauge, NY.

Ch. Karnovanda's Angeline, winning an extremely large Bred-by Class at the 1985 National Specialty Show. The sire was Ch. Karnovanda's Some Kind of Hew ex Ch. Innisfree's Morning Mist. Owner-handled and bred by Judith Russell.

Pittsburg
Siberian Husky Club of Greater Youngstown
Siberian Husky Club of Kentuckiana
Siberian Husky Club of Muncie
Siberian Husky Club of Northwestern Ohio
Siberian Husky Club of South Florida
Siberian Husky Club of Tampa Bay
Siberian Husky Club of Southeastern Michigan
Susquehanna Valley Siberian Husky Club

AREA 3:
El Paso Del Norte Siberian Husky Club
Heart of Texas Siberian Husky Club
Rocky Mountain Siberian Husky Club
Siberian Husky Club of Greater Chicago
Siberian Husky Club of Greater Kansas City
Siberian Husky Club of Greater

Oklahoma City
Siberian Husky Club of Greater Milwaukee
Siberian Husky Club of Greater Omaha
Siberian Husky Club of Houston
Siberian Husky Club of Metropolitan Dallas
Siberian Husky Club of San Antonio
Siberian Husky Club of the Twin Cities

AREA 4:
Bay Area Siberian Husky Club
Camino Real Siberian Husky Club
Northern California Siberian Husky Club
Siberian Husky Club of Anchorage, Alaska
Siberian Husky Club of Greater Phoenix
Siberian Husky Club of Hawaii
Siberian Husky Club of San Diego County
Siberian Husky Club of

Southern California Siberian Husky Club of Washington State

Since club secretaries change on a rather frequent basis, those wishing to join a club would be wise to write or telephone the American Kennel Club, 51 Madison Avenue, New York, NY 10010 to secure the name and address of the current secretary. They will be able to put you in touch with the proper person. A letter or call to them will also advise you on necessary procedures to join the group after application.

THE INTERNATIONAL SIBERIAN HUSKY CLUB

In spring, 1961, the Seppala Siberian Husky Club was formed in honor of the man whose name it bore. Charter members were Mr. and Mrs. Leonhard Seppala, Mrs. Louis Foley, Mr. and Mrs. Raymond Thompson, and Mrs. Virginia Emrich. However, in 1964 the name was changed to the International Siberian Husky Club. Its membership has grown to include over 500 members in 40 states, provinces of Canada and 5 countries.

By 1964, for the information of its members, the club published a bi-monthly newsletter edited by Mrs. Beth Murphy and Miss Jane Smith. In 1965, editor Arnie Hed was in charge and changed the publication to a quarterly. By 1966 it was a monthly publication and the editorship had passed to Miss Doris Lovrine.

In 1961, committees formed to serve their membership in specific categories. Among the noteworthy committees was the Research and Records

AmCan Ch. Tandara's Che Kodiak, CD, No. 10 Siberian Husky in the Kennel Review System in 1981. The sire was AmCan Ch. The Bastion's Palacheveyo; owned by Lynne Patterson, Tandara, Gio Harbor, WA.

> *"A special Outstanding Achievement Award is given to the dog which completed the championship requirements and raced in 20 heats of ten miles or more and finished in the upper half of the total number of entries."*

Committee headed by Mrs. Louis Foley. Mrs. Foley researched the breed and presented the club with a great deal of information on the early history of the Husky in Siberia. This committee was discontinued in 1965. In 1967, the ISHC Pedigree Directory was published under the guidance of Mrs. Peggy Hazlett; the directory presented a listing of various dogs, their pedigrees and their characteristics.

Also in 1967, the club held its first booster show in Toronto, Canada. An entry of 42 appeared, which was a record entry for the breed in Canada up to that time. Gunnar Allerellie and Mrs. Carol Sutliff were largely responsible for this initial effort.

The Award Committee was started in 1967, offering a number of achievement awards. Every dog which attained a championship or obedience title received a certificate of recognition. The racing award is presented to the Siberian which has raced on a team that has completed 20 single races or ten two-heat races of not less than ten miles. The team must have finished in the upper half of the total entries as well. An obedience award for CDX was given and a special award to CD dogs which won with scores of 190 or better on all three legs.

The Championship award was given to the Siberian Husky which earned the title with ten Bests or Bests of Opposite Sex in shows where three or more points were awarded. A special Outstanding Achievement Award is given to the dog which completed the championship requirements and raced in 20 heats of ten miles or more and finished in the upper half of the total number of entries. This dog must also meet certain obedience requirements.

There is also a Combination Achievement Award with slightly different requirements and members are advised to write the club for detailed requirements on all rules.

Of interest to those in—or getting into—the breed are the *International Siberian Husky Club News*, the official publication of this organization, and Cynthia Molburg's *Team and Trail*, the musher's monthly news, published in Center Harbor, New Hampshire.

THE FEDERATION CYNOLOGIQUE INTERNATIONALE

The Standard for the Siberian Husky was officially recognized by FCI in June 1966. The FCI is the top European organization in the world of dogs and was formed in the early 1930s. It is the central governing body and is composed of a few selected representatives and delegates of each of the national kennel clubs whose purpose it is to standardize breeds and shows. They establish the rules for the shows, select the recognized

FIRST
IN
GROUP

LEWIS-CLARK KENNEL CLUB
PILGRIM CLUSTER
NOVEMBER 23, 1984
JUDGE: MR. N. WALLACE

WORKING
GROUP

JUNE 3, 1984

Top: Ch. Zatmieniya Tyene winning a 4-point major and a Group First at the 1984 Lewis-Clark KC Show. This beautiful bitch finished for her championship with this prestigious win, piloted by handler Ollie Click. Bred by Walter and Nancy Belknap, she is owned by Marsha Folks. The sire was Ch. Cinnaminson Copper Prestige ex Reverlry's Titania.

Bottom: Ch. Toko's Four-Leaf Clover at age 9½ years, winning a strong Working Group under Sam Pizzino in 1984. He is one of 7 champions for the litter sired by Ch. Marlytuk's Red Sun of Kiska ex Ch. Fournier's Tiffany of Toko. Bred, owned and handled by Jean Fournier.

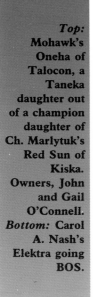

Top: Mohawk's Oneha of Talocon, a Taneka daughter out of a champion daughter of Ch. Marlytuk's Red Sun of Kiska. Owners, John and Gail O'Connell. *Bottom:* Carol A. Nash's Elektra going BOS.

Top: Beautiful head study of Marie Wamser's Fra-Mar's Koala Diavol. Whelped in 1981, his sire was Ch. Chuniek's Follow His Shadow ex Fra-Mar's Paata Diavol. *Bottom:* Ch. The Honey Bear of Troika, owned and handled by Patty Jones, Troika Kennels, Bonner Spring, KS. The sire was Ch. Marlytuk's Sachem of Canaan ex Ch. Kczar's Phoenix of Troika.

breeds, put them in their groupings, settle all disputes and disagreements which might arise within the establishing of International Championship titles. Their group consists of 21 member countries and 13 associate member countries. They issue points toward the title called the Certificate of Beauty and Aptitude.

The International Champion title is the highest award a dog can achieve. Before a dog can be called an International Champion, he must have received the CACIB certificate four times, at four different shows in three different countries (including his home country), and under three different judges. The CACIB certificate stands for Certificate of Ability to Compete for the Title of National Champion, and can be compared to the US Winners Dog or Winners Bitch wins, in that they are receiving

points toward their titles. CACIB wins are earned from the Open Classes.

While there is a Youth Class for dogs from ten to 15 months, the minimum age for Open Class is 15 months, so most European dogs are entered in the Open Class starting with their very first show at exactly 15 months of age. There are sometimes classes for braces or groups of the same breed, but no Specials Classes as we know them in the US. There is no Best of Breed or Group judging and there is no Best in Show award in Europe.

The Siberian Husky is judged in Europe by those judges qualified to judge all Northern dog breeds, or by an all-breed judge.

THE RALSTON PURINA INVITATIONAL

In the 1980s, the Ralston Purina Company began their

Ch. Karnovanda's Wolfgang, winning the Veteran Dog Class at the 1981 National Specialty Show at the age of 12½ years. This was the second time in a row for this dog to capture this prestigious win. Judge was Donald Booxbaum and trophy presenter was Anna Mae Forsberg. Handled by breeder-owner Judith Russell.

Arahaz Kaylee Konkon, CD, and Ch. Arahaz Tengri Khan, CD, another of the Kaylee Best in Show-winning braces. This picture taken at the First Independent Specialty (in 1972) of the SHCA. Owned and handled by Susanna W. Rodney of Baltimore, MD.

annual Purina Invitational dog show. This event was inaugurated by Purina to recognize the best dogs of the year or the top ten show dogs in each Breed or Variety for that particular year. Selection is based on the *Canine Chronicle* newspaper and their Rutledge Point system of top-winning dogs.

What makes the Invitational so exceptional is the phenomenal cash awards given at the show. A panel of top judges gets to give the $2500 Best in Show cash award with the winner's name inscribed on a sterling silver loving cup to be permanently displayed at the Dog Museum of America. Reserve Best in Show takes home a cash award of $1500 with Group wins of $500 for First, $250 for Group Second, $150 for Group Third, and $100 for Group Fourth. Rosettes are awarded to Best of Breed winners and all participants receive a Certificate of Participation.

This is not an American Kennel Club-sanctioned event and no championship points are awarded; it is also not an indication of an endorsement or testimonial for Purina dog foods. It is merely a special event supported by certain parties interested in the fancy. One of these is *Canine Chronicle*, on whose point system the top dogs are determined.

BUYING YOUR SIBERIAN HUSKY

"It is advisable that you become thoroughly acquainted with the breed prior to purchasing your puppy."

In searching for that special puppy, there are several paths that will lead you to a litter from which you can find the puppy of your choice. If you are uncertain as to where to find a reputable breeder, write to the parent club and ask for the names and addresses of members who have puppies for sale. The addresses of various breed clubs can be obtained by writing directly to the American Kennel Club, Inc., 51 Madison Avenue, New York, NY 10010. They keep an up-to-date, accurate list of breeders from whom you can seek information on obtaining a good, healthy puppy. The classified ad listings in dog publications and the major newspapers may also lead you to that certain pup. The various dog magazines generally carry a monthly breed column which features information and news

on the breed that may aid in your selection.

It is advisable that you become thoroughly acquainted with the breed prior to purchasing your puppy. Plan to attend a dog show or two in your area, at which you can view purebred dogs of just about every breed at their best in the show ring. Even if you are not interested in purchasing a show-quality dog, you should be familiar with what the better specimens look like so that you will at least purchase a decent representative of the breed for the money. You can learn a lot from observing show dogs in action in the ring, or in some other public place, where their personalities can be clearly shown. The dog show catalog is also a useful tool to put you in contact with the local kennels and breeders. Each dog that is entered in the show is listed

Four-week-old puppies at play at Innisfree.

along with the owner's name and address. If you spot a dog that you think is a particularly fine and pleasing specimen, contact the owners and arrange to visit their kennel to see the types of dogs they are breeding and winning with at the shows. Exhibitors at the dog shows are usually more than delighted to talk to people interested in their dogs and the specific characteristics of their breed.

Once you've decided that this is the breed for you, read some background material so that you become thoroughly familiar with it. When you feel certain that this puppy will fit in with your family's way of life, it is time to start writing letters and making phone calls and appointments to see those dogs that may interest you.

Some words of caution: don't choose a kennel simply because it is near your home, and don't buy the first cute puppy that romps around your legs or licks the end of your nose. All puppies are cute, and naturally some will appeal to you more than others. But don't let preferences sway your thinking. If you are buying your puppy to be strictly a family pet, preferences can be permissible. If you are looking for a top-quality puppy for the show ring, however, you must

The photograph that graced the cover of the author's first book on the Siberian Husky. Ch. Monadnock's Misty of Arahaz and Mischa of Arahaz. Owned by Rosemary Fischer of Beaver, PA.

evaluate clearly, choose wisely, and make the best possible choice. Whichever one you choose, you will quickly learn to love your puppy. A careful selection, rather than a "love at first sight" choice will save you from disappointment later on.

To get the broadest idea of what puppies are for sale and what the going market prices are, visit as many kennels as possible in your area and write to others farther away. With today's safe and rapid air flights on the major airlines, it is possible to purchase dogs from far-off places at nominal costs. While it is safest and wisest to first see the dog you are buying, there are enough reputable breeders and kennels to be found for you to take this step with a minimum of risk. In the long run, it can be well worth your while to obtain the exact dog or bloodline you desire.

It is customary for the purchaser to pay the shipping

charges, and the airlines are most willing to supply flight information and prices upon request. Rental on the shipping crate, if the owner does not provide one for the dog, is nominal. While unfortunate incidents have occurred on the airlines in the transporting of animals by air, the major airlines are making improvements in safety measures and have reached the point of reasonable safety and cost. Barring unforeseen circumstances, the safe arrival of a dog you might buy can pretty much be assured if both seller and purchaser adhere to and follow up on even the most minute details from both ends.

WHAT TO LOOK FOR IN YOUR DOG

Anyone who has owned a puppy will agree that the most fascinating aspect of raising him is to witness the complete and extraordinary metamorphosis that occurs during his first year of maturing. Your puppy will undergo a marked change in appearance, and during this period you must also be aware of the puppy's personality, for there are certain qualities

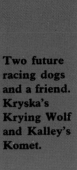

Two future racing dogs and a friend. Kryska's Krying Wolf and Kalley's Komet.

Top: Darling little puppy and future champion at the Sakonnet Kennels of Leroy and Leslie Simons, Leighton, IA. *Bottom:* A lazy summer afternoon at the Arlington Kennels in Staten Island, NY.

Top: **Charming photograph of Sylvia Roselli's Cin Cin and Krissy.** *Bottom:* **Three Kaylee puppies at their kennel yard in Baltimore, MD.**

Two-week-old promising litter whelped at Anne Bruder's Sunset Hills Kennels in Taos, NM.

visible at this time that will generally make for a good adult dog. Of course no one can guarantee nature, and the best puppy does not always grow up to be a great dog; however, even the novice breeder can learn to look for certain specifics that will help him choose a promising puppy.

Should you decide to purchase a six-to-eight-week-old puppy, you are in store for all the cute antics that little pup can dream up for you! At this age, the puppy should be well on its way to being weaned, wormed, and ready to go out into the world with its responsible new owner. It is better not to buy a puppy that is less than six weeks old; it simply is not ready to leave its mother or the security of the other puppies. By eight to twelve weeks of age, you will be able to notice much about the behavior and appearance of the dog. Puppies, as they are recalled in our fondest childhood memories, are amazingly active and bouncy—and well they should be! The normal puppy should be alert, curious, and interested, especially when a stranger is present. However, if the puppy acts a little reserved or distant, don't necessarily construe these acts to be signs of fear or

Eight-week-old Ta-Ra's Baron of Konik tells Santa what he wants for Christmas at the Konik Kennels of Janet and Gary Cingel of East Hampton, CT.

shyness. It might merely indicate that he hasn't quite made up his mind whether he likes you as yet. By the same token, though, he should not be openly fearful or terrified by a stranger—and especially should not show any fear of his owner!

In direct contrast, the puppy should not be ridiculously over-active, either. The puppy that frantically bounds around the room and is never still is not especially desirable. And beware of the "spinners." Spinners are the puppies or dogs that have become neurotic from being kept in cramped quarters or in crates and behave in an emotionally unstable manner when let loose in adequate space. When let out they run in circles and seemingly "go wild." Puppies with this kind of traumatic background seldom ever regain

full composure or adjust to the big outside world. The puppy which has had proper exercise and appropriate living quarters will have a normal, though spirited, outlook on life and will do its utmost to win you over without having to go into a tailspin.

If the general behavior and appearance of the dog thus far appeal to you, it is time for you to observe him more closely for additional physical requirements. First of all, you cannot expect to find in the puppy the coat he will bear upon maturity. That will come with time and good food and will be additionally enhanced by the many wonderful grooming aids which can be found in pet shops today. Needless to say, the healthy puppy's coat should have a nice shine to it, and the more dense at this age, the better the coat

Siberian puppy with a wonderful show-ring career ahead.

will be when the dog reaches adulthood. Look for clear, sparkling eyes that are free of discharge.

It is important to check the bite. Even though the puppy will cut another complete set of teeth somewhere between four and seven months of age, there will already be some indication of how the final teeth will be positioned.

Puppies take anything and almost everything into their mouths to chew on, and a lot of diseases and infections start or are introduced in the mouth. Brown-stained teeth, for instance, may indicate the puppy has had a past case of distemper, and the teeth will

remain that way. This fact must be reckoned with if you have a show puppy in mind. The puppy's breath should be neither sour nor unpleasant. Bad breath can be a result of a poor food mixture in the diet, or of eating low quality meat, especially if it is fed raw. Some people say that the healthy puppy's breath should have a faint odor that is vaguely reminiscent of garlic. At any rate, a puppy should never be fed just table scraps, but should be raised on a well-balanced diet containing a good dry puppy chow and a good grade of fresh meat. Poor meat and too much cereal or fillers tend to make the puppy grow too fat. Puppies should be in good flesh but not fat from the wrong kind of food.

Needless to say, the puppy should be clean. The breeder that shows a dirty puppy is one to steer away from. Look closely at the skin. Make sure it is not covered with insect bites or red, blotchy sores and dry scales. The vent area around the tail should not show evidences of diarrhea or inflammation. By the same token, the puppy's fur should not be matted with feces or smell strongly of urine.

True enough, you can wipe dirty eyes, clean dirty ears, and give the puppy a bath when you get it home, but these things are all indications of how the puppy has been cared for during the important formative first months of its life, and they can vitally influence the pup's future health and development. There are many reputable breeders raising healthy puppies that have been reared in proper places and under the proper conditions in clean housing, so why take a chance on a series of veterinary bills and a questionable constitution?

MALE OR FEMALE?

The choice of sex in your puppy is also something that must be given serious thought before you buy. For the pet owner, the sex that would best suit the family life you enjoy would be the paramount choice to consider. For the breeder or exhibitor, there are other vital

considerations. If you are looking for a stud to establish a kennel, it is essential that you select a dog with both testicles evident, even at a tender age. If there is any doubt, have a vet verify this before the sale is finalized.

The visibility of only one testicle, known as monorchidism, automatically disqualifies the dog from the show ring or from a breeding program, though monorchids are capable of siring. Additionally, it must be noted that monorchids frequently sire dogs with the same deficiency, and to knowingly introduce this into a bloodline is an unwritten sin in the fancy. Also, a monorchid can sire dogs that are completely sterile. Such dogs are referred to as cryptorchids and have no testicles.

Veleah's Justin Thyme, owned by Ernie and Pati Fleshman of Orlando, FL.

Top: Smile for the camera! Arlington Kennels.
Bottom: Little Bobby Levine with his pal Arahaz Margaritka. Olan Mills photo.

Opposite: A typical Snoking Kennels puppy, bred and owned by Richard and Jan MacWhade of Hinckley, OH.

An additional consideration in the male versus female decision for private owners is that with males there might be the problem of leg-lifting and with females there is the inconvenience while they are in heat. However, this need not be the problem it used to be—pet shops sell "pants" for both sexes, which help to control the situation.

THE PLANNED PARENTHOOD BEHIND YOUR PUPPY

Never be afraid to ask pertinent questions about the puppy, nor questions about the sire and dam. Feel free to ask the breeder if you might see the dam; the purpose of your visit is to determine her general health and her appearance as a representative of the breed. Also, ask to see the sire, if the breeder is the owner. Ask what the puppy has been fed and should be fed after weaning. Ask to see the pedigree, and inquire if the litter or the individual puppies have been registered with the American Kennel Club, how many of the temporary and/or permanent inoculations the puppy has had, when and if the puppy has been wormed, and whether it has had any illness, disease, or infection.

You need not ask if the puppy is housebroken; it won't mean much. He may have gotten the idea as to where "the place" is where he lives now, but he will need new training to learn where "the place" is in his new home! You can't really expect too much from puppies at this age anyway. Housebreaking is entirely up to the new owner. We know puppies always eliminate when they first awaken and sometimes dribble when they get excited. If friends and relatives are coming over to see the new puppy, make sure he is walked just before he greets them at the front door. This will help.

The normal elimination time for puppies is about every two or three hours. As the time draws near, either take the puppy out or indicate the newspaper for the same purpose. Housebreaking is never easy, but anticipation is about 90 percent of solving the problem. The schools that offer to housebreak your dog are virtually useless. Here again the puppy will learn "the place" at

Ruth Gregg with Arahaz Sin Koroleva.

Simba Tu and Shantue, puppies bred by Judi Anderson of Panuck-Denali Kennels in Laconia, NH. Shantue resided in Berlin, Germany, with a member of the American Embassy.

the schoolhouse, but coming home he will need special training for the new location.

A reputable breeder will welcome any and all questions you might ask and will voluntarily offer additional information, if only to brag about the tedious and loving care he has given the litter. He will also sell a puppy on a 24-hour veterinary approval basis. This means you have a full day to get the puppy to a veterinarian of your choice to get his opinion on the general health of the puppy before you make a final decision. There should also be veterinary certificates and full particulars on the dates and types of inoculations.

PUPPIES AND WORMS

Let us give further attention to the unhappy and very

Top: A young lady and her dog at Sylvia Roselli's Arlington Kennels. *Bottom:* Mr. Chip's "chip off the old block"; puppy owned by Angela Porpora by Jean Fournier's Ch. Toko's Mr. Chip of Yago, CD.

Eleven-week-old Hurricane's Camile of Grawyn. Owners, Deanna and Lou Gray, Woodstock, IL.

unpleasant subject of worms. Generally speaking, most puppies—even those raised in clean quarters—come into contact with worms early in life. The worms can be passed down from the mother before birth or picked up during the puppies' first encounters with the earth or their kennel facilities. To say that you must

The extent of the infection can be readily determined by a veterinarian, and you might take his word as to whether the future health and conformation of the dog has been damaged. He can prescribe the dosage and supply the medication at this time, and you will already have one of your problems solved.

Arahaz Kalinda, bred and owned by Rosemary Fischer, Beaver, PA.

not buy a puppy because of an infestation of worms is nonsensical. You might be passing up a fine animal that can be freed of worms in one short treatment, although a heavy infestation of worms of any kind in a young dog is dangerous and debilitating.

VET INSPECTION
While your veterinarian is going over the puppy you have selected, you might just as well ask him for his opinion of it as a breed, as well as the facts about its general health. While few veterinarians can claim to be breed-conformation experts,

they usually have a good eye for a worthy specimen and can advise you where to go for further information. Perhaps your veterinarian could also recommend other breeders if you should want another opinion. The veterinarian can point out structural faults or organic problems that affect all veterinarians that we can expect to reap the harvest of modern research.

Most reliable veterinarians are more than eager to learn about various breeds of purebred dogs, and we in turn must acknowledge and apply what they have proved through experience and research in their

Future First Lady Nancy Reagan during the first Reagan Presidential Campaign in 1980 in Laconia, NH, gets ready for a sled ride bearing Judi Anderson's Alaskan Parka and holding Mara, a Panuck-Denali puppy, while team dogs look on.

breeds and can usually judge whether an animal has been abused or mishandled and whether it is oversized or undersized.

I would like to emphasize here that it is only through this type of close cooperation between owners and field. We can buy and breed the best dog in the world, but when disease strikes we are only as safe as our veterinarian is capable—so let's keep him informed, breed by breed and dog by dog. The veterinarian can mean the difference between life and death!

THE CONDITIONS OF SALE

While it is customary to pay for the puppy before you take it away with you, you should be able to give the breeder a deposit if there is any doubt about the puppy's health. Depending on local laws, you might also postdate a check to cover the 24-four hour veterinary approval. If you decide to take the puppy, the breeder is required to supply you with a pedigree, along with the puppy's registration papers. He is also obliged to supply you with complete information about the inoculations and American Kennel Club instructions on how to transfer ownership of the puppy to your name.

For convenience, some breeders will offer buyers time payment plans if the price on a show dog is very high or if deferred payments are the only way you can purchase the dog. However, any such terms must be worked out between buyer and breeder and should be put in writing to avoid later complications.

You will find most breeders cooperative if they believe you are sincere in your love for the puppy and that you will give it the proper home and the show ring career it deserves (if it is sold as a show-quality specimen of the breed). Remember, when buying a show dog, it is impossible to guarantee what mother nature has created. A breeder can only tell you what he *believes* will develop into a show dog, so be sure your breeder is an honest one.

Also, if you purchase a show prospect and promise to show the dog, you definitely should show it! It is a waste to have a beautiful dog that deserves

Mr. William Creamer and his two Arahaz puppies, Kristi and Ciara.

recognition in the show ring sitting at home as a family pet, and it is unfair to the breeder. This is especially true if the breeder offered you a reduced price because of the advertising his kennel and bloodlines would receive by your showing the dog in the ring. If you want a pet, buy a pet. Be honest about it, and let the breeder decide on this basis which is the best dog for you. Your conscience will be clear and you'll both be doing a real service to the breed.

BUYING A SHOW PUPPY

If you are positive about breeding and showing, make this point clear so that the breeder will sell you the best possible puppy. If you are dealing with an established kennel, you will have to rely partially, if not entirely, on their choice, since they know their bloodlines and what they can expect from the breeding. They know how their stock develops, and it would be foolish of them to sell you a puppy that could not stand up as a show specimen representing their stock in the ring.

However, you must also realize that the breeder may be keeping the best puppy in the litter to show and breed himself. If this is the case, you might be wise to select the best puppy of the opposite sex so that the dogs will not be competing against one another in the show rings.

A friendly visit at Arlington Kennels, Staten Island, NY.

THE PURCHASE PRICE

Prices vary on all puppies, of course, but a good show prospect at six weeks to six months of age will usually sell for several hundred dollars. If the puppy is really outstanding, and the pedigree and parentage are also outstanding, the price will be even higher. Honest breeders, however, will all quote around the same figure, so price should not be a strong deciding factor in your choice. If you have any questions as to the current price range, a few telephone calls to different kennels will give you a good average. Reputable breeders will usually stand behind the health of their puppies should something drastically wrong develop. Their obligation to make an adjustment or replacement is usually honored. However, this must be agreed to in writing at the time of the purchase.

STATISTICS AND THE PHILLIPS SYSTEM

"The first annual Westminster Kennel Club show was held at Gilmore's Garden (Hippodrome) on Tuesday, Wednesday, and Thursday, May 8, 9, 10, in 1877."

SIBERIAN HUSKIES AT THE FIRST WESTMINSTER KENNEL CLUB

The first annual Westminster Kennel Club show was held at Gilmore's Garden (Hippodrome) on Tuesday, Wednesday, and Thursday, May 8, 9, and 10, in 1877. Charles Lincoln was the superintendent, and the bench show committee for the first event listed the names of famous pioneers of the fancy in the country. On the list were William M. Tileston, C. DuBois Wagstaff, H. Walter Webb, Dr. W.S. Webb, Louis B. Wright, and E.H. Dixon.

The catalogue, consisting of 49 pages of entries, featured Siberian or Ulm Dogs as listings 704 through 711. It is interesting to note that every entry but one, apparently a recent import, was listed as for sale. The catalogue read as follows:

704 J. Fortune, Marion
Jersey City Heights, NJ
Roman, ash and wh., 2 years 8 months, $100.

705 E. Bolenius
229 Bowery, NY
Guido, yellow and wh., 2 years. From the State of Wurtenburg, $200.

706 Lewis Lintz
West Winfield, Herkimer County, NY
Darling, mouse, 4 years; impt. $500.

707 Lewis Lintz
West Winfield, Herkimer
County, NY
Centennial, mouse, 8 months,
by *Darling* $75.

708 Max Borchardt
54 Garden Street, Hoboken, NJ
Ralph, bl. and wh., 2 years.
$25.

709 F. Bencing
27½ Christy Street, NY
Caesar, bl. and wh., 2½ years,
$150.

710 J.W. Jones
Plainfield, NJ
Bruno, grey and gl., 6 years
$150.

711 J.B. Miller
Box 170, Newburg, NY
Frank, wh. and brown, 2
years imported

FIRST SIBERIAN HUSKY CHAMPIONS

The first Siberian Husky champion of record in the United States was recorded in 1931. The dog's name was Pola. Another champion followed the next year, in 1932, and the name was Northern Light Kobuk. A few years went by (1936 to be exact) before another champion was to be listed, and the name was Shankhassock Lono. In 1938 and 1939, single championships were attained by dogs named

EuMor's Necia, owned by Scott Quirin. Necia is the foundation bitch for their Scoqui Kennels in Duluth, MN.

Cheenah of Alyeska and Togo of Alyeska respectively.

By the 1940s however, and in the years that followed, the number of championship Huskies increased. During the 1940s, 18 championships were entered in the American Kennel Club books, with the kennel names of Monadnock and Alyeska predominating. During the 1950s, no less than 63 Siberians included the Ch. before their names.

During the 1960s the total was 515 championships! From the 1960s until the present day, there are too many championships to be recorded here. The Siberian Husky had earned his place in the show ring with championship status—there is no doubt about it!

EARLY BEST IN SHOW WINNERS

The honor of being the first Siberian Husky to win a Best in Show was bestowed upon Ch. Monadnock's King, bred and owned by Lorna Demidoff. The show was the Mohawk Valley Kennel Club and the date was November 11, 1961. King was sired by Ch. Monadnock's Pando out of Monadnock's Czarina.

The date was October 19, 1964, at the Kokomo Kennel Club show, that another Monadnock dog won the second Best in Show honors; his name was Ch. Monadnock's Dmitri. Though owned by Dr. James Brillhart, Dmitri was also bred by Lorna Demidoff

and sired by Ch. Monadnock's Pando. The dam of Dmitri was Monadnock's Ekatrina.

1964 was obviously a good year for Siberian Bests in Show, since Ch. Frosty Aires Alcan King, owned and bred by Marie Wamser, also won a Best in Show that year at the Gambier, Ohio Kennel Club Show in October.

It wasn't until 1968 that another Siberian won a Best in Show; this was Marie Wamser's Ch Fra-Mar's Soan Diavol that got the top award at the Dan Emmett Kennel Club show. The breeder was Nina Fisher, and the sire was the winner of the 1964 Best in Show award, Alcan King. Soan Diavol was also a champion in Canada and Bermuda, and was a very popular stud as well. His dam was Ch. Fra-Mar's Misarah.

Earl and Natalie Norrises' Ch. Bonzo of Anadyr, CD, was the first all-breed Best in Show winner in Alaska, as well as the first Siberian Husky to win a CD title there.

THE WONDERFUL WESTMINSTER WINNER!

The ultimate was achieved on February 12, 1980, at Madison Square Garden in New York City when the beautiful Siberian Husky, Ch. Innisfree's Sierra Cinnar, with his beautiful handler Trish Kanzler, went all the way to the top—the coveted Best in Show award at the Westminster Kennel Club.

Judge Herman Cox set the

Top: Best of Sled Dogs, dog or bitch, at the SHC of Greater New York Specialty in 1985 was Alkas'Iber Kid Kreko, bred and owned by George and Ann Cook and Stephen Serafin. The sire was Manitou Timbucktoo ex Can Ch. Tokomac's Kashega. *Bottom:* The absolute dream in dogdom! Best in Show at Westminster Kennel Club in New York City. Trish Kanzler wins in 1980 with her Top-Producing champion in breed history, AmCan Ch. Innisfree's Sierra Cinnar. In addition to his 114 champion get, Cinnar has 30 Bests in Show and 15 Bests in Specialty. Pictured with daughters Trish and Sheila are Kathleen and Norbort Kanzler of the world-famous Innisfree Kennels.

scene by awarding Cinnar the Working Group; the crowning glory followed when Best in Show judge E. Irving Eldredge selected Cinnar for the top award. Needless to say, it was a popular win as it usually is when a family dog is shown by a member of the family and goes all the way. In this case, the breeder was Trish's mother, Kathleen Kanzler, whose dogs and kennel name have graced the ranks of top dogs in the breed for many years.

This was the first Garden winner for the breed and we can all be proud of this remarkable achievement; let it serve as an inspiration for the future.

THE SYSTEM AND THE SIBERIANS

The first five years of the Phillips System—1956-1961—no Siberian Husky placed in either the Top Ten of the Working Group or the Top Ten of the all-breed listings. But in the 1961 Phillips System issue of *Popular Dogs* magazine, a Siberian Husky was listed—not in the Top Ten in the Working Group, but as a Best in Show winner, a Specialty Show winner, and with Group Placements.

The dog was Ch. Monadnock's King, who had a total of 790 points. King had won a Best in Show, two Specialties, a Group First, a Group Second, and a Group Fourth. Siberians were on their way in the Phillips System!

1962

In 1962, Ch. Monadnock's King once again was mentioned as a member of the Working Group winners with 590 points for a Group First, two Thirds, and a Fourth. This was also the year that 24 dogs were cited for having sired 32 champion Huskies during that year.

But it is Ch. Monadnock's King that must be credited with being the first of the breed to appear in the Phillips System rating system. In fact, he did himself proud by doing it two years in a row.

1963

In 1963, *Popular Dogs* published the system finals in a slightly different manner. They featured the Top Ten all-breed winners and then listed the Top Three in each breed. Siberian Huskies qualified with three in this category. They were No. One, Ch. Ty Cheko of Baltic, CD, with 908 points for a Group First, two Seconds, two Thirds, and three Fourths; No. Two, Ch. Snow Ridge Rina with 270 points for a Group Third and a Group Fourth; and No. Three was Ch. Frosty Aires Peter, CD, with 144 points, Phillips System, for a Group Third.

1964

In 1964, another Monadnock dog headed the Top Three in the breed. His name was Ch. Monadnock's Dmitri and he garnered 720 points for a Best in Show win, and a Group First, Group Second, and a

Ch. Weldon's Beau Tukker, a famous Top-Producer from the past. Handled by Trish Kanzler for owner Kathleen Kanzler, Innisfree Kennels, Chateaugay, NY.

Group Third. Number Two was Ch. Snow Ridge Czar with 693 points for a Group First, two Seconds, and a Third. Ch. Frosty Aires Alcan King was No. Three with 455 points for a Best in Show, Group First, a Group Third, and a Group Fourth.

1965

In 1965, Ch Monadnock's Dmitri repeated in the No. One spot of the Top Three in the breed. This year he totalled an amazing 3136 points for his Best in Show, three Group Firsts, four Seconds, four Thirds, and a Fourth. This was the year that "System Fever" was catching on and competition began to run high. Number Two dog and No. Three dog were new to the scene. Ch. Colorado's State Badge was second of the three winners with 618 points for one Group First, Second, and Fourth. Ch. Kings Soloman was No. Three with 354 points for a Group Second and Third.

Ch. Jonathie Cin-R Citka v. Sno-Fame, owned by William and Linda Albright. Whelped in 1976, the breeders were Joyce Thiele and Ann M. Sullivan. The sire was Westminster Best in Show winner Ch. Innisfree's Sierra Cinnar ex Sno-Fame Jonathie O'Tara.

1966

As good as things were in 1965, three dogs were mentioned in 1966 among the significant winners. Chugachigimiut was listed as No. One with Niuski of Martha Lake, CD, No. Two, and Ch. Alakazan Marika O'Racecrest as No. Three.

1967

In 1967, *Popular Dogs* presented the Phillips System in a slightly different manner; compiling a list of the Top Fifty Dogs in the nation according to the Phillips System.

Unfortunately, there was no Siberian Husky among these winners, nor among the Top Ten in the Working Group.

1968

In 1968 we—by popular request—reverted to our Top Ten ratings, again with no qualifying Husky.

1969

In 1969 and again in 1970 there were no qualifying Siberians in either the Top Ten all-breed or the Top Ten Working Dogs, nor in 1971 or 1972. But there were two Best in Show winners in 1972 that bear mentioning.

Number One in the breed was Ch. Dudleys Tavar of Innisfree, owned by C. and G. Dudley. Tavar had a Best in Show, four Group Seconds, one Group Third, and two Group Fourths for a total of 3134 Phillips System points. Ranked No. Three with a Best in Show, three Group Thirds and a Group Fourth for 1535 points was J.M. Russell's Ch. Karnovandas Wolfgang. Number Two was another Karnovanda dog, Ch. Karnovandas Khan of Kiev with 2687 points for his Group Second, four Group Thirds, and four Group Fourths.

Number four dog was Wintersett Instant Replay, owned by J. Salaba, with 1316. Number Five was Ch. Omiks Quista with 1019, owned by J.M. Ensminger; No. Six dog was Ch. Alakazans Kio Kam of Snoana, owned by M.A. Piunti, with 805 points; and No. Seven was the Kanzlers' Ch. Weldons Beau Buck with 789 points. The No. Eight spot went to Ch. Yanas Erik the Red Viking,

Ch. Sodiax Double or Nothing, owned by Beverly Peterson. The sire was Ch. Innisfree's Pegasus ex Ch. Zodiac's Kara Bear.

owned by R. Patt, with 785 points. Number Nine was Ch. Wolfdens Copper Bullet who had 759 points; he was owned by B. Allen. Number Ten was Ch. Cinnaminsons Soaya Fournier, owned by A. Goldberg and Jean Fournier with 677 points.

1970s

By the mid-1970s, other systems began to evolve in other magazines, especially within the individual breeds.

Following the records based on the original rules of the famous Phillips System which appeared in these other publications, the purity of the rating systems began to spread too thin. Therefore, to assure consistency within a breed, it was wisest to consult the results within the individual breeds, which were kept by statisticians with the members of the breed or parent club. The most outstanding difference with the systems was that most of them did not jibe with the Phillips System, since they included Best of Breed wins, which threw the numbers off and many became confused. Many exhibitors began keeping their own records, and discrepancies began to arise which caused a certain amount of bad feeling when one system was pitted against another. This was regrettable, but true. Today, it is difficult to find a system that truly measures greatness, and the author cannot recall a single one that rings true or creates the fervor that the original Phillips System generated in the days when everyone competed against the same standards.

The 1982 Alaskan KC Show Best of Breed award went to Phyllis Castelton's AmCanBda Ch. White Fox's Blitzen.

On the right is Ch. Sunset Hill's Morning Glory shining for Anne Dussetschleger and Marietta H. Jones.

1980s

By the time we reached the 1980s, Siberian Huskies reached No.15 in popularity, with A.K.C. breed registrations just over 20,000. Litter registrations for 1980 were 7342, with a slight increase to 7618 for 1981.

In synopsis, the 1980s could be called a decade of stabilization, a period of slow, though steady, growth. The Husky closed the 80s with registrations of 21,430 and 21,875, and a rank of 18 and 19 for 1988 and 1989, respectively. While it did drop in rank, its numbers steadily grew.

It may be that this "slowing down" period was positive for the breed. Coming off the explosive growth spurt that occurred from the late 60s through the late 70s—during which time the breed nearly doubled in registration numbers—the more mellow 80s gave the fancy a time to focus on the details and gain greater perspective for the future of the breed.

1990s

The Siberian Husky opened the decade with registration numbers of 21,944 for 1990, and regained its rank of 18, which it held in 1988. There is a general sense among fanciers that the breed is on the rise again, with interest piqued around the globe. There is a concerned optimism among American fanciers, who hope for greater international cooperation and a continued pursuit of excellence by breeders. Much planning and deliberation went into the 1992 National Specialty, a five-day spectacular featuring over 10 breeder-judges and the finest dogs in North America. It will surely be interesting to watch Siberian statistics as the breed trots into the 21st century.

SHOWING AND JUDGING THE SIBERIAN HUSKY

"After all this, the dog is expected to turn on its charm once inside the ring, fascinate the crowds, captivate the judge, and bring home the silverware and ribbons."

Ever since I started judging dogs, I never enter a show ring to begin an assignment without thinking back to what the late, great judge Alva Rosenberg told me when we discussed my apprentice judging under his watchful eye. His most significant observation, I find, still holds true for me today—that a judge's first and most lasting impression of a dog's temperament and bearing will be made the moment it walks into the ring.

It has always been a source of amazement to me the way so many exhibitors ruin that important first impression of their dog before the judge. So many are guilty of dragging their dogs along behind them, squeezing through the ringside crowds, and snapping at people to move out of the way, just to arrive in the ring with a dog whose feet have been stepped on by people pushing to get closer to ringside and whose coat has been ruined by food and cigarette ashes. After all this, the dog is expected to turn on its charm once inside the ring, fascinate the crowds, captivate the judge, and bring home the silverware and ribbons! All this on a day that is invariably either too hot or too cold or too rainy. Not to mention are the hours of standing rigidly, while being sprayed in the face and all over the body with a grooming substance that doesn't smell or taste too good, and then brushed and trimmed until dry to their handler's satisfaction. Add to this the lengthy bath and grooming session the day before the show and the bumpy ride to the show grounds, and, well, Alva Rosenberg had a point! Any dog that can strut into the ring after what could be regarded as a 48-hour torture treatment *does* have to have an excellent disposition and a regal bearing. How fortunate we are that so many of our dogs do have such marvelous temperaments in spite of our grooming rituals.

There is no reason why an exhibitor cannot allow sufficient time to get to ringside, with a few minutes to spare, in order to wait calmly somewhere near the entrance to the ring. They need only walk directly ahead of the dog,

Ch. Kirkacha's Suzi Skyhope winning the Working Group at a 1985 show, owner-handled by Mickey Zinger, Kirkacha's Siberians, Arlington, TX.

Ch. Indigo's Honest Injun, bred and owned by David Qualls of Jacksonville, FL. Sire was Ch. Innisfree's Foxzie ex Ch. Innisfree's Newscent's Niavar.

politely asking the people along the way to step aside with a simple statement to the effect that there is a "dog coming through." It works. Spectators promptly step aside, not only to oblige this simple request when politely stated, but also to observe the beauty of the show dog passing by. Those owners of small breeds who prefer to carry their dogs, and know how to do it without disturbing the dog's coat, can make the same request for the same result.

The short waiting period at ringside allows time for the dog to gain his footing and perspective, and it gives the exhibitor time to get his armband on securely so it won't drop down the arm and onto the dog's head during the first sprint around the ring. These few spare moments will also allow a great deal of the "nervousness" that travels down the lead to your dog to disappear, as the realization that you have arrived at your class on time occurs to you, and you and your dog can both relax.

ENTERING THE RING

When the ring steward calls out the numbers for your class, there is no need for you to try to be first in the ring. There is no prize for being first. If you are new at the game, you would do well to get behind a more experienced exhibitor or professional handler, where you can observe and perhaps learn something about ring behavior. The judge will be well aware of your presence in the ring when he makes a small dot or a small check mark in his judge's book as you enter. The judge must also mark all absentees before starting to evaluate the class, so you can be sure no one will be overlooked as he "counts noses."

Top: Judge Quenten LaHam gives Jean Fournier's Ch. Toko's Mr. Chip of Yago, CD, the Stud Dog Class at the 1985 Yankee SHC Specialty. His get, Aquilla's Silver Belle O'Toko, owned by Yvonne Lewis, and Ch. Toko's Misty Dawn of Northsea were shown by Angela Porpora and are co-owned by Janet Linnehan. *Bottom:* Ch. Itaska's Marvelous Marvin winning the Puppy Dog Class on the way to championship, under Jean Fournier at the AKC Centennial Show in 1984. Bred and owned by Wendy Willhauck, Mansfield, MA.

Simply enter the ring as quickly and calmly as possible with your dog on a loose lead, and at the first opportunity, make sure you show your armband to the judge. Then take a position in the line-up already forming in the ring (usually at the opposite side from the judge's table). Set your dog up in the show pose so that once the judge has checked in all the dogs in the class, he will have an immediate impression of the outline of your dog in show stance. This is also referred to as "stacking" your dog.

The judge will then go up and down the line of dogs in order to compare one outline with another while getting an idea of the symmetry and balance of each profile. This is the time when you should see that your dog maintains the show stance. Don't be nervously brushing your dog, constantly adjusting his feet, tilting his head, primping his tail, etc. All of this should have been done while the judge was walking down the line with his eyes on the other dogs in the class.

By the time the judge gets to your dog, it should be standing as still as a statue, with your hands off it if at all possible. Far too many exhibitors handle

Kristara's Sno-Fame Echo, owned and handled by Lynne Kester, and co-owned and bred by Ann M. Sullivan, winning the 1982 Bronx County KC Show under Robert Forsythe. Echo not only went on to win the Breed over Specials, he went on to a Group Second at this same show.

Sandra Porter's Ch. Keraseva's Harlequinade qualifying for her CD title.

show dogs as if they were puppets with strings attached to all the moving parts. They are constantly pushing the dog in place, prodding it to the desired angle for the judge to see, and placing the head, tail, and feet according to their idea of perfection. More often than not their fingers are covering the dog's muzzle or they are employing their thumbs to straighten out a topline or using a finger to tilt a tail to the proper angle. Repeatedly moving a dog's feet tends to make the judge believe the dog can't stand correctly by itself. If a dog is standing incorrectly the judge might assume that it just happened to be standing incorrectly at that moment, that the exhibitor couldn't imagine such a thing and therefore never noticed it.

Fussing over a dog only calls attention to the fact that the exhibitor either has to do a lot to make the dog look good or is a rank amateur and is nervously mishandling the dog. A free, natural stance, even when a little "off base," is still more appealing to the judge than a dog presented with all four feet barely touching the ground. All dogs are beautiful on their own, and unnecessary handling can only be regarded as a distraction—not as indulgence—on the part of the exhibitor. Do not get the mistaken idea that if the judge thinks you are working hard with your dog, you deserve to win.

MOVE THEM OUT

Once the judge has compared the outlines (or profiles) of each dog, he will ask the exhibitors to move the dogs around the ring so that he might observe them in action. This usually means two complete circles of the ring, depending on the size of the ring and the number of dogs competing in it. This is

AmCan Ch. Kohoutek's Kia of Krislands, bred by Bob and Chris Landers and owned by Alice J. Watt of Salem, OR. Sire was Krisland's Kopper Kohoutek ex Marlytuk's Natasha of Sunny.

the time when the judge must determine whether the dog is moving properly or if it is limping or lame. The judge will check the dog for proper gait and observe if the dog is moving freely on its own—not strung up on the end of a lead with the handler holding the head high.

In the limited time and space you have to show the judge how your dog moves, be careful not to hamper your dog in any way. This means gaiting on a loose lead. Move next to your dog at a safe distance so that you do not step on him while going around corners or pull him off balance on turns. You must also keep in mind that you should not get too close to the dog ahead of you, and that you must keep far enough ahead of the dog behind you so that your dog doesn't get spooked, or so that you don't break the gait.

Once the judge has had time to observe each dog in motion, the signal will be given to one person to stop at a specific spot in the ring, forming the line-up for closer inspection of each dog individually. At the judge's discretion, the individual evaluation can be done either in place or for small breeds, on a table placed in the ring. Whether the judge chooses to evaluate each dog on the ground or on a table, he must go over each one completely in order to evaluate it in accordance with the Standard for its breed.

CLOSE EXAMINATION

As the judge approaches your dog, he will get his first close look at the expression. The judge will want to see the eye color and will want to check the stop, the muzzle, the occiput, the ear leather and set, and the head in its entirety for excellence. During this examination, the exhibitor must make sure the dog remains perfectly still and in correct show stance. Since the dangers of various viral infections and contagious diseases that can be passed from dog to dog at the shows have been made known to us, hopefully the judge will ask that each exhibitor show his own. However, some judges prefer to open the dog's mouth themselves, especially if they have reason to believe there is a

Kossok's Flower Child, bred and owned by Alice Watt, Kossok Kennels. Sire was Kaila's Beau Bleu of Rusojhn ex Ch. Kossok's Good As Gold.

fault. The judge will also evaluate the head from straight on, as well as in profile.

Next, the neck and shoulders will be checked. Shoulders play an important part in the proper placement of the front legs and pasterns. Running his hands down the front leg, the judge will go all the way to the foot, picking it up and checking the foot pads and nails and paying particular attention to whether the dog puts its foot down correctly in place when released.

The judge will check the brisket and the tuck-up, as well as the topline. At this point, with his hands going over the dog, the judge can determine the proper texture of the coat and the general weight of the dog. Judging the hindquarters should prove the dog's legs are sturdy, well placed, and strong enough to provide the strength for proper gait and movement. This is also the time when the judge will check to see that on male dogs both testicles are present and descended.

Once the judge has gone over the dog completely, he will usually take a step or two away from the dog to give it a final over all view, keeping a complete picture of it in his mind to make the comparison with the dog he has judged just before and will judge after yours. This is the time you must still keep your dog "on his toes" so that when the judge glances ahead or behind, your dog is not sitting down, chasing butterflies, or lifting his leg on the number markers. Remember, training is done at home—*performance* is required in the show ring at all times.

INDIVIDUAL GAITING

Once the judge has gone over each dog individually, he will go to the end of the ring and ask each handler to gait his dog. It is important at this point to pay strict attention to the judge's instructions as to how this is to be done. Some judges require the "T" formation, others the half-triangle. Further observation of your dog may bring a request for you to repeat the pattern, especially if your dog did not show well during the first trip. It is important that you hear whether the judge wants you to repeat the entire exercise or merely to gait your dog "down and back" this time.

When each dog has been gaited, the judge will want a last look at all of them lined up together before making this final decisions. Usually the procedure will be to, once again, present the left side of your dog as the judge weaves in and out of the line to check once more the fronts or rears or other individual points of comparison. Some dogs may be asked to gait a third time or to gait side by side with one of the other dogs, should the judge want to "break a tie" as to which dog is the better mover. Because such deciding factors cannot be predicted or anticipated, it is necessary for the handler to always be ready to oblige once the request is given by the judge.

After the decisions are made, the judge will point to his four placements and those four will set their dogs up in front of the designated number markers on the side of the ring. Be ready at this point to show the numbers on your armband so that the judge can mark his judge's book. The judge then will present the winners with the appropriate color ribbons and any trophies won, and you may leave the ring.

Contrary to popular opinion, it is not necessary or even correct to thank the judge for the ribbon. It is to be assumed that the dog *deserved* the ribbon or the judge would not have awarded it. Handing you the ribbon is part of the procedure and does not warrant a thank you. The club, not the judge, is responsible for the donation of the trophies. It is not called for that the exhibitor speak to the judge, but if the win is significant enough so that you feel compelled to say *something*, a simple and not overly exuberant "I'm so pleased that

Ch. Indigo's Grand Illusion, bred by Dr. and Mrs. David Qualls and owned by John Brock. She is shown here winning at a 1984 show.

Ch. Arahaz Shali, bred and owned by Rosemary Fischer.

you like my dog," or something similar, is still more than is necessary.

The thank you for the ribbon has, on occasion, become what some exhibitors like to think of as a "weapon." At ringside you can sometimes hear words to the effect that, "I didn't even thank him for that rotten red ribbon!" As if the judge had even noticed! However, it *is* expected that you take with you from the ring a ribbon of *any color*. To throw it on the ground or leave it behind in the ring so that the steward is obliged to call you back into the ring for the judge to hand it to you again is most unsportsman-like. You must play the game according to the rules. Your entry fee is to obtain the opinion of your dog by the judge. You must take the opinion of your dog by the judge. You must take the opinion and behave

accordingly. If you do not like it, do not give them another entry, but you owe the judge the courtesy of respect for that title.

After this judging procedure is followed in the five classes for dogs, and Winners Dog and Reserve Winners Dog have been determined, the bitches are judged in this same manner. After Winners Bitch and Reserve Winners Bitch awards have been made, the Best of Breed judging follows. Once the judge has completed his assignment and signed his judge's book, it is permissible to request any photographs that you may wish to have taken of your wins. At this time it is also permissible to ask the judge his motives in his judging of *your* dog. If you wish to, it should be done in a polite and calm manner. It must be remembered that the judge is not going to make comparisons, rating one dog against another, but can, if he chooses, give a brief explanation as to how he evaluated your dog.

It is helpful to remember that "no one wins them all." You will win some and lose some no matter how good your dog is. Judges are human and, while no one is perfect, they have earned the title of "judge" for some mighty good reasons. Try to recall that this is a sport and it should be fun—tomorrow is another day.

THE GAMES PEOPLE PLAY

If you are new to the game of dog-show exhibiting there are a few things you should know about, such as how to protect yourself and your dog so that you do not get too discouraged and disillusioned right at the start.

There may be an occasion where your dog is winning a great deal and jealousy will arise from others competing in the ring with you. It has been

Ch. Shalimar's Velika Noga, Karl and Jo Geletich's first champion and stud dog at their Shalimar Kennels. He is winning the Breed at a Golden Gate KC show under H.M. Cresap.

known that some of these bad sports will try to get between you and the judge so the judge cannot see your dog at his best. Others may try stepping on your dog, breaking his gait so that he cannot be adequately judged, bringing bitches in season into the ring, throwing bait around to distract your dog, and so on. Needless to say, most judges are aware of these nasty tricks people play and will not tolerate them. Just be on your guard. Do not leave your dog alone or leave it in the care of others. Thefts have been known at dog shows, as have poisoning and physical abuse. Watch your dog at all times, and be safe rather than sorry.

CHILDREN IN THE SHOW RING

No one is more approving than I of children learning to love and to care for animals. It is beautiful to see a child and an animal sharing complete rapport and companionship or performing as a team in the show ring. Those of us who have been around dog shows for any length of time have

Lois Lippincott and Rosemary Fischer own this handsome dog, Ch. Arahaz Vishii Samets by Ch. Dudley's Vaarska ex Arahaz Barkhata.

Count Boris of Cedarwood winning Best of Breed award. Bred and owned by Rosemary Fischer.

been witness to some remarkable performances by children and their dogs. Junior Showmanship is one example; dogs caring for or standing guard over babies and infants is another example.

There is nothing "cute," however, about a child being allowed to handle a dog where both the welfare of the child and the general public are in danger. Dogs have been known to pull children to the ground with resulting injury to either child, dog, or both. I have seen frightened children let go of leashes or become tangled up in them in the middle of dog fights that left all three participants injured.

If a child shows the natural desire to exhibit a dog after having attended handling classes where he is taught how to properly show a dog, he must also be taught ring procedure. It is not fair to expect other exhibitors to show patience while a judge or the steward informs the child where to stand or waits for him to gait the dog several times before it is done in the formation requested. Lack of knowledge or repeated requests delay the judging, look bad to the ringside crowds, and certainly don't make the dog look good.

If necessary, parents might stay after the dog-show judging and actually train the child in an empty ring. Parents should also sit ringside with the children to explain the judging procedures to them so they will know what to expect when they enter the ring. Many match show appearances should precede any appearance in a point show ring also. Certainly no parent could possibly expect a judge to give them a win just because they are a cute pair— even though they are!

BAITING

No matter how one feels about baiting a dog in the ring, we must acknowledge that almost everyone at one time or another has been guilty of it. Certain breeds are particularly responsive to it, while others show little or no interest with so much going on all around them.

There is no denying that baiting can be an aid to basic training, but in the show ring some judges consider it an indication that the training of the dog for the show ring is not yet complete. It becomes obvious to the judge that the dog still needs an incentive to accomplish what other dogs do in the name of performance.

Frequently, tasty morsels of food are used to bait dogs in the show ring; however, squeaky toys will work as well. Using conversation and pet nicknames in trying to encourage the dog is inappropriate.

Ch. Medvezhi's Indigo Invader, owned by Richard and Gayle Atkinson.

Ch. Bunda's Pumpkin Pisces, bred by Dr. and Mrs. Gabriel Mayer and co-owned by David Qualls and Jann Campbell. Pumpkin is a classic combination of Marlytuk and Innisfree lines and producer of champion get.

DOUBLE HANDLING

You may be sure that a competent judge becomes aware of any double handling, to which some of the more desperate exhibitors may resort.

Double handling is both distracting and frowned upon by the American Kennel Club, nonetheless, some owners go to all sorts of ridiculous lengths to get their apathetic dogs to perform in the ring. They hide behind trees or posts at ringside or may lurk behind the ringside crowd until the exact moment when the judge is looking at or gaiting their dog and then pop out in full view, perhaps emitting some familiar whistle or noise. They may even wave a hat or something similar in hopes that the dog will suddenly become alert and a bit animated.

Don't be guilty of double handling. The day may come when you finally have a great show dog, but the reputation of an owner guilty of double handling lives on forever! You'll be accused of the same shady practices and your new show dog is apt to suffer for it.

APPLAUSE, APPLAUSE!

Another "put-on" by a less secure exhibitor is the practice of bringing his own cheering section to applaud vigorously every time the judge happens to cast an eye on his dog.

The judge is concentrating on what he is doing and will not pay attention to this, nor will he be influenced by the cliques set up by those trying to push their dogs to a win, supposedly by popular approval. The most justified occasions for applause are during a Parade of Champions, during the gaiting of an entire Specialty Best of Breed Class, or during the judging awards for Stud Dog,

". . . to try to prompt a win or stir up interest in a particular dog during the normal course of class judging is amateurish."

Brood Bitch, and Veterans Classes. At these thrilling moments the tribute of spontaneous applause—and the many tears—are understandable and well received, but to try to prompt a win or stir up interest in a particular dog during the normal course of class judging is amateurish.

If you have ever observed this practice, you will notice that the dogs being applauded are sometimes the poorest specimens, whose owners seem to subconsciously realize they cannot win under normal conditions.

SINS WHEN SHOWING DOGS

- **Don't** forget to exercise your dog before entering the ring. Do it before grooming if you are afraid the dog will get wet or dirty after his grooming session.
- **Don't** ever take a dog into the show ring that isn't groomed the very best you know how.
- **Don't** take a dog into the ring if there is any indication that he sick or not *completely* recovered from a communicable disease.
- **Don't** drag the dog around the ring on a tight lead that destroys his proud carriage or disposition or chances

of becoming a show dog in the future, if not that particular day.

- **Don't** talk to the judge while you're in the ring. Watch him closely and follow instructions carefully. Don't speak to those at ringside, and don't talk to your dog in an excessive or loud manner.
- **Don't** strike or in any way abuse your dog before, during, or after the judging. The time and place for training and discipline is at home, not in public. Always use the reward system, not punishment, for the most successful method of training a dog.
- **Don't** be a bad loser. You can't win em all, so if you win today, be gracious; if you lose, be happy for the dog who won.
- **Don't** shove your dog in a crate or leave him on the bench alone until it's time to leave the show grounds. A drink of water or something to eat and a little companionship will go a long way toward making dog shows more enjoyable for him, so that he will show even better the next time.

Top: Can Ch. Grawyn's Whistlin' Dixie winning in a 1985 show. Handled by Lou Gray, who co-owned and bred with Deanna Gray. The sire was Ch. Innisfree's Pagan Sinner ex Grawyn's Ravin' Beauty. *Bottom:* Ch. Almaring's Chopaka Talapus, handled by Ollie Click. Bred and owned by Ingrid Brucato of Almaring Kennels.

335

THE DOG SHOW WORLD

Let us assume that after a few months of tender loving care you realize your dog is developing beyond your wildest expectations and that the dog you selected is very definitely a show dog. Of course every owner is prejudiced, but if you are sincerely interested in going to dog shows with your dog and making a champion of him, now is the time to start casting a critical eye on him from a judge's point of view.

There is no such thing as a perfect dog. Every dog has some faults, perhaps even a few serious ones. The best way to appraise your dog's degree of perfection is to compare him with the Standard for the breed or when he is before a judge in the show ring.

Keep in mind that dog show terminology varies from one place to another and even from one time to another. If you plan to show your dog, it always makes sense to check with your local or national breed club or with the national dog registry for the most complete, most up-to-date information regarding dog show regulations. In Great Britain, for example, match shows are known as limit shows. Age limit also differs, as dogs less than six months old may not be shown in Britain. Additionally, Britain has no point system for dogs, rather the dogs compete for championship certificates (C.C.s). Thus, point shows are known as championship shows in Great Britain.

MATCH SHOWS

For the beginner there are "mock" shows, called match shows, where you and your dog go through many of the

BEST OF OPPOSITE | WINNERS BITCH

ESSEX COUNTY KENNEL CLUB

NEW CHAMPION

Can Ch. Arahaz Varlina, bred by Rosemary Fischer. Varlina is also pointed in the USA.

procedures of a regular dog show but do not gain points toward championship. These informal events are usually held by kennel clubs, annually or semiannually, and much ring poise and experience can be gained there. The minimum age limit at most matches is usually two months, in order to give puppies four months of training before they compete at the regular shows when they reach six months of age. (It should be noted, however, that at some match shows the minimum age requirement varies, so be sure to inquire about this before you fill out the entry form.) Classes range from two to four months, four to six months, six to nine months, and nine to twelve

months. Puppies compete with others of their own age for comparative purposes. Many breeders evaluate their litters in this manner, choosing which is the most outgoing, the most poised, the best showman, and so on.

For those seriously interested in showing their dogs to full championship, match shows provide important experience for both the dog and the owner. Class categories may vary slightly, according to number of entries, but basically include all the classes that are included at a regular point show. There is a nominal entry fee and, of course, ribbons and trophies usually are given for your efforts as well. Unlike the point shows, entries can be made on

Marlytuk's Natasha of Sunny winning Brood Bitch Class at the 1980 ISHA Area II Match Show in Asheville, NC, with Phylis Secrist handling. Her get are son Ch. Majula's Russlan with Jim Babb handling, and daughter Majula's Melody with Joni Barnhardt handling. The judge was Robert Messinger.

the day of the show right on the show grounds. Matches are unbenched and provide an informal, congenial atmosphere for the amateur, and this helps to make the ordeal of one's first adventure in the show ring a little less nerve-wracking.

THE POINT SHOWS

It is not possible to show a puppy at an American Kennel Club sanctioned point show before the age of six months. When your dog reaches this eligible age, your local kennel club can provide you with the names and addresses of the show-giving superintendents in your area who will be staging the club's dog show for them, and they can tell you where to write for an entry form.

The forms are mailed in a

pamphlet called a premium list. This also includes the names of the judges for each breed, a list of the prizes and trophies, the name and address of the show-giving club and where the show will be held, as well as rules and regulations set up by the American Kennel Club.

A booklet containing the complete set of show rules and regulations, *Rules Applying to Registration and Dog Shows,* may be obtained by writing to the American Kennel Club, Inc., 51 Madison Avenue, New York, NY 10010.

When you write to the dog-show superintendent, request not only your premium list for this particular show, but ask that your name be added to their mailing list so that you will automatically receive all

Aldona Levine's Arahaz Margaritka wins the Breed and Group at a Puppy Match under Marie Moore in 1983.

premium lists in the future. List your breed or breeds and they will see to it that you receive premium lists not only for all-breed shows, but for specialty shows as well.

Unlike the match shows where your dog will be judged on ring behavior, at the point shows he will be judged on conformation to the breed Standard. In addition to being at least six months of age (on the day of the show) he must be purebred for a point show. This means both of his parents and he are registered with the American Kennel Club. There must be no alterations or falsifications regarding his appearance, for example, no dyes or powders may be used to enhance or alter the natural color, the shade of natural color, or the natural markings of the dog's coat. Females cannot have been spayed and males must have both testicles in evidence. Any lameness, deformity, or major deviation from the Standard for the breed constitutes a disqualification.

With all these things in mind, groom your dog to the best of your ability in the specified area for this purpose in the show

Top: Ch. Karnovanda's Sasha Groznyi winning at 1979 show. Later Sasha was sold to Ann Bruder. The sire was Ch. Karnovanda's Viktor Groznyi ex Ch. Karnovanda's Rally. *Bottom:* Four generations of Tawny Hill breeding and winning. All bitches, Tanja of Monadnock, Molina, Gamyun, and Melaphre—all bearing the Tawny Hill prefix and all champions. Adele M. Gray, breeder and owner.

Top: Ch. Indigo's Indian Summer, bred and owned by Dr. and Mrs. David Qualls. "Indie" finished for championship at less than 8 months of age. *Bottom:* Rosemary Fischer's Arahaz Tovari at the South Hills KC show in 1977.

hall and *exercise your dog before taking him into the ring!* Too many dog show people are guilty of making their dogs remain in their crates so they do not get dirty, and the first thing the animals do when they are called into the ring is to stop and empty themselves. There is no excuse for this. All it takes is a walk *before* grooming. If your dog is clean, well groomed, *empty*, and leash-trained, you should be able to enter the show ring with confidence and pride of ownership, ready for an appraisal by the judge.

The presiding judge on that day will allow each and every dog a certain amount of time and consideration before making his decisions. It is never permissible to consult the judge, regarding either your dog or his decision, while you are in the ring. An exhibitor never speaks unless spoken to, and then only to answer such questions as the judge may ask—the age of the dog, the dog's bite, or to ask you to move your dog around the ring once again.

However, before you reach the point where you are actually in the ring awaiting the final decisions of the judge, you will have had to decide in which of the five classes (five for each sex) your dog should compete.

POINT SHOW CLASSES

The regular classes of the AKC are: Puppy, Novice, Bred-By-Exhibitor, American-bred, and Open; if your dog is

undefeated in any of the regular classes (divided by sex) in which it is entered, he or she is *required* to enter the Winners Class. If your dog is placed second in the class to the dog which won Winners Dog or Winners Bitch, hold the dog or bitch in readiness, as the judge must consider it for Reserve Winners.

• THE PUPPY CLASS shall be for dogs which are six months of age and over but under twelve months, and which are not champions. Classes are often divided, thus: six and (under) nine, and nine and (under) 12 months. The age of a dog shall be calculated up to and inclusive of the first day of a show. For example, a dog whelped on January 1 is eligible to compete in a Puppy Class on July 1, and may continue to compete up to and including December 31 of the same year. He is not eligible to compete January 1 of the following year.

• THE NOVICE CLASS is for dogs six months of age or over, whelped in the USA or Canada, which have not, prior to the closing entries, won three first prizes in the Novice Class, a first prize in Bred-by-Exhibitor, American-bred or Open Class, nor one or more points toward a championship title.

• THE BRED-BY-EXHIBITOR CLASS is for dogs whelped in the USA (or, if individually registered in the AKC Stud Book, for dogs whelped in Canada) that are six months of age and over, that are not

WINNERS
BITCH
GILBERT PHOTO

Ch. Kimik's Anya of Yeti, co-owned by David Carlson and Joy Messinger. She is pictured winning a 3-point major under judge J. Council Parker at the 1974 Great Barrington KC Show.

champions, and that are owned wholly or in part by the person or by the spouse of the person who was the breeder or one of the breeders of record. Dogs entered in the BBE Class must be handled by an owner or by a member of the immediate family of an owner, i.e., the husband, wife, father, mother, son, daughter, brother, or sister.

● THE AMERICAN-BRED CLASS is for all dogs (except champions) six months of age or over, whelped in the USA by reason of a mating that took place in the USA

● THE OPEN CLASS is for any dog six months of age or over, except in a member specialty club show held for only American-bred dogs, in which case the class is for American-bred dogs only.

● WINNERS DOG and WINNERS BITCH After the above male classes have been judged, the first-place winners are then *required* to compete in the ring. The dog judged "Winners Dog" is awarded the points toward his championship title.

● RESERVE WINNERS are selected immediately after the Winners Dog. In case of a disqualification of a win by the AKC, the Reserve Dog moves up to "Winners" and receives the points. After all male classes are judged, the bitch classes are called.

● BEST OF BREED or BEST OF VARIETY COMPETITION is limited to Champions of Record or dogs (with newly acquired points, for a 90-day period prior to AKC confirmation) which have completed championship requirements, and Winners Dog and Winners Bitch (or the dog awarded Winners if only one Winners prize has been awarded), together with any undefeated dogs which have been shown only in non-regular classes; all compete for Best of Breed or Best of Variety (if the breed is divided by size, color, texture, or length of coat hair, etc.).

● BEST OF WINNERS: If the WD or WB earns BOB or BOV, it automatically becomes BOW; otherwise they will be judged together for BOW (following BOB or BOV judging).

Best of Opposite Sex is selected from the remaining dogs of the opposite sex to Best of Breed or Best of Variety.

Other Classes may be approved by the AKC, such as Stud Dogs, Brood Bitches, Brace Class, Team Class; classes consisting of local dogs and bitches may also be included in a show if approved by the AKC (special rules are included in the AKC Rule Book).

● THE MISCELLANEOUS CLASS is for purebred dogs of such breeds as designated by the AKC. No dog shall be eligible for entry in this class unless the owner has been granted an Indefinite Listing Privilege (ILP) and unless the ILP number is given on the entry form. Application for an

Four littermates who took Best of Breed, Winners Dog, Winners Bitch and Reserve Winners Dog all at the same show in 1981 at the New Brunswick KC event. Bred by Ann M. Sullivan.

BEST OF
OPPOSITE
SEX

HODGES
FORT GARRY
K.C.

RESERVE
WINNERS
BITCH

Top: AmCan Ch. Yeti's Serendipity of Sundana, winning Best of Opposite Sex at the 1979 National Specialty at the SHC of Canada event. She is the dam of a Specialty winner and 2 champions. Bred and owned by Robert and Joy Messinger. *Bottom:* The Siberian Husky Club of America 50th Specialty Show found White Fox's Sik-Sik Reserve Winner from the 9–12-Month Puppy Class. Owned and shown by Phyllis Castelton of Anchorage, AK.

Top: Ch. Arahaz Tengri Khan, CD, wins under Kitty Drury. Owner-handled to this Breed win by Susanna Windsor Rodney. *Middle:* The initial training for a weight- or sled-pulling dog. Dogs are put in full harness and allowed to drag heavier and heavier loads during practice sessions. *Bottom:* Ch. Indigo's The Wizard of Id, bred and owned by Dr. and Mrs. David Qualls.

Top: Ch. Indigo's Poison Ivy, bred and owned by Dr. and Mrs. Qualls. Ivy is a multi-Best of Breed winner. *Bottom:* Ch. Almaring's Karmina winning the Breed at 12 years old! Bred by Ingrid Brucato, she is handled here by owner Phyllis Willis. The sire was Ch. Monadnock's Akela ex Monadnock's Tatiana.

Ch. Karnovanda's Rally with 10-year-old Natalie Russell winning in Junior Handling Class. Rally is the dam of Ch. Karnovanda's Blak Jack, Sasha Groznyi and Vela Groznyi.

ILP shall be made on a form provided by the A K C and when submitted must be accompanied by a fee set by the Board of Directors.

All Miscellaneous breeds shall be shown together in a single class except that the class may be divided by sex if so specified in the premium list. There shall be *no* further competition for dogs entered in this class. Ribbons for 1st, 2nd, 3rd, and 4th places shall be rose, brown, light green and gray, respectively.

OBEDIENCE TRIALS

Some shows also offer Obedience Trials, which are considered as separate events.

These give the dogs a chance to compete and score by performing a prescribed set of exercises intended to display their training in doing useful work.

There are three obedience titles for which they may compete: First, the Companion Dog or CD title; second, the Companion Dog Excellent or CDX; and third, the Utility Dog or UD. Detailed information on these degrees is contained in a booklet entitled *Obedience Regulations* and may be obtained by writing to the American Kennel Club.

JUNIOR SHOWMANSHIP

Junior Showmanship

competition is for boys and girls in different age groups who handle their own dogs or ones owned by their immediate family. There are four divisions: Novice A (10 to 12-year-olds) and Novice B (13 to 17-year-olds) for competitors with no previous Junior Showmanship wins, Open A (10 to 12 year-olds) and Open B (13 to 17-year-olds) for competitors with one or more JS awards.

As Junior Showmanship at the dog shows increased in popularity, certain changes and improvements had to be made. The American Kennel Club issues a pamphlet, *Regulations for Junior Showmanship,* which may be obtained by writing to the AKC at 51 Madison Avenue, New York, NY 10010.

DOG SHOW PHOTOGRAPHERS

Every show has at least one official photographer who will be more than happy to take a photograph of your dog with the judge, ribbons, and trophies, along with you or your handler. These make marvelous remembrances of your top show wins and are frequently framed along with the ribbons for display purposes. Photographers may be paged at the show over the public address system if you wish to obtain this service. Prices vary, but you will probably find it costs little to capture these happy moments, and the photos can always be used in various dog magazines to advertise your dog's wins.

ALL-BREED VS. SPECIALTY

There are two types of dog shows licensed by the American Kennel Club. One is the all-breed show which includes classes for all of the AKC recognized breeds and groups of breeds, i.e., all Terriers, all

Ch. Aslanlar's Nefis Eshek winning National Stud Dog honors at the 1974 SHCA Specialty in Oakland, CA. Judge was Donald Booxbaum. Grey Baron and Vinehills Novaya of Aslanlar are Eshek's get. Owner, B. Sue Adams.

Toys, etc. Then there are the specialty shows, for one particular breed, which also offer championship points.

BENCHED VS. UNBENCHED SHOWS

The show-giving clubs determine, usually on the basis of what facilities are offered by their chosen show site, whether their show will be benched or unbenched. A benched show is one where the dog show superintendent supplies benches or cages dogs. Each bench is numbered and its corresponding number appears on your entry identification slip which is sent to you prior to the show date. The number also appears in the show catalog. Upon entering the show, you should take your dog directly to the bench where he should remain until it is time to groom him prior to judging. After he has been judged, he must be returned to the bench until the official time of dismissal from the show. At an unbenched show, the club makes no provision whatsoever for your dog other than an enormous tent (if an outdoor show) or an area in a show hall where all crates and grooming equipment must be kept.

Benched or unbenched, the moment you enter the show grounds, you are expected to look after your dog and have it under complete control at all times. This means short leads in crowded aisles or when getting out of cars. In the case of a benched show, a "bench chain" is needed. It should allow the dog to move around but not get down off the bench. Please refrain from having small tots lead dogs around the show grounds where they might be dragged into the middle of a dog fight. Show dogs should be supervised at all times by a responsible adult or adolescent, never by a young child.

IF YOUR DOG WINS A CLASS

Study the classes to make certain your dog is entered in a proper class for his or her qualifications. If your dog wins his class, *you are required*—for no additional fee—to enter classes for Winners, Best of Breed and Best of Winners. No eligible dogs may be withheld from competition. It is not mandatory that you stay for group judging, *if your dog wins a group*, however, *you must stay for Best in Show competition.*

THE PRIZE RIBBONS

No matter how many entries there are in each class at a dog show, if you place in the first through fourth positions you will receive a ribbon. These ribbons commemorate your win, and when collected and displayed they can be impressive to prospective buyers when and if you have puppies for sale or if you intend to use your dog at public stud.

All ribbons from the American Kennel Club licensed dog shows will bear the AKC seal, the name of the prize, the name of the show-giving club,

Top: Ch. Kadyak's Arctic Raider, also a sled-dog champion winning at a 1983 show in Fairbanks, AK. Owner-handled by Ardene Eaton. The sire was Ch. Innisfree's Red Roadster ex Ch. Kadyaks Kopper Kyan. *Bottom:* Best in Show for AmCan Ch. Innisfree's On The Road Again in 1985. Owners, Richard and Jan MacWhade, Snoking Kennels.

Many times Best Brace in Show are Alkas'Iber Steely Dan and Konik's Silver Bullet. These "cousins" are co-owned by George Cook, G. Cingel, and S.A. Serafin. The judge at this show was well-known dog breeder and judge Shirley Thomas.

the date of the show, and the name of the city or town where the show is being held. In the classes the colors are blue for first, red for second, yellow for third, and white for fourth. Winners Dog or Winners Bitch ribbons are purple, while Reserve Winners Dog and Reserve Winners Bitch ribbons are purple-and-white. Best of Winners ribbons are blue-and-white, Best of Breed and Best of Variety of Breed are purple-and-gold, and Best of Opposite Sex ribbons are red-and-white.

In the groups, first prize is a blue rosette or ribbon, second placement is red, third is yellow, and fourth is white. The Best in Show rosette is either red, white, and blue or incorporates the colors used in the show-giving club's emblem.

QUALIFYING FOR CHAMPIONSHIP

Championship points are given for Winners Dog and Winners Bitch in accordance with a scale of points established by the American Kennel Club, based on the popularity of the breed in entries and the number of dogs competing in the classes. This scale of points varies with the breed, its sex, and the geographical location of the show, but the scale is published in the front of each dog show catalog. You may win additional

Top: Ch. Indigo's Super Imposed, owned by Mark and Barbara Mullins, bred by David Qualls. *Bottom:* Ch. Innisfree's Benchmark, bred and owned by Kathleen Kanzler, handled by Trish Kanzler, going Winners Dog at the 1985 parent club National Specialty Show under Helen Miller Fischer. The sire was Ch. Innisfree's Red Roadster, CD, ex AmCan Ch. Canadian Mist.

Top: Ch. Beorthwulf Boreas Re Tymen, CDX, and Umiat's Bluwulf of Shalimar winning at the Reno KC Show.
Bottom: Ch. Poli's Toka Tu, one of the Top Ten Siberian Huskies in the nation for 1977–1980. Bred and owned by Frank and Michele Polimeni.

Top: Ch. Whispering Oak's Dushinka handled by Betty Jean Orseno for owner Susan Vosnos of Barrington, IL.
Bottom: Ch. Sno-Fame Sequoia Chiaro Mikko, bred and owned by Ann M. Sullivan, was sired by Ch. Jonathie's Sequoia of Sno-Fame ex Donasha's Lady of the Wind.

Arahaz Vzriv winning the Breed under judge Beryl Allen. Co-owner-breeder, Rosemary Fischer; owner-handler, Susanna Rodney.

points by winning Best of Winners, if there are fewer dogs than bitches entered, or vice versa. Points never exceed five at any one show and a total of 15 points must be won to constitute a championship. These 15 points must be won under at least three different judges, and you must acquire at least two major wins. Anything from a three-to-five point win is a major, while one and two point wins are minor wins. Two major wins must be won under two different judges to meet championship requirements.

PROFESSIONAL HANDLERS

If you are new in the fancy and do not know how to handle your dog to his best advantage, or if you are too nervous or physically unable to show your dog, you can hire a reliable professional handler who will do it for you for a specified fee. The more successful or well-known handlers charge slightly higher rates, but generally speaking there is a uniform charge for this service. As the dog progresses with his wins in the show ring, the fee increases proportionately. Included in this service is professional advice on when and where to show your dog, grooming, a statement of your wins at each show, and all trophies and ribbons that the dog accumulates. Usually any cash award is kept by the handler as a sort of "bonus."

When engaging a handler, it is advisable to select one who does not take more dogs to a show than he can properly and comfortably handle. You want your dog to receive his individual attention and not be rushed into the ring at the last moment because the handler has been busy with too many other dogs in other rings. Some handlers require you to deliver the dog to their establishment a few days ahead of the show so they have ample time to groom and train him. Other handlers will accept well-behaved and trained dogs that have been groomed by their owners at ringside—if they are familiar with the dog and the owner. This should be determined well in advance of the show date. *Never* expect a handler to accept a dog at ringside that is not groomed to perfection!

There are several sources for locating a professional handler. Dog magazines carry their classified advertising. A note or telephone call to the American Kennel Club will also put you in touch with several in your area.

DO YOU REALLY NEED A HANDLER?

The answer to that question is sometimes yes, sometimes no. However, the answer that must be determined first of all is, "Can I *afford* a professional handler?" or "I want to show my dog myself. Does that mean my dog will never do any big

Happy To Be Innisfree, dam of Ch. Kontoki's Natural Sinner, winning under Charles Hamilton in 1976. Owned by Thomas Oelschlager and Marlene DePalma of Kontoki Kennels.

winning?''

Do you *really* need a handler to win? If you are mishandling a good dog that should be winning and isn't because it is made to look bad in the ring by its owner, the answer is yes. If you don't know how to handle a dog properly, why make your dog look bad when a handler could show it to its best advantage?

Some owners simply cannot handle a dog well and wonder why their dogs aren't winning in the ring no matter how hard they try. Others are nervous, and this nervousness travels down the leash to the dog and the dog behaves accordingly. Some people are extroverts by nature, and these are the people who usually make excellent handlers. Of course, dogs that do all of the winning at the shows usually have a lot of "show off" in their nature, too, and this helps a great deal.

THE COST OF CAMPAIGNING A DOG

At present, many champions are shown an average of 25 times before completing a championship. In entry fees at today's prices, that adds up to a few hundred dollars. This does not include motel bills, traveling expenses, or food. There have been dog champions finished in fewer, say five to ten, shows, but this is the exception rather than the rule. When and where to show

Stu Galka winning with Kolyma's Igloo Pak Keyan and Sherry Galka with Kolyma's Sierra Silver Tomari, CD. Their Kolyma's Racing Siberian Kennel is in Sonora, CA.

Tandara's Tikaani Bublichki winning in the show ring. Bred and owned by Lynne and Bonny Patterson, Tandara Kennels, Gio Harbor, WA.

should be thought out carefully so that you can perhaps save money on entries. This is one of the services a professional handler provides that can mean considerable savings. Hiring a handler can save money in the long run if you just wish to make a champion. If your dog has been winning reserves and not taking points and a handler can finish him in five to ten shows, you would be ahead financially. If your dog is not really top quality, the length of time it takes even a handler to finish it (depending upon competition in the area) could add up to a large amount of money.

Campaigning a show specimen that not only captures the wins in his breed but wins Group and Best in Show awards gets up into the big money. To cover the nation's major shows and rack up a record as one of the top dogs in the nation usually costs an owner thousands of dollars a year. This includes not only the professional handler's fee for taking the dog into the ring, but the costs of conditioning and grooming, boarding, and advertising him in magazines and so forth.

There is great satisfaction in winning with your own dog, especially if you have trained and cared for it yourself. With today's enormous entries at the dog shows and so many worthy dogs competing for top wins,

AmCan Ch. High Country's Hyper Holly with Margaret Cook winning Brood Bitch Class at the 1984 Delaware Valley KC Specialty. Paul Willhauck has Ch. Itaska's Marvelous Marvin and Janet Roberts handles Teeco's Tweet Rockin Robyn.

many owners who have said "I'd rather do it myself!" and meant it have become discouraged and have eventually hired a handler anyway.

However, if you really are in it just for the sport, you can and should handle your dog if you want. You can learn the tricks by attending training classes, and you can learn a lot by carefully observing the more successful professional handlers as they perform in the ring. Model yourself after the ones who command respect as being the leaders in their profession. But, if you find you'd really rather be at ringside looking on, do get a handler so that your worthy dog gets his

deserved recognition in the ring. To own a good dog and win with it is a thrill, so good luck, no matter how you do it.

DOG CLUBS

In addition to getting involved with the parent club for your breed, it is advisable for owners to join other clubs if they wish to keep informed and abreast of all the latest information pertaining to the fancy.

It is wise to belong to an all-breed club in your area, as well as to dog training clubs, if you are interested in obedience work. These clubs can usually be located through your telephone book listing in the Yellow Pages.

Rontu's Gamay going Best of Winners under judge Duvella Kusler at a dog show in 1985. Owned by Jo Geletich and C. Smith.

There is also the Owner-Handler Association of America, Inc. Founded in 1967, this group has members throughout the United States (including Puerto Rico) and Canada. Their objectives are to encourage and promote the sport of owner-handling and the training of purebred dogs and to communicate with and educate purebred dog fanciers.

Membership is open to all who advocate these principles.

Any interested group of 15 or more members may form a chapter in their area with the approval of the Board. Chapters hold training classes in obedience and show training, offer educational programs, and hold symposiums of benefit to the fancier.

SIBERIAN HUSKY
BEST IN SHOW WINNERS
1955-1985: The Formative Years

Name	Color	Date	Owner
Ch. Bonzo of Anadyr, CD	G/W	April 1955	Natalie Norris
Ch. Tyndrum's Chynik	G/W	Nov. 1960	Hank and Lorna Buege
Ch. Monadnock's King	B/W	Nov. 1961	Lorna Demidoff
Monadnock's Dimitri	B/W	October 1964	James Brillhart
Ch. Frosty Aires Alcan King	B/W	October 1964	Marie Wamser
Ch. Fra-Mar's Soan Diavol	B/W	August 1968	Marie Wamser
Ch. Darbo Domeyko of Longs Peak	G/W	August 1969	Edward Samberson
Ch. Karnovanda's Wolfgang	B/W	May 1972	Judith Russell
Ch. Innisfree's O'Murtagh, CD	B/W	July 1972	Milton Dohn
Ch. Dudley's Tavar of Innisfree	B/W	Nov. 1972	Clarence & Gladys Dudley
Ch. Lobo Rey	B/W	Sept. 1973	Sylvia Gambosh
Ch. Weldon's Beau Phunsi	G/W	May 1974	Rev. & Mrs. John Jones
Ch. Oomik's Quista	G/W	June 1974	Joseph Ensminger
Ch. Wintersett's Instant Replay	B/W	October 1974	Dave & Judy Salaba
Ch. Chotovotka's Ms. Kitty Russell	B/W	October 1975	Robert & Dorothy Page
Ch. St. Nicholas of Blackwatch	B/W'	January 1976	Robert & Kay Bair
Ch. Innisfree's Sierra Cinnar	R/W	May 1976	Kathleen Kanzler
Ch. Dudley's Varska	B/W	Sept. 1976	Clarence & Gladys Dudley
Ch. Fra-Mar's Rayle Diavol	B/W	June 1976	Carolyn Pietrack
Ch. Innisfree's Jasmine Jewell	G/W	March 1978	Karen & Charles Bowers

Ch. Innisfree's Targhee	B/W	July 1978	Don Egan & Kathleen Kanzler
Ch. Innisfree's Fonzie	B/W	Sept. 1978	Gail & Richard Atkinson
Ch. Kontoki's Natural Sinner	B/W	June 1980	Tom Oelschlager
Ch. Sierra's Hawkeye	R/W	June 1980	Carol & David Vogt & M. Burnside
Ch. Toko's Mr. Chip of Yago, CD	G/W	June 1981	Jean Fournier & Pat Giteles
Ch. Innisfree's Gilpak Macho	B/W	January 1982	Virgil & Mary Gilbreaith
Ch. Gilpak's Kris Kringl of Grawyn	B/W	August 1982	Deanna & Lou Gray

Best Brace in Working Group at the Yukon KC in Alaska went to Phyllis Castelton's CanBda Ch. White Fox's Tatiana Kazankina and Can Ch. White Fox's Kayakin of Anadyr, CD.

Ch. Kadyak's Ms. Kishwin	R/W	June 1982	Ardene Eaton
Ch. Oaklyf's Batchelors Button	B/W	June 1982	Robert & Pat Lanaghan
Ch. Maridel's Turk-Kei of Desha	R/W	May 1983	Michael Burnside
Ch. Innisfree's Pagan Sinner	B/W	May 1983	Sandra James
Ch. Aazar's Sure Hit	R/W	June 1983	Larry & Susan Govedich & Carolyn Duryea
Ch. Foxlair's Foxcroft of Alpaws	G/W	Sept. 1983	William & Joanne Kreckmann & Anna Bain
Ch. Rysalka's Tabitha	B/W	October 1983	Glenda Seidelman & Betty Ware

AmCan Ch. Gerick's Gypsy Fantasy. "Fanci" is co-owned by Dick and Gerry Dalakian and Doug and Joan Hurst of Flemington, NJ.

Teeco's Tweet Rockin Robyn winning her first 2 points at the 1985 Saw Mill KC Show. Paul Willhauck handled for owner Margaret Cook under Mrs. Ed Bivin.

Ch. Maridel's El Cid of Innisfree	R/W	April 1984	Mike & Karen Burnside & Kathleen Kanzler
Ch. Aazar's Nordique of Terried	B/W	Sept. 1984	Carolyn Duryea
Ch. Pole-land's Regulus W.O.W.	B/W	March 1985	Chuck & Carolyn Weber & Al Ferreira
Ch. Innisfree's On The Road Again	R/W	March 1985	Richard & Jan MacWhade
Ch. Kiev's The Magician	B/W	June 1985	Howard & Bonnie Miller
Ch. Kontoki's One Mo Time	G/W	August 1985	J & S Munsey & Marlene DePalma
Ch. Veleah's Silver Patriot	G/W	Sept. 1985	H. Level Leahy

SIBERIAN HUSKIES IN OBEDIENCE

"Obedience training and tests for dogs were an immediate success from the moment those first 150 spectators saw the dogs go through their paces."

Dog shows and conformation classes had a big head start on obedience. It was in 1933 that the first obedience tests were held in Mount Kisco, New York. It was Mrs. Helene Whitehouse Walker who inaugurated these initial all-breed obedience tests that she had brought from England. Along with her kennel maid at that time, Blanche Saunders, they were responsible for the staging of the first four obedience tests held in the United States.

Obedience training and tests for dogs were an immediate success from the moment those first 150 spectators saw the dogs go through their paces.

Mrs. Walker was instrumental in getting the American Kennel Club to recognize and even sponsor the obedience trials at their dog shows, and her discussions with Charles T. Inglee (then the vice president of the AKC) ultimately led to their recognition. In 1935, she wrote the first booklet published on the subject called simply "Obedience Tests." These tests were eventually incorporated into the rules of the AKC obedience requirements in March 1936. It developed into a 22-page booklet that served as a manual for judges, handlers, and the show-giving clubs. The larger version was called "Regulations and Standards for Obedience Test Field Trials."

Mrs. Walker, Josef Weber (another well-known dog trainer), and Miss Saunders added certain refinements, basic procedures, and exercises, and these were published in the

April 1936 issue of the *American Kennel Gazette*.

On June 13 of that same year, the North Westchester Kennel Club held the first American Kennel Club licensed obedience test in conjunction with their all-breed dog show. At that very first show there were 12 entries for judge Mrs. Wheeler H. Page.

The exercises for Novice and Open classes remain virtually unchanged today—almost half a century later. Only Tracking Dog and Tracking Dog Excellent have been added in the intervening years.

By June 1939, the AKC realized obedience was here to stay and saw the need for an advisory committee. One was established and chaired by Donald Fordyce, with enthusiastic members from all parts of the country willing to serve on it. George Foley of Pennsylvania was on the board. He was one of the most important of all men in the fancy, being superintendent of most of the dog shows on the Eastern seaboard. Mrs. Radcliff Farley, also of Pennsylvania, was on the committee with Miss Aurelia Tremaine of Massachusetts, Mrs. Bryand Godsell of California, Mrs. W. L. McCannon of Massachusetts, Samuel Blick of

Ch. Veleah Keemah of Jeuahnee on her way to Best of Breed and a Group Fourth. Owner Vel Leahy handling.

Maryland, Frank Grant of Ohio, as well as Josef Weber and Mrs. Walker. Their contribution was to further standardize judging procedures and utility exercises.

A little of the emphasis on dog obedience was diverted with the outbreak of World War II, when talk switched to the topic of dogs serving in defense of their country. As soon as peace was declared, however, interest in obedience reached new heights. In 1946, the American Kennel Club called for another Obedience Advisory Committee, this time headed by John C. Neff. This committee included Blanche Saunders, Clarence Pfaffenberger, Theodore Kapnek, L. Wilson Davis, Howard P. Calussen, Elliott Blackiston, Oscar Franzen, and Clyde Henderson.

Under their leadership, the obedience booklet grew to 43 pages. Rules and regulations were even more standardized than ever before and there was the addition of the requirements for the Tracking Dog title.

In 1971, an obedience department was established at the American Kennel Club offices to keep pace with the growth of the sport and for constant review and guidance for show-giving clubs. Judge Richard H. D'Ambrisi was the director until his untimely death in 1973, at which time his duties were assumed by James E. Dearinger along with his two special consultants, L. Wilson Davis for Tracking and

Up, up and away! Trivalent Siberians' Can Ch. Yasha of Kolyma River, CDX, clears the barrier with ease. Yasha is owned by Richard and Mutsuko Punnett of Tonawanda, NY.

Reverend Thomas O'Connor for Handicapped Handlers. The members of this 1973 committee were Thomas Knott of Maryland, Edward Anderson of Pennsylvania, Jack Ward of Virginia, Lucy Neeb of Louisiana, William Phillips of California, James Falkner of Texas, Mary Lee Whiting of Minnesota, and Robert Self of Illinois, co-publisher of the important *Front and Finish* obedience newspaper.

While the Committee functions continuously, meetings of the board are tentatively held every other year, unless a specific function or obedience question comes up, in which case a special meeting is called.

During the 1975 session, the Committee held discussions on several old and new aspects of the obedience world. In addition to their own ever-increasing responsibilities to the fancy, they discussed seminars and educational symposiums, the licensing of Tracking clubs, a booklet with suggested guidelines for obedience judges, schutzhund training, and the aspects of a Utility Excellent Class degree.

Can Ch. Yasha of Kolyma River, CDX, during a practice session in the backyard. Owned by Richard Punnett.

Through the efforts of succeeding Advisory Committee members, the future of the sport has been insured, as well as the continuing emphasis on the working abilities for which dogs were originally bred. Obedience work also provides novices an opportunity to train and handle their dogs in an atmosphere that provides maximum pleasure and accomplishment at minimum expense—which is precisely what Mrs. Walker intended.

When the Advisory Committee met in December 1980 many of the familiar names were among those listed as attending and continuing to serve the obedience exhibitors. James E. Dearinger, James C. Falkner, Rev. Thomas V. O'Connor, Robert T. Self, John S. Ward, Howard E. Cross, Helen F. Phillips, Samuel W. Kodis, George S. Pugh, Thomas Knott, and Mrs. Esme Treen were present and accounted for.

As we look back on almost a half century of obedience trials, we can only surmise that the pioneers, Mrs. Helene Whitehouse Walker and Blanche Saunders, would be proud of the progress made in the obedience rings.

It was a sad day when we learned that Mrs. Walker died on March 11, 1986, at the age of 86. She will be missed—and remembered.

THE SHUMAN SYSTEM
Just as the Phillips System mushroomed out of the world of show dogs, it was almost inevitable that a system to

measure the successes of obedience dogs would become a reality.

By 1974, Nancy Shuman and Lynn Frosch had established the "Shuman System" of recording the Top Ten All-breed obedience dogs in the country. They also listed the top four in every breed if each dog had accumulated a total of 50 points or more according to their requirements. Points were accrued in a descending scale based on their qualifying scores from 170 and up.

THE DELANEY SYSTEM

In 1975, *Front and Finish,* the dog trainer's news, published an obedience rating system compiled by Kent Delaney to evaluate and score the various obedience dogs which had competed during the previous year. The system was devised primarily to measure the significance of a win made over a few dogs against those made over many dogs.

Points were given for both High in Trial or Class placements, as recorded and published in the *American Kennel Gazette* magazine. The dog that scores the highest in the trial receives a point for each dog in competition, and first place winner in each class receives a point for each dog in the class. The dog placing second receives a point for each dog in the class less one, the third place winner a point less two, the fourth place winner a point less than three.

Ch. OTCH Firesides Takgamy of Omayok, UD, doing what he does best!

TO TRAIN OR NOT TO TRAIN

There are those obedience buffs who will tell you that the Siberian Husky is strictly meant to be a sled dog in a cold climate and you are wasting your time trying to train it in obedience. Nothing could be further from the truth. The records prove that it can be done. You must simply decide if you and your dog would make a great team together and whether or not he would enjoy the training as much as you would.

It is very true that all dogs should have some obedience training if only to make their manners in the house and with people better! Especially the larger breeds, such as the Siberian Husky, which might require some extra handling and strength to keep them under control at all times. The high intelligence of the Siberian Husky makes it a probable candidate for obedience work so why not go for it? If your dog enjoys it, the experience can turn out to be very enjoyable and rewarding.

If you are going for a degree, there will always be the doubt lingering in the back of your mind as to whether or not your dog will perform in the ring for the test, even though he does well in class. This is great fun for those of us who love a challenge!

More and more Siberians are earning their titles all the time, and more training methods and devoted owners are succeeding where others have failed,

Tazza Sioux Av Karnik, CDX, owned and trained by Larry Govedich, Apparition Siberians, Port Matilda, PA, pictured at a 1979 obedience trial in which he was High Scoring Dog at a Specialty of the SHC of Delaware Valley.

Working dog and loving it. Harvey's Vashka working the dumbbell.

proving that it can be done. While it is not advisable to force a dog into working toward a degree, basic training for him will pay off in general good manners if in nothing else. If the natural ability is there, you may wish to go on to higher degrees to give your dog the opportunity to display his natural desire to please his owner.

HUSKIES AS OBEDIENCE DOGS

The intelligence of the Siberian Husky is beyond doubt. Its willingness to work in the obedience ring is something else again! A Siberian knows what he is supposed to do once he has been taught, but he doesn't always want to do it, and if he doesn't want to, he seldom will!

Just how much your Siberian Husky learns is up to you, or the trainer, and your ability to communicate with the dog, plus the degree of patience and time you or the trainer is willing to spend toward the

Opposite:
Arahaz
Rumyana, CD,
bred and
owned by
Rosemary and
Edward
Fischer. The
sire was Count
Boris of
Cedarwood
ex Panda of
Cornell.

ultimate achievement of that CD, CDX, or any other title.

Each year there are more and more obedience Siberian Husky title holders in all classes in both the United States and Canada, and an impressive number of CDX, UD, and even UDT dogs—so it can be done. Those who know the breed realize that the great innate desire to run straight out ahead of a sled is the complete opposite behavior to the constrained discipline which must be displayed in the obedience ring. And once that degree has been won the victory is twice as sweet, since the challenge has been twice as great!

To achieve the **Companion Dog** degree, your Siberian Husky must compete and earn a total of 170 or more points out of a possible 200 under three different judges at three different trials. The novice obedience degree is based on the performance given in six exercises as follows: The Heel on Leash, 35 points; Stand for Examination, 30 points; Heel Free, 45 points; Recall, 30 points; Long Sit, 30 points; and Long Down, 30 points.

The first Siberian Husky to earn a Companion Dog (or CD) title was named King, and the year was 1941. Since 1941, there have been many others who have worked willingly and well to earn their titles.

There are seven exercises which must be executed to achieve the **Companion Dog Excellent** degree. Candidates must qualify in three different obedience trials and under three different judges and must have received scores of more than 50% of the available points in each exercise, with a total of 170 points or more out of the possible 200. At that time they may add the letters CDX after their name. The first CDX title was awarded to Ch. Chornyi of Kabkol in 1947.

The **Utility Dog** degree is awarded to dogs which have qualified by successfully completing six exercises under three different judges at three different obedience trials, with a score of more than 50% available points in each exercise, and with a score of 170 or more out of a possible 200 points.

These six exercises consist of: Scent Discrimination, with two different articles for which they receive thirty points each if successfully completed; Direct Retrieving, for 30 points; Signal Exercise, for 35 points; Directed Jumping, for 40 points; and a Group Examination, for 35 points. The first Husky to complete the UD title was Ch. Chornyi of Kabkol in 1948.

Snow Valley Flicka, UD

One of the most outstanding all-around Siberian Huskies in the breed is Don Carlough's Doncar's Snow Valley Flicka, UD. Bred by C.B. Hitchins, Flicka was sired by Cognac's Snow Lad of Koryak out of Vyesna Pulchrissimo Kindera. Flicka got off to a remarkable

start in the obedience field. She received her CD title, as a nine-month-old puppy, in her first three trials. By the time she reached a year-and-a-half, she had won her CDX title, also in three consecutive shows. At two-and-a-half she was a Utility Dog title holder and was being used in obedience demonstrations in the area. She was also a member of an all-breed obedience team which used lighted lanterns in their routine.

Flicka was a member of the Garden State Obedience Demonstration Team which performed at the National Specialty Show in 1972. Flicka was active in competition in obedience brace class and was a member of a Scent Hurdle Relay Race Team in northern New Jersey. She trained in tracking, and was cited by *Chips*, the national dog obedience magazine, as the top-ranking Siberian Husky in

obedience in the United States for the year 1970.

Schutte

Jane Schutte is the owner of Windy IV, UD, and is mighty proud of her. Windy is co-owned by George Schutte of Rowland Heights, California.

The Schuttes do not have a kennel—Windy is their only Siberian—but Jane is very active in the fancy. She teaches obedience, and has judged at match shows and obedience matches as well.

Windy IV, UD, took a high in trial in Open A with a score of 199. Her last two legs on her UD were scored at 198 and 196. With these scores, she won first place honors.

Tracking Dog Degree

The Tracking Dog trials are not held, as the others are, with the dog shows, and need be passed only once. The dog must work continuously on a strange track at least 440 yards long and with two right angle turns. There is no time limit; the dog must retrieve an article laid at the other end of the trail. There is no score given; the dog either earns the degree or fails. The dog is worked by his trainer on a long leash, usually in harness.

There are comparatively few dogs in any breed which attain this degree, so the Siberian Huskies which have earned it are to be especially commended. We are pleased to note that several Siberians have earned this title.

1949
Ch. Chornyi of Kabkol
1966
Ch. Chuchi of Tinker Mountain
1969
Juno's Lad CD

Chornyi and Chuchi are entitled to use the letters UDT after their names which includes their UD title. Lad uses TD for Tracking Dog only.

Ch. Aazar's Sure Hit, Best in Show-winning Siberian owned by Larry and Susan Govedich. This win was at the 1983 Rubber City KC Show.

SIBERIAN HUSKY CLUB GR. CLEVE. APRIL 19, 1980

HIGH IN TRIAL

POOLE

Chornyi of Kabkol, UDT

We live in an age of great progress and achievement, and we all know that records are made to be broken. But there is a great deal to be said for those who set the records that we must strive to break in the name of progress. Such is the story of Ch. Chornyi of Kabkol, the first UDT (Utility Dog Tracking) Siberian Husky in the history of the breed. Others may follow, but Chornyi will always remain first!

The H. Richard Garretts of Washington DC obtained Chornyi in April 1946, and he earned his CD degree by December of that same year. With Mr. Garrett handling the dog exclusively, he had earned his CDX title less than one year later, by September 1947. By December, 1947 he had won his championship in the show ring and within four months of championship won his Utility Dog degree (in April, 1948). A year later he was the first UDT dog in our breed's history.

During this time Chornyi was winning friends for the breed and setting records at the same time. In earning his CD title, he finished in three

Black Oak's Winter Breeze, CDX, bred by the Black Oaks Kennel and owned by James and Elizabeth Phillips of Hixson, TN. Trained by Elizabeth Phillips.

Top: Kryska's Khokolate Knoah and Kryska's Khokolate Kamelot. Owners, James and Maureen Kent.
Bottom: Storm King of Siberia, UD, is owned by Eleanor and Weldon Fulton. Breeder, Janet Cantrell.

"Chuchi acquired her CD in October, 1960, her CDX by October, 1961, her UD by September, 1963, and the record of being the second Siberian to earn the Utility Dog title."

consecutive shows, the second CD Husky on record. He was the first Siberian to finish for a CDX degree, and on April 8, 1948, he finished first in his class, earning his UD title. The tracking test was granted on the first try.

Through the years, Chornyi got to putting his training to good purpose. He not only has performed at hospitals and schools and before church groups but also has used his remarkable tracking ability to help the police on two occasions. The first time he located a boy's body, wedged between rocks and out of sight of the rescue team, and on the second occasion he was instrumental in saving an old woman lost in the woods.

Chornyi, whelped in 1945, died in 1959, after having lived a full and useful life with his devoted family.

Chuchi of Tinker Mountain, UDT

Chuchi came to live with the H. Richard Garretts as a champion at the age of four years. So sorely did they miss their beloved Chornyi that they decided they must have another Siberian Husky to obedience train, love, and use to bring attention to the breed in the same favorable way that Chornyi had. They obtained Chuchi from Louis Foley and Jimmy Whitfield, and they made her the second Siberian Husky and first Siberian Husky bitch to become a dual champion in breed and obedience.

Chuchi acquired her CD in October, 1960, her CDX by October, 1961, her UD by September 1963, and the record of being the second Siberian to earn the Utility Dog title. In 1965, she acquired her Tracking Dog title and the honor of being the second UDT Siberian Husky in the history of the breed. Her good long life was from 1956 to 1970.

The Garretts are most pleased and proud of their achievements with their two Siberians. They were teachers of obedience in the Washington DC area and obedience was always their prime interest and pleasure.

OTCh. Storm King of Siberia

OTCh. Storm King of Siberia is owned by Eleanor and Weldon Fulton of Big Bear Lake, California, and he was the first Siberian Husky to earn this coveted American Kennel Club title.

Storm earned his CD degree in September, 1974, and the CDX by April, 1975. That same year, in September, he had his UD title; he was also the youngest Siberian to have earned his UD degree, at just one year and eight months of age. When he finished, he had 108 points and a fourth High in Trial with 199 in Utility.

Whelped January 3, 1974, Storm retired from competition in 1982; he continued running around the mountains in Big

Bear Lake. The Fultons remain active with memberships in the Southwest Obedience Club of Los Angeles, the Camino Real Siberian Husky Club, and the Siberian Husky Club of America. It is their sincere hope that Storm's

Number One was Keno XIX, CD, with 144 points; No. Two was Karnovandas Alexei Puschkin with 140. R. Garrison was the owner of Keno, while Alexei was co-owned by G. Wilson and B. Newcomb. Number Three was Mr. and

Talocon's Arctic Aurora, CD, bred, owned, and shown to obedience title by John and Gail O'Connell.

accomplishments will inspire other Husky owners to participate in obedience training and competition.

1975

In 1975 there were ten Siberian Huskies that qualified.

Mrs. J. Sharbek's Misty Sheba of Mikita with 138; No. Four was Dees Babe of Manahtok, CD, owned by K. Karsch with 83 points; and No. Five was Shel E Jo, owned by B. and D. Yanley with 78 points. L.

Govedich's Yama Av Karnik, CDX, had 77 points; while the Munroe's Lei Kus Frosty Mist, R. Ripley's Ripleys Enoch, and Sivaks Akim of Hobik all had 76 points. Number Ten was Lady Tanya of South Mountain, CD, owned by C. and S. Waitkus with 65 points.

In 1975, there were a total of 41 all-breed show obedience trials and 174 licensed all-breed obedience trials; 507 all-breed trials held by show clubs in connection with their shows; and 265 Specialty trials held by clubs in connection with their Specialties. This adds up to an impressive 722 all-breed obedience trials and 276 Specialty obedience trials. By 1976 every one of these categories showed an increase and the obedience systems were on their way.

1976

There were no Siberian Huskies in the Top Ten obedience working breeds in the Shuman System in 1976, but four qualified in the breed rankings. Storm King of Siberia, UD, owned by E. and W. Fulton, amassed 98 points by the year's end. Dees Babe of Manahtok, owned by K. Karsch, was a repeater from 1975 listings with 43 points;

No. Three was Prince Igor XXV, owned by A.K. Madier and V. Cobb, had 42 points. Number Four was L.W. Govedich's Yama Av Karnik and had 39 points.

1977

Winners here again were four in number with first place going to Storm King of Siberia, UD, owned by E. And W. Fulton, with 124 points. Number Two dog was Prince Igor XXV, UD; Dee's Babe of Manahtok, UD, had 50 points to her credit. Number Four was R.H. Buzzard's Nicholas XXX, with 30 points, Shuman System.

1978

1978 was the year a Siberian Husky not only made second on the list of Top Ten Working Dogs, but captured the No. Seven spot with an all-breed win, Shuman System. This honor went to Rogers Arctic Star, UD, owned by D.I. Deaver. He had earned 340 points.

Rogers Arctic Star, UD, put in another appearance in the No. Two spot with 197 points, followed by Storm King of

Alkas'Iber Dig It Deeper, CD, taking High in Trial at a 1984 obedience trial with co-breeder-owner, George Cook at the Yankee SHC Show. "Aldi" also runs lead dog on George Cook's team. The sire was Can Ch. Channikko's Nordic Digger, Am CD, Can CDX, and Can TD.

At the 1983 Windward Hawaiian Dog Fanciers Show, Bonnie Duarte shows her Ch. Sunset Hills Don Ho-Beau, a multi-Group winner, No. 1 Siberian Husky, No. 4 in the Working Group, and No. 8 all-breed.

Siberia, UD, with 57, and Misty Sheba of Mikita, 51 points.

1979

In 1979, Siberians fell from the Top Ten all-breed and the Top Ten Working Dog ranks, but they held their own within the breed. Once again, Storm King of Siberia, UD, topped the list with 258. Three newcomers followed. Number Two went to L. and S. Govedich's Apparitions

Genghis Khan with 51 points; No. Three to a tie, with 42 points for both J. Anderson's Northern Lights Tonya and S. Ichikawa's Palos Verdes Kiskamo.

1980

In 1980, no Siberian qualified in the all-breed or working group listings, but there were ten within the breed ranks. Storm King of Siberia, UD, had 268 points, Delaney System; with 150 points for R. and D. Hoase's Northernlights Chief Zodiac in the No. Two spot. L. Baker's Garlis Tanya II had 134 to rank third, and J. Shaw's Ayavriks Ruska Karovin had 103 points to rate No. Four. Kus Camas The Sundance Kid, owned by G. Cropsey and B. Jacobi, was fifth with 164 points. Number Six went to Apparitions Genghis Khan, CDX, with 93 points; and No. Seven with 90 points was P. Swaney's Kimshas Tosca of Kamiakin. Number Eight and No. Nine tied with 67 points, and they were M. and K. Murtha's Murts Ebony Streaker and C. Koegel's and T. Boitano's Niko. Number Ten was Tawny Hills R.J., owned by D. and K. Dupuis, with 64 points.

1981

In 1982, the *American Kennel Gazette* published a list of the Top 25 Obedience Trial Champions that had earned points during 1981. No Siberian Husky made the list, but the Shuman System listed four Siberian Huskies. Number One, with 165 points, went to

Jane Schutte's Windy IV, UD, trained by owner and co-owner, George Schutte. Windy took first place honors with scores of 198 and 196 (out of 200) on the last 2 legs of her UD title.

L. Lucas's Sula, CDX. In the No. Two spot we found a repeater—but with an additional title! This was OTCh. Storm King of Siberia, owned by E. and W. Fulton, 86 points. Number Three, with 40 points, was the Govedich's Apparitions Genghis Khan, CDX; and No. Four went to D.M. Larson's Hodgendells Rocky Road, UD, with 40 points also.

1985
By the mid-1980s, Siberians were still holding their own— and then some. Number One in the Top Ten Working dogs, according to *Front and Finish*, with 193 points was J. and L. Pagini's Timbermists Regent, UD. Number Two, on the list of the Top Four, was Lojans Very Special Sula, UD, owned by L. Leonard, with 176 points. Number Three was Ch. Artka Truk of Innisfree, owned by R. Canada with 41 points; and No. Four was Tasha Tikki Jo, with 36 points, owned by J.T. Ditmer.

HISTORY OF HUSKY RACING

"Life for a working sled dog is a demonstration of the survival of the fittest in its most extreme context."

HARDSHIPS OF EARLY TEAM DOG LIFE

In the wilds of the North, the Siberian Husky team dogs were completely different from those we see in more modern times. They were scrappy and vicious, and brutal fights among the dogs were commonplace. All life was a challenge; a defense against the elements or a cruel master, the winning of a female, a fight for food, territory, or status among the rest of the dogs. If there was a fight for pack leadership between two dogs, it would be a fight to the death. The entire pack would swarm around eagerly waiting to demolish and devour whichever dog turned out to be the loser.

No amount of beating on the part of the owner can hold off the pack when the loser in a dog fight goes down. The same applies when, for some reason, the pack ostracizes a dog in its midst. It may lag behind the rest at first, but sooner or later the pack will gang up on it, close in, and finish it off. And what's more—the dog will know it is a goner and will do little to defend itself. The lead dog realizes this as well. The moment it shows the first sign of weakness, illness, or oncoming age, it must be replaced immediately or it will meet the same fate as the outcast dog. Life for a working sled dog is a demonstration of the survival of the fittest in its most extreme context.

These represent a few reasons why geldings were used more and more frequently on the teams. They ate much less food, did not fight as much among themselves, and could be quartered together in small places. The dogs were gelded with an iron knife, and at times, only the lead dog on a team was a whole male, making his job of maintaining law and order much easier. Geldings frequently suffered the additional indignity of having their tails cropped, since the Kamchadal and Koryak tribes believed that this added to their speed.

The first sleds or komiatics were made from whale bone or driftwood gathered from ice floes or from the tundra during the thaws. The runners were usually wooden, preferably hickory, and extended from five to 30 feet in length, with 12 feet being the average. Reindeer antlers tied to the sled with strips of walrus hide were sometimes used as handle bars. The baskets were made of seal or walrus hide; on some sleds, when wood was not available, runners were made from parts of the jawbones of whales. In an emergency, sleds could be

Ready and waiting—Ch. Indigo's Ismarelda, though born and bred in Florida, does well on the snow-covered paths of the North. Margaret Cook is the owner of this fine bitch.

made from cuttings of ice, frozen together and carved to individual needs.

There were basically three kinds of harnessing in ancient times, as there are today. One type of harnessing was attaching the dogs in pairs on both sides of a main line that was attached to the middle of the front of the sled. This was, of course, the ideal method of hauling large, heavy loads.

The second method of harnessing the dogs was with them attached singly, alternately placed on a single tow line to the sled. They used about six or seven dogs on this single team haul. The logic behind the single line was to avoid excessive loss in crevasse accidents and to prevent dogs from going over the precipices during snowstorms.

The third harnessing method was the fan attachment, where several dogs ran side by side, being attached at a single point and with a single tow line to the sled. This method was satisfactory only on clear, wide-open terrain.

Harnessing began when the puppies were a few months old, sometimes as early as two months. It was not uncommon to see entire litters of puppies tied up behind their mother, learning to pull in unison even at this early age. These teams often made the best and most efficient workers. The Koryaks put their new-born puppies in underground dugouts and kept them there in total darkness until they were old enough to

be harnessed, the result being that the moment the puppies saw daylight for the first time, they were so exuberant that there was no holding them.

On occasion there were dogs which could never make the team. These dogs were killed and probably eaten. Quarrelsome dogs had their teeth pulled out or the points broken off. By the time they reached 18 months of age, the new young dogs were ready to join the teams in prominent positions, and the older dogs were weeded out.

With this eventual and complete turnover every so

often you can readily understand the importance of the lead dog. He leads; the rest follow *him*, not the driver. The team is only as good as the lead dog. It was perfectly possible for a lead dog to bring that team home, when the driver was lost on the trail, against the most unbelievable odds. They may have turned up snowblind during a blizzard, but they've kept to the trail and have gotten the team home safely.

Well-treated, well-fed Huskies take great pleasure in their work, and the closer the relationship between the driver and the lead dog, the better the team will function. Winning drivers in racing events never forget this!

Seven years was about the limit of service for a sled dog, though some of the stronger dogs were used for a dozen or more years. It was, however, strictly downhill from about seven years on. Many dogs, especially older ones, were lost to frostbite, hunger, accidents on the trail, dog fights, ending up second best in a bout with a bear, another animal, or disease. More still fell victim to their owners' cruelty and neglect.

Driver Sharlene Lawson and her Aurora Siberian Husky team at a Flagstaff, AZ, race in 1982.

WHELPING IN THE WILDS

Unless the women took pity on them, bitches often were pulling sleds up to the moment of delivery. If their puppies were born while they were out on the trail they were usually destined to die. If the puppies were born at home, the wives would frequently care for them as well as take pity on the dam. The Eskimo women have been known to take it upon themselves to nurse the puppies along with their own babies if the dam were to die or be unable to perform this vital function herself.

Since the bitches were smaller and could not pull the weight the dogs could, they were

usually not put in a lead position. However, if a male team was reluctant to pull, a bitch in season would be put in the lead to give the males the needed incentive to get up and move. Bitches in season were sometimes tethered out, where male wolves would have access to them, when owners felt it was necessary to reintroduce wolf blood into their pack to strengthen the stock.

many of the tribes treated their dogs horribly. Dogs which became ill or wouldn't run up to standard were abandoned on the trail and left to die, the rare exception being an extraordinarily good runner, who might be forgiven and put on the sled for the ride home.

Some dogs which were disobedient had their tails cut off on the spot, leaving a trail of blood along the way. Obedience

The wide open spaces on the lower Yukon headed up the river to Grayling, AK. Marcia Hoyt drives the Norris' team at the 1985 Iditarod Race in Alaska.

Otherwise, the lead dogs were given first opportunity to cover the bitches for breeding purposes.

TREATMENT OF THE DOGS

In ancient times, just as today, treatment of dogs varied from person to person, family to family. While all tribes were aware of the importance of the dogs to their very existence,

was taught with a stick, and many severe beatings had to be endured before the dogs came to realize what was expected of them. Sticks used were usually four feet long and thick enough to brake the sled, a usual secondary purpose for them.

Some drivers preferred whips. These were vicious instruments, with a lash reaching anywhere from 18 to 24 feet, with a one-foot handle.

With this, the driver, by cracking it on either side of the lead dog, while shouting and repeating certain guide words, could pretty well hold the team in complete control. These whip handles were frequently used on the heads of the dogs if they didn't shape up.

Other disobedient dogs would have a rope, with a knot in it, tied around their throats; the rope would be pulled tight until they fell senseless. Dogs that chewed their harness were hung up until they lost consciousness, and then the tips of their rear molars were knocked off so they could no longer chew. While this method was terribly brutal, we must recall that in olden times the teeth of the dogs and the wolves were a great deal larger and sharper. Domestication has reduced the size and sharpness of teeth.

While these Esquimaux dogs were virtually slaves to their owners rather than allies and help-mates, their hard work and bitter treatment did, at times, make them refuse to move. If there was an especially heavy load and the dogs were badly treated by the drivers, women were frequently called upon to entice the dogs to move. The women, having played with the dogs as puppies, cared for them when they were sick and, in general, just treated them better, could often get them to give their all.

Driver Wayne Curtis at the 1986 Seven-Dog Class at the Baldwin, Michigan, competition.

Ready to go! James and Maureen Kent's team in fall training near Bow, NH. These Kryska Kennel dogs at the starting line in November 1985.

At times a woman would walk ahead of the sled, throwing bits of animal skin which had first been placed in her mouth, ahead of them in the snow. The dogs would think it was food and move ahead. Certain tribes even harnessed the women and young girls, who helped pull right along with the dogs.

It was only when the explorers began to arrive in the North, and demonstrated to the Eskimos that better results could be achieved through training and humane treatment, that the Eskimos began to look at their teams in a different light and the brutality and cruelty began to subside. It was the beginning of a man and dog relationship, rather than just man's will and dominance over a wild animal.

The tribes that treated their dogs kindly went to other extremes at times. The children were allowed to play with them, the women played a part in the upbringing of the puppy, and some tribes would build outdoor shelters for their dogs' protection against the elements.

Although some tribesmen built shelters for their dogs, others merely staked them out somewhere near their housing. In the face of violent storms or raging blizzards, the dogs were set free to avoid their being buried in the snow drifts or freezing to death for want of exercise. In summer, the dogs were set free to fend for themselves. They would dig holes in the ground to keep cool or lie in water to avoid the mosquitos. Some did well for themselves, especially if the seal

"Licking the snow caused less contraction of the stomach and avoided cramping and distress; it relieved the hunger pains caused by these contractions."

hunters were successful and threw scraps to them, while others were good at fishing and managed to survive on their own skill. Others had to scrounge for their food, and still others succumbed to starvation.

FEEDING IN ANCIENT TIMES

Food was always ravaged by these half-starved dogs, and, of course, more food was required by a dog living and working in a cold climate than those in a temperate zone. Instinctively, however, the Eskimo knew his dogs would be in trouble working on a full stomach or after drinking large quantities of water, so dogs were fed after the day's work was done. Instinctively, the dogs knew that licking snow was a substitute for water. Licking snow caused less contraction of the stomach and avoided cramping and distress; it relieved the hunger pains caused by these contractions. Many of the dogs came back from the long hauls not having been fed for days; they were often weak and hungry and would die of pneumonia or starvation.

The diets of the Eskimos consisted largely of seal, whale, or walrus meat and whatever scraps of meat or blubber were left over would get tossed to the dogs. If they were putrid so much the better. When food was scarce, the dogs would devour whatever came in front of them in the way of solid food; they were known to have chewed up their own harness or the thongs that tied the sleds together.

The farther south the dogs were, the better they fared. If fishing was good, they survived quite nicely on whole dried fish. The dogs got along on very little food, since their owners knew if they got too heavy they could not pull as well or as much. As winter approached, the drivers watched to see that the dogs lived off their own fat if they had eaten well over the summer months. During the winter, when the dogs were cared for, they might be fed a sort of soup, made from dried salmon bones with a piece of blubber thrown in, slopped in a trough. It is a wonder the dogs survived at all, much less that they were capable of pulling the great burdens they were expected to haul!

RACING IN ALASKA

The turn of the century marked the era of the great Alaskan Gold Rush. By 1906, a little village named Nome had burst into a boom town! It was the leading gold mining town in the world but, once winter set in and froze the Bering Sea, it had little more than the telegraph and native dog teams with which to keep in contact with the rest of the world.

Dog teams suddenly became an essential means of transportation for the natives as well as the members of the mining companies. In order to

Top: Gwynn Quirin of Scoqui Kennels skijoring in northern Minnesota. *Bottom:* One of the Kents' racing teams in a practice run.

Lupita and LupoTu, bracemates bred, owned and handled by Judi Anderson, Panuck-Denali Kennels, Laconia, NH.

assure the stamina and performance of the dogs, the Nome Kennel Club was organized in 1907. The man responsible was a lawyer named Albert Fink, who was to serve as the first president of the club. The All-Alaska Sweepstakes races were devised to create interest in the dogs.

A race course between Nome and Candle on the Seward Peninsula was drawn, which would represent a 408-mile trail round trip with a $10,000 first prize! It was to be run each April, the exact date depending on the weather conditions. The course was to follow as closely as possible the Nome to Candle telephone line, and it presented every possible kind of terrain. During the heyday of the Sweepstakes, winning of this race was so important that the drivers would feed and bed down their dogs before considering their own comforts. In extremely cold weather, the dogs were rubbed down with alcohol; sometimes they were given flannel moccasins for the feet and eye covers to prevent snowblindness.

In 1908, a Russian fur trader named Goosak imported a team of small dogs from Siberia; driven by a man named Louis Thustrup, this team won third place in this running of the Sweeps, in spite of 100 to one odds against them! There was great speculation that Thustrup might have done better if he had not become snowblind before reaching the finish line.

At this time a young Scotsman named Fox Maule Ramsay, in Alaska to supervise (with his two uncles, Colonel Charles Ramsay and Colonel Weatherly Stuart) his family's investments in the gold fields, showed up on the scene. The second son of the Earl of Dalhousie, he was fascinated by the excitement of the races and chartered a schooner for $2500 to cross the Bering Sea. He brought back 70 dogs of mixed breeding (several of which he claimed swam out to the ship to meet him) in the Siberian settlement named Markova, 300 miles up the Anadyr River.

He had driven his own team of dogs in the 1909 event and had not placed, so on the advice of his friend Ivor Olsen, he trained his new mixed breeds and entered three teams in the 1910 event. He drove one team himself and placed second. One of the two other teams, entered in the names of his uncles, placed first. He hired John "Iron Man" Johnson to drive one of the teams, and Johnson won in the record time of 74 hours, 14 minutes, and 37 seconds. Third place went to the mixed breed Malamute team entered by Allen and Darling.

After the race, Ramsay turned the dogs over to the drivers, never to compete again; he eventually returned to Scotland, where he succeeded to the Earldom of Dalhousie upon the death of his older brother.

1911 saw the entry of two Siberian dog teams, one by Johnson and Madsen and driven by Charles Johnson. Scotty Allen won the race with

Sy Goldberg and his five-dog team coming in from a race. The team of all champion dogs finds Am. and Can. Ch. Tanya of Cinnaminson in the lead position; right point, Ch. Koryak's Black Charger; left point, Ch. Mischa of Chaya, C.D., right wheel, Ch. Tokco of Bolshoi and left wheel Ch. Chachka of Cinnaminson.

Top: Ch. Koyma's Red Tannu of Mayhill, CDX, closing in for first place in the weight pull at Bear River, CA. Owned by Stu and Sherry Galka of Sonora, CA.
Bottom: Marcia Hoyt's team at Rainy Pass during the freeze at the 1985 Iditarod Race. Earl Norris photo.

his mixed-Malamute team entered by Allen and Darling; second position went to another mixed Malamute team driven by Coke Hill, who later became US district judge for the fourth Judicial Division. Charles Johnson and his team of Siberian Huskies were third. Iron Man Johnson with his team of Huskies did not place in the top three this year; it was rumored that he had thrown the race, since there was so much money bet on the outcome of this one due to his remarkable record the year before.

Enthusiasm waned the next year—only four teams entered the 1912 All-Alaska Sweepstake Race. Scotty Allen won with the Allen-Darling mixed-Malamute team, and Alec Holmsen, also with a mixed-breed team, placed second. Charles Johnson and his Siberians placed third.

The sixth running of the Sweepstakes, in 1913, was won by the mixed-breed entry of Bowen and Delzene, driven by Fay Delzene. Iron Man Johnson and his Siberians took second place and Scotty Allen was third with the Allen-Darling team. 1914 was Iron Man Johnson's year once again; the Allen-Darling team was second, and third spot went to Fred Ayer with an entry of half-Malamute and half-Foxhound team. This was also the year a stalwart young man named Leonhard Seppala arrived on the scene with his mixed-breed team, although after several misfortunes he was obliged to drop out of the competition.

The 1915 All-Alaska Sweepstakes was a different story, however, Leonhard Seppala entered and won with his Siberians. Second to Seppala was a mixed-breed entry of Bowen and Delzene,

Racing in Vermont in January 1986. Leonard Bain driving a 10-dog team consisting of: right lead, Turick's Final Conflict; left lead, Kimlan's Alpha Centauri; right point, Winslow's Chelsea Girl; left point, Winslow's Simply Simon; right swing, Turkick's Remington Steele; left swing, Permafrost's Uganda; right wheel, Turick's Overdrive; and left wheel, Turick's Totl Eclipse O'Heart. Nancy Wolfe photo.

driven by Fay Delzene, and third was the Fred Ayer Malamute-Foxhound team.

This triumphant and satisfying win by Seppala in 1915 was one which he repeated in 1916 and again in 1917. He probably would have done it again in 1918 but the War had hit Nome hard, and the greatest dog team races ever run at this annual Alaskan event came to a sad end.

Even today, Alaska considers sled dog racing as its very own sport and features two of the world's most famous races, North American Championship Race, held in Fairbanks, and the Fur Rendezvous, or the Rondy, in Anchorage. The Fur Rendezvous became a virtual festival for everyone, with a fur auction, parties, dances, and exhibitors all being held at the one gathering place. But from the beginning, dog racing was the main event, and today the 75-mile race still is! The schools close on the Friday of the Rendezvous, and the city turns out *en masse* to watch the four-dog team demonstrations which became the regular feature in 1946. The North American race is 70 miles in length; both events are run in three heats which divide the distance in three parts, over three days. After the third day, the winner

Richard and Jan Walker's first family of Siberians, at their Shihoka's Kennels in Ogden, UT. It includes Rocky Mountain Caribou, Ch. Rockies Rhett Butler, CD, and Ch. King of the Rockies.

Out over the polar ice during the 1984 Iditarod Race. This is Kari Skogun's team.

is announced and the celebrating begins anew!

There are also state championship races held in Kenai and Soldotna, and also one in Tok. Racing in Alaska, which had diminished during World War II, picked up again with new enthusiasm in the late 1940s, when the Alaska Dog Musher's Association was formed in Fairbanks. There were few members, however, who bred pure Siberian Huskies; the dogs were mostly mixtures. But the Earl Norrises, Hortense Landru, Jack and Sid Worbass, and Don and Virginia Clark were dedicated breeders for several years.

In 1949, in Anchorage, the Alaska Sled Dog and Racing Association was organized. This club had several members who bred Siberian Huskies and they formed the Alaska Siberian Husky Club from within the ranks of member of ASDRA. They joined the parent club and held several AKC-recognized dog shows. This club worked diligently to advertise the Husky as a race and show dog, and the Siberian Husky was a top dog during the 1950s.

Ch. Bonzo of Anadyr, CD,

was the first Siberian Husky to win Best in Show in the Alaska all-breed show and was 'Best in Match at their first sanctioned obedience trial; he was the first Siberian Husky to earn his CD in Alaska. Ch. Tyndrum's Oslo, CDX, was the first and, to date, the only winner of this title. Both of these dogs were famous racing lead dogs as well.

The Huslia Heritage and Hustlers

The Athabascan Indian village named Huslia, which has given to the racing world in Alaska so many of its top dogs and drivers, is situated 260 miles northwest of Fairbanks on a river about one mile from the Koyukuk. The village remains very remote, still steeped in its Indian culture, but with modern ways and communications now gradually creeping up on it.

Jimmy Hunington was originally a trapper but gained fame for borrowed dogs, got a team together and by mushing and getting a ride on a mail plane (along with his 14 dogs!) arrived in Fairbanks to race in the North American Race, intent on winning enough money to open his own trading post in Huslia. He placed fourth but went home broke because he was unable to collect his prize money.

The desire to race stayed

George and Ann Cook's team, being driven by George. Lead dogs are Can Ch. Tokomac's Kashega, and Tokomac's Aivilik Pacesetter; point dog is Tokomac's Makushkin Nunatak; and wheel dogs are Tokomac's Punuk Qooyanasat and Shonko's Daring Tugger.

AmCan Ch. Black Oaks Crescendo, AmCan CD, is owned by Ward and Don Young.

Top: Libby Riddles and Joe Garni at the finish line in Nome, AK, in 1985 at the Iditarod Race. Riddles was the first woman to win the Iditarod, and was named Athlete of the Year and Woman Athlete of the Year for this remarkable feat.

Middle: The 5-dog racing team of Vern and Olivia Harvey, Tucson, AZ.

Bottom: Jim Kent and his Kortar's Kranberry Kaptain, CD, photographed in 1980

with him, and in 1956 the villagers urged him to try again and loaned him their best dogs; he emerged the winner of the North American Race in Fairbanks and the Fur Rendezvous in Anchorage. He thereby became known as The Huslia Hustler, until 1958, when George Attla, Jr. also from Huslia, appeared on the scene; George carried the title as well! Looking at the line-up of any big Alaskan race today, you'll probably find either a winning team of dogs and/or drivers from Huslia!

In 1958 George Attla, Jr. appeared in his first Rondy Race and won handily with a 12-dog team. He owned only one of them, his lead dog named Tennessee. The rest of the dogs belonged to members of his family.

George Attla was born in 1933, one of eight children born

Carol Nash of Plaistow, NH, driving her 5-dog team in Rangeley, MN, in March 1985. Dogs are Ch. Sheliko's Brendon of Canaan, Ch. Canaan's Rollicking Raven, Canaan's Go Diva, Canaan's P.T. Barnum, and Canaan's Resurrected MacInri.

to George and Eliza Attla. A form of tuberculosis caused the fusing of the bones in George's knee, but the defect in no way stopped him from sled racing; in addition to four Rondy wins, he has captured the number one spot in just about every other major race in Alaska.

George is also known as a great dog trainer. In addition to training his own dogs, he sometimes trains dogs for his competition! He excels in training lead dogs which have made winning teams for many of his competitors in the major races—some of which have beaten his team!

George authored a book entitled *Everything I Know About Training and Racing Sled Dogs,* in collaboration with Bella Levorsen, a racing enthusiast in her own right, which reveals George's secrets of success as a world champion racer four times to date! His 1972 racing records at Bemidjii and Ely, Minnesota; Kalkaska,

Kamikhan Kennel's Ch. Blue Shadow Marshall, CD, owned by Raymond and Irma Marshall of Crownsville, MD. Shadow earned his CD title owner-handled and placed in the ribbons 2 out of 3 qualifying legs.

Top: Turick's Damien of Yeso Pac, top stud dog at Carolyn Kaiser and Leonard Bain's Turkick and Winslow Kennels in Acworth, NH. Bred and owned by Carolyn Kaiser. *Bottom:* Black/white, copper/white Siberian Huskies by Robert Pearcy.

Top: A team of champion Siberian Huskies from Alaska, and Ardene Eaton and daughter Kim. Kim was Top Junior Handler 2 years in a row. *Bottom:* Kolyma's Racing Siberian award-winning team on the move. Left lead is Kolyma's Kokoda of Igloo Pak; right lead, Kolyma's Shasta of Igloo Pak. Left swing dog is Kolyma's Kobuk of Igloo Pak; right swing dog, Igloo Pak's Lobo. Left team dog is Igloo Pak's Midget; right, Igloo Pak's Lucky. Left wheel dog, Kolyma's Tuolumnhe Igor; right, Kolyma's Kino of Igloo Pak. All dogs on the team, with the exception of Igor, are of Dr. Lombard's breeding.

Top: Judith Russell's Karnovanda's Innisfree Mist and Zinka Raven competing in a 6-dog class in 1984, with 15-year-old Ethan Russell driving.
Bottom: Kimlan's Alpha Centauri, lead dog owned by Leonard Bain and bred by D. and R. Hooker.

Michigan; Anchorage, Nenana, Fairbanks, Tok, and Tanana, Alaska, earned George Attla the Gold Medal from the International Sled Dog Racing Association's first annual competition for a Point Champion.

The Iditarod

Organized by Joe Remington, "Father of the Iditarod," the first Iditarod Trail Race was held in 1967. Celebrating its silver anniversary in 1992, this trek of endurance along the historic gold trails is surely the "granddaddy of 'em all."

The Iditarod is the longest sled dog race in the world, totalling 1049 miles in racing distance. There are at least twenty checkpoints through which the teams have to pass, and, of course, there are designated rest periods to ensure the welfare of both dog and driver. All mushers carry sleeping bags, survival equipment, and two sets of boots for each dog. It is a most challenging and demanding race, and many a contestant has

Haglund's racing team at the Paul Bunyan Sled Dog Race in Bemidji, MN: Amaroq's Snow Speeder, CD; Alaskan's Tundra of Anadyr, SC; Northome's Sugar Bear, SD; Shjegge Manns Lobo of Amaroq, SD; Shjegge Manns George; Shjegge Harvey.

Top: One of the most famous of all racing men, Doc Lombard, with Kari Skogun at the 1984 Iditarod checkpoints. *Bottom:* Earl Norris crossing the finish line during the 1985 Iditarod Race.

suffered frostbite, fatigue—or worse.

Men and women alike have won the Iditarod. The first female victor was Libby Riddles, who won the event in 1980. Since that time, Susan Butcher has raced to the forefront of women mushers, winning the Iditarod several times, which, among other things, earned her the title of Women Athlete of the Year. One of the top men in today's competition is Martin Boser, also a multiple winner of the race.

On average, two or three all-Siberian teams are entered in the race every year. Perhaps the singlemost significant contributors to this aspect of the breed are Earl and Natalie Norris of Willow, Alaska. The Norrises have long participated in the race, both in person and by putting up teams for other drivers.

The contemporary European counterpart to the Iditarod is known as the Alparod, a 1000-plus-mile race through five European countries. It is an international event in which each participating country is invited to send two teams.

THE AMERICAN DOG DERBY

1917 was the first year of the American Dog Derby in Ashtown, Idaho. The event featured several events in different towns each year. A ten-mile course is held for each of the two different days. The Derby is now a far cry from the first races, when a half-dozen teams of mixed breeds raced from West Yellowstone, Montana, to Ashtown, Idaho, a distance of 75 miles.

WORLD CHAMPIONSHIP SLED DOG DERBY

Laconia, New Hampshire, is the site on the Eastern seaboard for this event. The racers take over the main street and use snow-making machines if Mother Nature does not oblige with the real thing. There is a Musher's Ball, a Beauty Queen, and much fanfare for this popular event.

SLED DOG RACING IN MINNESOTA

The St. Paul, Minnesota, Winter Carnival in 1962 was the site of the first sled dog race in the state, in conjunction with special events at the State Fair.

In 1965, the North Star Sled Dog Club, Inc., was started as a racing club, and by 1969, the club decided to sponsor a major national racing event at the Winter Carnival called "East Meets West." A total of 55 teams competed that year in St. Paul, representing 11 states and Canada. The event was a major breakthrough for racing enthusiasts and has been growing in popularity and competition ever since. The purses get larger each year and the number of spectators increases notably as well.

ALL AMERICAN RACES

Each year the All American Championship Sled Dog Races

Top: A 3-dog racing team featuring three Whispering Oaks' dogs: Ch. Dushinka, Lightfoot and Cayenne. Owned by Susan Vosnos of Barrington, IL.
Bottom: Aus Ch. Chukchii Yukon Lad getting ready to practice racing with his young trainer, Wayne Baker, in Victoria, Australia.

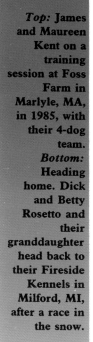

Top: James and Maureen Kent on a training session at Foss Farm in Marlyle, MA, in 1985, with their 4-dog team.
Bottom: Heading home. Dick and Betty Rosetto and their granddaughter head back to their Fireside Kennels in Milford, MI, after a race in the snow.

are held in Ely, Minnesota, and feature mutt races as part of the special events program. These mutt races are usually held following a torch-light parade, and are run for boys and girls from six to eight years of age, eight to ten years of age, and from ten to twelve years of age. Each child runs a single hitch, and the one dog may be of any type or breed. The only differential is that they separate the experienced and trained sled dogs from the amateur dogs and run them in separate categories.

There is no entry fee and, of course, trophies are provided for the winners. This is always a popular event with racing enthusiasts of all ages.

Riddles takes first place in Nome at the 1985 Iditarod Race.

Saturday sees the first heats of the All American Championship Sled Dog Race. Usually over 100 teams compete. Saturday night there is a banquet and entertainment, and on Sunday the second heats are run; prizes are awarded at the completion of the day's events.

There is over $5000 in prize money awarded to the racers as well as hundreds of dollars' worth of trophies to the winners who manage to triumph on one of the finest racing trails in the world. The best known racers from all over the United States (including Alaska, of course) and Canada manage to show up to compete.

Because of the great beauty of the dogs, and the excitement of the chase, there is always a great deal of spectator enthusiasm as well as newspaper, radio, and television coverage and stories in major magazines all over the world. Over 20,000 fans show up to cheer on their favorite dog teams. The Chamber of Commerce of Ely, Minnesota, can be proud of their Expo-Mini Sports Show and Sled Dog Races which are the biggest winter sports events in northern Minnesota.

The sled dog gathering usually opens with a community center show which features the latest in sleds, equipment, accessories, and demonstrations of anything and everything pertaining to racing, including items which can be purchased.

This is followed on Friday night by a torchlight parade, the beauty queen, sleds, snowmobiles, floats, and the like. The parade is followed by

Gary Cingel and his 6-dog team 12 miles out in Marmora, Ontario, Canada. Left lead, Konik's Silver Streak; right lead, Konik's Silver Bullet; left point, Konik's Silver Belle; right point, Toko's Chase; left wheel, Markova's Mirkwood Desperado; and right wheel, Tokomac's Sasha of Konik.

Top: Judy Russell driving her all-Karnovanda-bred 8-dog team with Karnovanda's The Replica in left lead.
Bottom: Amaroq's Snow Speeder, CD, SD, on his way to winning the Dakota Championship Weight Pull in Fargo, ND. Owners, Roger and Margaret Haglund.

417

Top: Dog Sled with wheels. Courtesy of Larry Freas, Lar-Anne Dog Training School, West Berlin, NJ. *Bottom:* Vel Leahy with Ch. Highpoint's Black Eyed Susie and Highpoint Veleah Quicksilver in Vel's lap. Veleah Siberians are located in Archer, FL.

the special events program, which features weight pulling contests, celebrity races, ski-joring, a scramble race, a beard contest, and the kids' mutt races. Entertainment of the indoor variety follows the activities in these categories.

WOMEN MUSHERS

It seems women have always shared their husbands' interest in driving dog teams and racing. We are all familiar with the successes of Short Seeley, Lorna Demidoff, and Louise Lombard, who in 1949 was the only woman entered in the 90-mile Ottawa, Canada, Dog Sled Derby, competing right along with her husband.

Mrs. E.P. Ricker, now Mrs. Nansen, was driving dog teams in 1928 and placed second at the Lake Placid fourth annual Sled Dog Derby in 1931. Bunty Dunlap, Mrs. Ricker's daughter, went on to follow in her mother's footsteps and became a top sled dog driver. And don't let us forget Jean Bryar, winner of the North American Women's Championship in Alaska, the first woman from the States to do it. She also gave a good account of herself in many of the gruelling Canadian races, not to mention New Hampshire events. Millie Turner was active at the New England events in the 1930s and 1940s, and Natalie Norris and Joyce Wells have been active at the

Desmond and Mary Cole's racing team photographed at Diamond Lake in 1985. Photo by Tom Watson.

Andrea Russell and her Top Junior Team for 1976. Andrea is the daughter of Judith Russell, Karnovanda Kennels, Davisburg, MI.

Rondy races.

1953 was the first year of the Women's World Championship Sled Dog Races in Alaska, an event that has been run every year since, except for 1956. The same rules apply to the women's races as apply to the regular races, and the women train their own dogs. The teams usually average 9 or 11 dogs, and there are on an average of ten to fifteen teams competing for the purse and the title of top female musher in Alaska—and the world!!

JUNIOR RACERS

While discussing mutt racing and the wide range of ages which can be found competing, we cannot fail to mention the former junior who made such a name for herself in racing circles. I refer to Darlene Huckins of Tilton, New Hampshire.

Darlene began racing at the age of ten with a three-dog team which she raised and trained herself. By the time she was 15 she had won just about every prize a junior could win

Kari Skogun finishing the 1984 Iditarod, running as the all-Siberian team from the Norris' Alaska/Anadyr Kennels.

with her splendid dogs. Later she became the youngest woman ever to enter the World's Championship Sled Dog Derby in Laconia, New Hampshire. On the first day she placed ninth, and after three days of racing was in 19th place, having won a higher position than many other older and more experienced drivers. In 1968 she finished 16th in the placings and won a trophy for having the best conditioned team in the event. In 1970 she received the Jonathan Allen Memorial Trophy as the top scoring former junior racer. Darlene's success set a marvelous example for other juniors who love to race and win with their own teams.

At the end of each December in Anchorage, Alaska, the Junior Alaskan Sled Dog and Racing Association opens its season. The club holds a meeting each Friday night to discuss weather and trail conditions and to draw for starting positions for the race at the Anchorage Tudor Track. Races are held each week throughout the month of January.

These juniors must adhere to all the rules and regulations followed by the adults. The races are held on the same trails as the adults run and are often eight to twelve miles long. To be a junior musher, the child must be from six to 18 years of age. There are five classes of junior races consisting of one-, two-, three-, five-, and seven-dog teams. The one-doggers race for a quarter of a mile on a

straight track, while the two-dog class and most of the three-dog classes run three miles. The five- and seven-dog classes increase the mileage still farther, running a six-mile trail for the opening race with a vote determining the length of future races.

It was inevitable that the children in the US would also become involved in the sport of racing. Most every club today has events for the children with lots of competition and lots of fun. Racing is a wonderful family sport and excellent training for the future. The kids bring out the crowds, and the rooting for them is inspiring.

AmCan Ch. Arctic Thor of Innisfree owned by Kathleen Kanzler.

RACING IN CANADA

There are two major races in Canada and they are taken very seriously and given special importance, since the trails are tough and the purses high.

The major race is the PAS held in Manitoba. This race is not widely known but is acknowledged to be the longest and the toughest in the world. The dogs cover a distance of anywhere from 100 to 150 miles during this three-day race. The Quebec race, while not as long, covers a 100-mile distance.

RACING IN FINLAND

1969 was the year that sled dog racing began in Finland. The first race, organized by Mr. P. Uimonen, was held in January of that year, with four teams participating. The Finnish races use the American ISDRA rules, but they limit the number of dogs to five in the A class. Four teams took part in the Class A event of 16 miles, and six teams competed in the Class C event of about three miles with three dogs.

The Siberian Husky Club of Finland held its fifth race of the season in February, 1969 on the Kuurile estate, with trails made by ski-doo machines and over a course running through forests, fields, and over ice-covered lakes. Most of the dogs used are Siberian Huskies; some were mixed or other breeds. Each year the number of dogs competing increased.

Finland has strict quarantine laws, but borders are open between Norway, Sweden, and Finland, and the drivers and their teams travel quite freely between those countries. Interest is keen, and the number and kind of races depend largely on the weather conditions at the time.

Top: Mrs. Sylvia Roselli and one of her 9-week-old homebreds. *Bottom:* Checkpoint at the 1984 Iditarod Race.

TODAY'S RACING DOG

Today's racing Siberian Husky is a far cry from those of ancient times and of the early days of this century. Just as a good "nose" is almost always hereditary with a Beagle, so is the desire to run usually inherent in the Husky. If Siberians are to be good racers they are *usually* well-angulated, with longer legs and lighter bones than those we see in the show ring (though this is not always the case). They are usually under 60 pounds with good feet and an innate desire to run!

EARLY TRAINING FOR THE RACING DOG

There is probably no better breed for racing or pulling than the Siberian Husky, because of his stamina and sustained power over long distances. Whether your dog will just race, or race and pull weight, training should start around two or three months of age. Start with a soft harness and let him drag a small log or board around. Judge the weight of the log by the weight of the dog. Don't let it be so heavy that the puppy could not possibly move it without a struggle; if you do that, he'll lose interest or get discouraged. By the same token, don't let it be so light that it will catch up with him on a down grade, or he'll never learn the meaning of what it is to "pull." Try what you think is just right, and then observe the puppy's behavior with it for a while; make any necessary adjustments at this time and, of course, as the puppy continues to grow.

At this time, while the puppy is learning to pull, he should be encouraged to pull along a given path, so that the idea of a trail can be established in his

mind should you wish to enter competition in the future.

We have stressed how important it is that each Husky destined to race have the innate desire to run and to win. This eagerness to compete will enable the trainer to start his harness training at an earlier age and thereby give a head start to the dog on the training as well as conditioning him to his purpose of running and pulling.

If you are fortunate enough to live in snow country, your sled, harness, and towline will be your initial equipment for

Top: **James and Maureen Kent's first Siberian Husky. "Chinook" is his name, and he is pictured here at their Kryska Kennels in Bow, NH.** *Bottom:* **Race training session at Lynne and Bonny Patterson's Tandara Kennels in Gio Harbor, WA. The 12-year-old Tandara's Zarenna Tatiana, CDX, teaches 4½-month-old Tandara's Runamuck Parmigan the "ropes."**

training. If you live in a comparatively snowless area you will need a three-wheeled balanced substitute for training. Training should be a serious matter and in no way the same as or comparable to playtime. Start with each dog individually pulling some weight. This individual training will help you determine which of the puppies has the strongest desire to pull ahead in spite of the weight. You will invariably find that the dog with the strongest desire to pull will make the best lead dog by the time your training nears completion.

One of the most difficult aspects of training will be finding the proper place to train the puppies. If you do not live in the country, it will be necessary to locate a park or wooded area, or better still, a local race track where the dogs can run a distance with minimum danger of interruption by uncertain terrain. Too many distractions in populated areas will throw puppies or young dogs off until they know what is expected of them. With too many spectators around there is always the danger of having the team bowl them over if they get in the way. Therefore, until the puppies get used to running and keeping on the trail, bridle paths, fields, and farm lands are the best places to work out. Remember the safety of others when tearing down a path with a team of Huskies! Under no circumstances should you train your dogs on the street or a concrete surface. The irritation

Arahaz Velvet Hammer, owned by S. Windsor Rodney, Kaylee Kennels. The sire was Arahaz VO Dudley ex Arahaz Barkhata.

Top: Innisfree's Maeve, bred and owned by Kathleen Kanzler, Innisfree Kennels. *Bottom:* Aus Ch. Kolyma Czarina Tasha and her mother, Aus Ch. Frosty Pine Anya, winners at the 1983 Royal Melbourne Show. Owned by Rex and Edna Harper, Kolyma Kennels, Victoria, Australia.

Top: IntCanBel Ch. Arcticlights Quincy was also the 1985 Vice World Champion. Bred by Eric and Nancy Van Loo, he is owned by Mr. and Mrs. F. Lizin of Belgium, where he was No. 1 Siberian for 1985. The sire was Telemark's Tok ex Can Ch. Arcticlight's Kirnova. *Bottom:* Ch. Talocon's Arctic Echo is a dual purpose dog—an awesome lead dog for owners, John and Gail O'Conner.

to the pads of the feet prevents the dogs from reaching out to their full stride, so they never become good distance runners in a race. Ideal conditions are snow or sand, but if such surfaces are not available, train on dirt surfaces to prevent the hackneyed gait of the dogs which are trying to preserve their own feet, or which will pull up with bloody pads if forced to run on pavement.

As the puppies grow and begin working together, you will undoubtedly have joined a club in your area where members are equally interested in racing. You will learn a great deal from your association with other members, and it is advisable to take full advantage

Can Ch. Almaring's the Native, AmCan CD. Bred by Michele Thie and Ingrid Brucato, Native is owned by Joanne Dixon of Jangley, Canada.

of their advice, knowledge, and experience. But there are still going to be many hours of training on your own where a few essential rules will apply.

Important to remember in your training is this: do not teach too many commands. Young puppies can not retain too many words, and expecting too much of them too soon will only confuse them and perhaps make them lose interest entirely. Remember to praise them lavishly for their good work and efforts. Remember to keep your puppies and dogs in top racing condition so that they will be able to give what is expected of them without draining every last bit of energy. Remember common sense rules which apply to racing as well as obedience or show training; namely, do not feed or water immediately before training, and exercise the puppies before starting the training so there will be no interruption. And perhaps most important of all, do not go on to another command or lesson until the dog has already learned the last one!

You will find that your puppy can cover a mile comfortably by the time he is eight months old, which should increase to 15 or 16 miles at the peak of his training and performance at two years of age.

FORMING YOUR TEAMS

One of the determining factors in selecting your team will be each dog's disposition. The training may have gone

Arahaz Charisma, 1 year old, and Arahaz Margaritka, 3 months old, waiting on the porch for their walk. Bred by Rosemary Fischer and owned by A. Levine.

along very well, but if the dog is a "scrapper" and will be undependable when harnessed with other dogs in a team, you will eventually run into trouble. While it is allowable to remove a dog from a team during a race, it would make more sense to have all members of your team able to finish if you really want to win and need that full team to do it!

When we talk about Huskies being smart in their own special way, we must explain that at times there is an almost obvious "holding back" or lack of complete communication between you and the dog, which manifests itself noticeably in the training for racing competition. When a Husky is being trained to race, he will usually pace himself to fit the distance he must cover on his own. Therefore, it is

wise when training the dog for the race to steadily increase the distance each day, rather than varying the ground mileage to be covered from one day to the next. Increasing distance each day will increase his desire to always "go further," and to the end of the race.

A tenet in animal behavior studies acknowledges that there is a leader in every pack. So it is with a racing team. Your lead dog must be the most respected member of your kennel or the other dogs simply will not give their all and "follow the leader." Whatever the sex of the lead dog, put your next two fastest dogs behind the lead dog and your biggest or strongest two at the wheel positions.

While your lead dog will assert himself to keep order in the pack, to maintain a good team you must have harmony

"Lacy" at 9 months of age, bred and owned by Verla McFayden and Frank and Michele Polimeni of Westminster, CA. Lacy's full name is Poli's Spirit of the Wind.

Head study of Stu and Sherry Galka's lead dog, Igloo Pak's Jib. The sire was Igloo Pak's Kaltag ex Igloo Pak's Teslim.

Ch. Nicholas of Toko, 1 of 7 champions from Jean Fournier's Ch. Fournier's Tiffany of Toko, one of the breed's Top-Producing bitches.

among all members of the team. Drivers will find that, on occasion, if they buy dogs from other teams to add to their own, the new dog is apt not to pull and will be dragged by the rest unless he feels he has been accepted by the other dogs as a member of the pack. Puppies from the same litter, trained together, often make the best teams for this reason. They "grow into the saddle."

Practice makes perfect, as the saying goes, and hours of practice and training are necessary to get all your dogs working together as a team. There is no easy way to accomplish this other than hard work. It is a magnificent challenge.

FEEDING THE RACING SIBERIAN HUSKY

While the Husky is known to be capable of extreme drive over long distances, a relatively simple diet is required.

Owners who race their dogs—including real professionals who have been in the racing game for a long time—will tell you that the basic diet is a good dog meal and that the average amount of food for a racing dog of average size is approximately a one-pound coffee can full. Most Siberian Huskies have voracious appetites and will overeat if permitted to do so, so try to establish the correct amount for keeping each of your racing dogs in proper flesh, and then stick to it.

This ration of a good dog meal, plus drinking water, are all that is really required for a proper and balanced diet, even if your dog races. However, there are those who choose to supplement a racing dog's diet in the belief that the "extras" add to the all-around good health of the animal. Alaskans, for instance, might add moose meat or other wild game meat to the diet; they also use fish as

A splendid portrait of AmCanMexInt Ch. Ma-Ri-An Wind's Storm Prince and the 3-month-old Ma-Ri-An Wind's Storm Sparkle. Owner, Mrs. Roselind M. McEnroe.

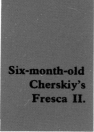

an added ingredient. And when we mention fish, we mean to say the *entire* fish—inside and out, head and tail included! Some owners of racing teams will supplement with liver, or keep their dogs on vitamins mixed in with the meal or feed. They might even use the vitamin tablets as treats or as a reward. Still others feed the added vitamins a few days

Six-month-old Cherskiy's Fresca II.

before a racing schedule begins. On the day of the race, some drivers feed lumps of sugar or add Karo syrup to the ration. But those "in the know" will tell you that while it will not harm the dog, sugar and Karo syrup are instant energy and are burned up so quickly it will in no way sustain a dog throughout the entire distance of the race. Therefore, the proper basic diet is still the best way to fully condition a dog for racing without having to rely on last-minute superficial extras.

This same principle applies to the vitamin B shots, which some owners of racing dogs believe to be of help. A dog that has been properly and substantially fed will not need any additional vitamin or energy supplements. There is always the risk of diarrhea when a diet is suddenly supplemented to any marked degree. Those that do add meat—or anything else for that matter—to the diet before racing their dogs do so for several days ahead of time so that the dog has time to adjust to it.

It is possible to buy huge frozen blocks of beef for the team and add it to the ration on a regular basis so it will not shock the dog's system. It is an unpleasant experience to have a racing dog with diarrhea, and diarrhea can certainly throw a dog off his performance and thereby hold back an entire team.

The correct procedure is to feed the dog his customary

Lovely candid shot of Ch. Talocon's Arctic Echo at 9 months of age.

diet, to have him in the peak of condition, and use a suppository about an hour before the race if the dog has not emptied himself entirely without prompting.

Just as it is not wise to feed before a race, it is not wise to let a racing dog drink too much water before a race. Watch the water intake carefully. If the dog is still thirsty as race time approaches, he usually will lick snow, but it is not wise to offer any water immediately before or immediately after a heat.

Lovely head study of Ch. K.C. Jones of Troika.

SECURING RACING INFORMATION

If you have decided that you wish to enter a team in a race, you must write to the race-giving club well in advance asking for all pertinent information along with an entry blank. Ask the race marshall for specific information regarding not only the race, but information on joining the club, which you will want to do eventually, if you haven't already. State the size of your team, and ascertain at this time if it is necessary to be a member of the club in order to enter the race. With some clubs this is a requirement.

While waiting for this information to reach you, consider once again whether or not you are *really ready* to enter your first race. Ask yourself whether your dogs are sufficiently trained, run well together, fight in harness, stick to the trail, tangle with other teams, can be distracted by people or other animals on the sidelines, and perhaps most important of all, are all the dogs equal in strength and endurance, and do they all really want to run more than anything else?!?

THE DAY OF THE RACE

You've entered your first race and have received your notification and rules regarding the race, time, place and requirements. Needless to say, the beginner should arrive early to observe the procedures others follow and to have plenty of time to ask questions. Be sure you park in the correct area, stake your dogs out in the proper area, exercise them, and determine within plenty of time when the drivers' meeting will be held so that you can attend it.

While you are waiting for the

Sheila Kanzler and Ch. Innisfree's Red Hugh, owned by Kathleen Kanzler.

meeting to begin, take the time to reread the rules of the race. As a beginner you may forget— and knowing what to do when and where can make a difference! Always check your equipment before this meeting.

Always include a complete substitute for your harness and tow lines, collars, leashes, etc., in your tack box. Accidents do happen, and it would be a shame to miss your first experience because a break left you without complete equipment. Don't be afraid to ask questions or to ask for help. Remember that everyone else was once a beginner, and most people remember how much it meant to have a helping hand or a genuine good word of advice.

Remember good manners during the race. Don't spoil someone else's chances because of your mistake or mistakes. They will be watching out for you if they know you are new at the game, but it is your responsibility not to spoil the race for others. You are expected to know the passing rules, re-passing rules, etc., and you will gain more respect for your sportsmanship and knowledge than you will for trying to stick it out when you should get out of the race. No one expects you to win your first race anyway! But whether you win or lose, once you've

Kryska's Kamelot and Khokolate Kalypso, owned by James and Maureen Kent.

Sherry Galka's lead dog from 1973–75, "Kori"; formally, Kolyma Mayhill Silver Koryak, CD.

gotten into the competition you will become addicted to the sport, and sooner or later you will win if your dogs are good and properly trained.

PROFESSIONAL RACING TEAMS

You must realize that racing for fun and pleasure, or in local club meets or contests, is entirely different from the professional racing meets where the stakes and purses are high and the owners and drivers are out to win. Professional racing teams mean serious business, and it is a completely different world for the professional racing dog!

The trainers and drivers of the professional teams are usually those dedicated to doing nothing else but training and racing the dogs. It is their profession; the lives of the dogs are dedicated to racing and winning.

This purpose begins with the picking of the dogs which show—above all else—the natural desire to run and to

win. The training is more rigorous, the culling more ruthless, and the proper rearing and selection of the dogs even more essential. Professional team owners will spare no expense and will travel the globe to acquire the right dog to enhance their team. The study of pedigrees becomes almost a science, and the health, care, and feeding of their teams is of major concern.

While the purses for the winners of the big races are large, so are the costs of maintaining a professional team. The costs far exceed the winnings, and before one considers getting into the professional aspect of the sport, financial considerations must be taken into account.

With professional racing teams there is also a more strict, concentrated training schedule. The dogs must be kept in top racing condition all the time, not just before racing seasons, which means they must not become overweight. Bad dispositions are weeded out at the first moment of discovery, grooming and training are on a regular schedule and more frequent, and the serious racing training begins in earnest at six or seven months of age. Most racing dogs are staked out at about three to four months old, and the confined conditions seem to heighten their desire to run.

While there are more Siberian Huskies on professional racing teams now than ever before, there are not as many as one would expect. There are reasons for this—the owners of the professional teams are interested to a great extent in the money prizes and will use any dog—purebred or otherwise—if the dog will run to win. Expenses are high to maintain and breed purebred Huskies exclusively while waiting for the top ones to come along. Trained sled dogs can cost from $600 to $5000, depending on their ability and past performances. Mixed breeds offer more opportunities to buy up the fastest dogs in spite of their ancestry, giving the owners a "faster team faster"! So unless money is no object, many pros will not stick to one breed, but will shop around. Though price may be no object, there is a time limit involved. It is only the dedicated Siberian Husky lover who can afford to support a team of purebreds, who brings out a matched team that has a good chance of winning!

A GLOSSARY OF RACING TERMS

ALASKAN HUSKY—A name applied to any Arctic-type cross-bred dog, usually a Husky, Malamute, Samoyed, or Eskimo cross

ALASKAN MALAMUTE—Used more for hauling than racing because of its great size and endurance

ATTITUDE RUN—A short "fun" race

BABICHE—Strips of raw hide used to join the parts of a sled

BACKLINE—A line from the harness to the towline. Sometimes referred to as a tugline

BASKET—The section of the sled which carries either passenger or cargo

BRAKE—The metal fork stepped on by the driver to bring the sled to a halt; a fork on the underside of the sled which hits the ground and stops the sled

BRIDLE—The collection of ropes gathered with a ring to which the towline is attached

CART TRAINING—When there is no snow, training dogs with a three or four wheel cart is undertaken. Carts also are used in racing in warm climates that do not have snow.

CHAIN—Lengths of chain are used to stake a dog outdoors; usually about six feet in length and attached with snaps at the dog's collar and to the stake

CHIEF STEWARD—Chief steward takes the other stewards out to their posts. He remains at the start and finish lines

CHUTE—The first several feet behind the starting line are referred to as the chute

DNF—Letters standing for Did Not Finish, which means a racer did not finish the race

DOG BOX—The compartment mounted on a truck in which the dogs are transported to and from the racing site

DRAGGING—When a dog is dragged along by his neckline, either after he falters, or if he is merely lagging behind

GANGLINE—Center line fastened to the sled and to which the dogs are hitched. Also known as towline

GEE—A term used with the dog to indicate a right turn

GO—Same as start, begin, etc. Response to this word can mean the difference between getting off to a head start or merely starting along with the others

HANDLE BAR—Topmost portion at the rear of the sled on to which the driver holds

HARNESS—The canvas or nylon webbing which covers the dog and is attached to the lines

HAW—Term used to indicate a left turn

HEAT—A heat is one race

HOLDING AREA—A section near the racing site where dogs are staked until race time

HOOK OR SNOW HOOK—A metal hook attached to the bridle of the sled by a line to hold the team in place. It can be driven into the ground or attached to a stationary object

HOOK-UP AREA—Same as holding area— a place where the dogs are held until race time

INDIAN DOG—A dog bred and owned by an Indian in an Indian village

JINGLER—A collection of bells or noisy trinkets used to get the attention of the dogs and spur them on

LEAD DOG—The dog at the head of the team, usually the fastest, most experienced, and best trained

LEADER—The same as a lead dog

LOWER 48 OR LOWER 49—Term used when referring to racing in any of the United States other than Alaska

MARSHALL—A term used when referring to the racing official in charge of the race

MUSH—Originally a French term meaning to walk or to march. While mush can be a term used for starting a team, more often "let's go!" or "take off!" work just as well; usually only drivers in the movies yell "Mush!"

MUSHER—The term applied to the driver of a team.

NECKLINE—A light line that hooks the dog's collar to the towline

NO—Word used to keep the dogs on the trail should they start to veer off course, or to stop them from chewing on the line, to ward off a scrap or fight, etc.

PEDALING—When the driver keeps one foot on the runner of the sled and pedals or pushes with the other

PUMPING—A term used meaning the same as pedaling

PUNCHING THROUGH—When the dog's feet break through the crust of ice on top of the snow, they are said to punch through. The term "punchy" is the word used for snow

RACE MARSHALL—Man in charge of the races

RIGGING—All the lines collectively to which the dogs are hooked

RUNNERS—Two bottom strips of wood on which the sled runs and are covered with steel or plastic strips called runner shoes

SIBERIAN HUSKY—Purebred dog used extensively in sled racing

SKI-JORING—A short race with the driver on ski s rather than with a sled. Line is attached around his waist with a slip knot

SLED BAG—The canvas bag which holds items necessary to the race and is usually carried in the basket

SNOWBERM—The ridges of snow made along the side of the road by snow plows

SNOW FENCE—Fencing made of wooden upright slats fastened together with wire used to mark off areas or to prevent heavy drifting of snow to mar the trail

SNOW HOOK—A hook used to stake a team temporarily

STANCHIONS—Vertical parts of a sled

STARTER—The man who starts the race

STAY—Same as "Whoa," "Stop," or "Halt." Used to stop the dogs at the end of the race or for any other reason. Choose one and stick with it

STEWARD—One of the officials placed along the trail to avoid trouble at traffic spots, sharp curves, etc. He must stay on the trail until the last team has passed

STOVE UP—When a dog pulls up lame or stiff

SWING DOG—Dog that runs directly behind the leader either on the right side of the tow line (right swing dog) or on the left side (left swing dog)

TEAM DOGS—Dogs hitched into the team between the swing dogs and the wheel dogs

TO MUSH DOGS—To drive a team

TOWLINE OR GANGLINE—The center line fastened to the sled and to which the dogs are hitched

TRAIL—Term shouted by mushers to ask another driver for the right of way

TUGLINE OR TUG—Line from harness to the towline, same as backline

VET CHECK—Before each race, a veterinarian checks over each dog to see that it has not been drugged, if it is in good health and running condition, etc.

WHEEL DOGS—The two dogs directly in front of the sled which determine the direction of the sled

WHIP—Usually whips are not permitted, but if they are, they must be under three feet in length so that they cannot touch the dogs

WHOA—With dogs, as with horses, this means "Stop!"

Ch. Kossok's Kiska of Oakcrest. Breeder/owner, Alice J. Watt.

THE SIBERIAN HUSKY AS A PACK DOG

"Pack trips are becoming very popular . . . as more and more Husky owners learn to enjoy mountain hiking with their dogs."

Strong, sure-footed, and steady in all kinds of weather, the Siberian Husky can be counted on as a first-rate pack dog. In the far north, Siberian Husky pack dogs are used when there is not adequate snow for sleds, and are also used by fur trappers and hunters to bring pelts back in their packs, rather than on the sleds, when snow is scarce. Pack trips are becoming very popular in this country as more and more Husky owners learn to enjoy mountain hiking with their dogs.

EARLY TRAINING

Training a dog to pack is relatively simple, with the main concern being the addition of the pack and the weight it carries. Start your early training with an empty pack, of course, and once the dog is used to the feel of it on his body, fill it with something to get the dog used to the sensation of weight. Many packers suggest a light but bulky load right from the beginning to get the dog used to the feel and the "swing" of the pack. Naturally, you will not overload your dog, especially not at the beginning of the training.

Ten pounds is an ideal weight for the average size Husky, though there are those who will pack almost one half the dog's weight (only if properly packed and the dog properly conditioned). You will find the dog will take to the pack quite easily and will eventually get rather protective of it, guarding it when you make camp and take the packs off!

In temperate climates during very cold weather, if you are hiking it may become necessary to have moccasins for the dogs. At any rate, in cold weather and on very rough terrain, check the dogs' feet for cut pads or ice balls between the toes. After you've made a few hikes their feet may toughen, but it is always best to be careful. It's a long way to carry them back home!

Since Siberian Huskies are such natural outdoor dogs, you will find they love to charge ahead of you along the trail. At a very early age, you must train your Huskies to return promptly when called when they are off lead. Some packers use whistles, but in any case, make sure you and your dogs understand each other completely on this point to avoid unfortunate disappearances. The reward system will really pay off on this point.

Siberian Huskies show a great deal of good sense when it comes to identifying trails and summits, and Joanne Rudnytsky, whose Wissahickon Beowulf, CD, is a member of the Appalachian Mountain Club's 4000 Footer Club, is a veteran at backpacking with her dogs over the years. Mrs. Rudnytsky claims that they never go too far away on circular hikes, but now and then on hikes, which are just

WESTERN PENN. BEST IN SHOW

Susanna Windsor Rodney's winning team takes Best in Show at the Western Pennsylvania event. Arahaz Kaylee Konkon, CD, Kaylee Kitkit Kulik, Kaylee Kitkit Kayikay and Ch. Arahaz Tengri Khan, CD. Owner-handled as usual.

"Two of the chief worries when backpacking with dogs are encounters with skunks and porcupines."

"up and back," they tend to run off. She tells of just such a happening on a climb when the day was particularly warm and one of her dogs, Tala, took off. She returned to the car after the trip down the mountain and found Tala lying in its shade—this proves you must keep a close eye on your dogs and be sure to have them wear their identification tags on their collars.

THE PACK DOG

It is not a good idea to feed the dog before starting on a trip. Feed at night before bedding down, when the dog can relax and properly rest while digesting his food. Water is essential for the pack dog; you will find they require much more water than they usually consume, and generally twice as much as a thirsty person. Since they do not drink out of canteens, remember to take along Sierra Club cups or aluminum dishes for them!

Dry foods, or semi-moist foods, carried in plastic bags are best and should be of the concentrated varieties which are high in protein for extra energy. Make sure everything is wrapped tightly, in double plastic with wire twists, so no water gets into the food in case you cross streams along the trail. You especially do not want water to get into the first aid kit! The first aid kit is something else that hikers are sure to want to take along.

Two of the chief worries when backpacking with dogs are encounters with skunks and porcupines. Again, a voice of experience in the person of Joanne Rudnytsky states that you are wise to carry alligator-nose pliers along to remove porcupine quills if necessary. Tweezers are equally essential for the removal of ticks, and alcohol and swabs go hand in hand with both afflictions! A past issue of *Field and Stream* magazine advocated the use of a solution of two teaspoonsful of ordinary baking soda mixed with one cup of vinegar, patted on all exposed portion of each quill; after a ten-minute wait, repeat the procedure. In another ten minutes you should be able to remove the quills painlessly, since the combined action of the soda and vinegar softens the quill to the point where it shrinks and can be removed. It is surely worth a try—but we sincerely hope the occasion will not arise! Death has been known to occur as a result of a dog's tangling with a porcupine, so do your best to steer clear of them. Confrontations with skunks are less dangerous but certainly no more pleasant. A bath with strong soap and several rinses with tomato juice when you get home are about the only remedy for this.

Training can start at about four months of age and should consist of the simple initial obedience training work for heel, sit, sit-stay, down, down-stay, and the extremely important recall! The recall can be either vocal or whistle or, as

Top: The 1980 Best Brace in Show at the SHC of Anchorage Specialty under judge Jean Fournier. The dogs are CanBda Ch. White Fox's Tatiana Kazankina, and Can Ch. White Fox's Kayakin of Anadyr, CD. *Bottom:* Teamwork! Ch. Talocon Nova's Calypso and Ch. Talocon Nova's Taneka at 6 months winning Best Brace in Show at the 1977 SHC of Greater New York Specialty. Bred and owned by J. and G. O'Connell.

Arahaz Kalinda and Arahaz Katina are an armful for breeder Rosemary Fischer, Beaver, PA.

Joanne Rudnytsky has advocated, two different whistles, one whistle to mean return immediately and another whistle to mean that the dog should merely show itself on the trail to establish visual contact. A reward for a return is in order. Vocal commands can be taught in the backyard, whistle training on walks in the woods near home before starting on longer hikes in the mountains.

It is best to take the puppies along with older dogs, which set an example and will help teach the puppies what trailing is all about.

Make sure these first trips are not difficult or dangerous ones and *not too long*, which will tire the puppies and perhaps discourage them from future enjoyment. Start them off on the trail with empty packs on home ground or on long walks. Then begin stuffing the packs with crumpled newspaper or magazines in increasing amounts until their capacity load has been attained. Then they will be ready for the longer, rougher trails in the mountains.

The pack is made of heavy canvas, leather, and ripstop nylon. It is in several parts: there is a heavy canvas saddle with a leather cinch, and sewn to the saddle are two ripstop nylon bags. The bags have a breast strap and a belly strap, and are usually bright red in color to help hikers identify and spot their dogs at a distance.

The bag is placed on the dog as far forward as possible so that it rides over the withers. The cinch is secured firmly as far forward on the brisket as possible so that it rides over the withers. The cinch is secured firmly as far forward on the brisket as possible, but not so tightly that it in any way restricts the breathing or will be a discomfort to the dog. The breast and belly straps are loosely secured to help keep the bag in place, so that it does not shift too much when the dog is going up or down steep inclines.

There are eight D-rings sewn on the bag: one on top, one forward, one rear, and one low on each bag. A wrap-around strap is passed through the D-rings to further hold the pack in place. The wrap-around is long, with an O-ring on one end. This passes over, under, in front of, and under the belly and back to the O-ring, where it is secured by a squaw hitch.

These packs come in three different sizes and styles and can be obtained from Wenaha Dog Packs, 14421 Cascadian Way, Lynnwood, WA 98036. There are also many other sources of supply. Since one of the rules of backpacking is to try not to go alone, you may be able to ask the other party for other places from which you can obtain any supplies.

Best Brace in Working Group at the 1979 Eastern Dog Club Show was Carol Nash's Ch. Marlytuk's Elektra and Ch. Marlytuk's Sachem of Canaan. Judge was Chet Collier. This impressive duo was Second in the Group at this show the year prior.

Top: Siberians at play at the Innisfree Kennels in Chateaugay, NY. *Bottom:* Maureen Kent and three of her dogs, Kaptain, Krystal and Katie, at their Bow, NH, kennel. *Opposite:* Bred by Sandra Porter, Skrimshaw's Sheet Charity, co-owned by breeder and Darlene Hawkins; and Skrimshaw's Windjammer, owned by George and Kathi Dorvee of Ballston Lake, NY. The sire was Ch. Sno-Fame Solo's Mr. J.W. Chips ex Ch. Keraseva's Harlequinade, CD.

be made at any time during one's lifetime. The climber is provided with a form which lists the name of the mountain, its height, and the date which the climber enters upon his ascent; the form also includes a record of his trip companions. Mrs. Rudnytsky's three Siberian Huskies, Wissahickon Beowulf, CD, Wissahickon Natala, and Wissahickon Zephyr Fournier, are all members! Beo has climbed all 46 peaks, accompanied by Tala and/or Zeph.

Perhaps one of the most famous of the pack-trained dogs is the Siberian Husky bitch belonging to Don Carlough of Suffern, New York. Doncar's Snow Valley Flicka, UD, is her name, and she is not only pack-trained for mountain and trail hiking, but is trained in ski-joring as well.

Timber and Pumpkin, bred by Jean Fournier and Robyn Mott and co-owned by Jean and Angele Porpora. This photo won first place in the parent club photo contest and was published in the October 1985 issue of the *American Kennel Gazette*. The sire was Tokorock's Aquila Hi-O Silver ex Ch. Toko's Misty Dawn of Northsea.

Top: Kossok's Favorite Son, bred and owned by Alice Watt, Salem, OR. *Bottom:* Four of Leroy Simons' Siberians in the exercise pen, waiting to go into the show ring.

SIBERIAN EVALUATION PERFORMANCE PROJECT

"Fearing the loss of the original working qualities of the breed, SEPP was founded."

One of the newest organizations in the breed is the SEPP program, dedicated to preserving the working dog qualities of the Siberian Husky. The Siberian Evaluation Performance Project was formed in July, 1982, by a group of concerned owners of working Siberians. Since the Siberian became known to the general public, the breed has achieved enormous popularity because of its striking beauty and pleasant temperament. This very popularity has worked against the original purpose for which this breed was treasured—that of a strong, hearty, and very competitive sled dog. Fearing the loss of the original working qualities of the breed, SEPP was founded.

The purpose of SEPP was to develop a testing program of the highest caliber to locate and identify those Siberians who could still perform on a world class level. Once identified, these few dogs would be available as the core breeding stock to re-establish the Siberian as a superior racing dog.

The four original racing evaluators were Dr. Charles Belford, veterinarian and outstanding driver from the 1930s through the 1970s; Richard Moulton, arctic explorer and famed dog driver, who went with Admiral Richard Byrd to the Antarctic in 1939; Dr. Roland Lombard, veterinarian and eight-time winner of the World Championship Sled Dog Race in Anchorage, Alaska; and Harris Dunlap, two-time

Camelot's Snowplow winning at just 7 months of age from the Puppy Class at the 1984 Rio Pocos KC Show. Owner-handled by Dr. William Miranda.

winner of the Gold Medal given for best overall performance throughout a season by the International Sled Dog Racing Association.

SEPP is governed by a Board of Directors and these Evaluators. The membership of SEPP is drawn from the United States, Canada, and Europe. Two corporate sponsors, Allen Products Company (ALPO) and Tuffy's Pet Foods have made considerable contributions to the success of the evaluations. ALPO has provided the speakers at some events; Tuffy's underwrote the entire expenses of the fourth evaluation, held in Minnesota.

The first skeletal measuring evaluators were Leigh and Susan Gilchrist from Ontario, Canada. The AKC show judges, who evaluate the participants according to the breed standard, vary from year to year and have included Vincent Buoniello, Jean Fournier, and Don Reynolds.

The first four founding, SEPP evaluations were in 1982 in Voluntown, Connecticut; 1983 and 1984 in Warrensburg, New York; and 1985 in Ely, Minnesota. In these four evaluations approximately 220 dogs were tested, with about 60 dogs passing. Of those 60, only seven achieved the highest rating of Superior/Excellent. Dogs have come from all the New England states, Delaware, Pennsylvania, New Jersey, New York, Maryland, California, Minnesota, Wisconsin, Illinois, Iowa, and Ontario and Quebec in Canada.

To enter a dog in a SEPP evaluation, the dog must be a

"The results of the three evaluations are made available to all those who enter, along with a set of pedigrees for each passing dog."

registered Siberian, AKC or CKC, with no serious genetic faults which would be detrimental to a breeding program. They must have at least 75 miles of training since September for the late October/early November testing weekend. Dogs who are over standard in height are allowed to enter, but this fact is noted on their breed standard evaluations.

The Siberians are evaluated in groups of six, hitched behind six or eight dogs from established world class teams provided by kennels with proven records. Dogs are judged on speed, gait, honesty of working attitude, temperament, and endurance.

On Saturday, the dogs are evaluated on raw speed over a short course of about three miles in length. One evaluator rides the rig and another rides in a pick-up truck following immediately behind the team. Both evaluators must approve a dog before it is asked to run again on Sunday. Speeds on those short runs often exceed 20 miles per hour for the flat and downhill stretches. Two different evaluators judge the dog on Sunday's run, an endurance trial of about five miles. Both evaluators again must rate the dog for a final rating of good, good/superior, superior, or superior/excellent.

At an average evaluation of 80 entrants, about 20 are asked to run twice, and only ten to 15 are passed.

After the trial testing on Saturday, the dogs are evaluated twice more: by an AKC judge to the breed standard, and by the skeletal measuring team, who carefully measure bone lengths, proportions, and balance with reference to the known measurements of some of the finest world class Siberians and Alaskans from top racing kennels.

The results of the three evaluations are made available to all those who enter, along with a set of pedigrees for each passing dog. The results are published in several national breed and racing magazines, and any interested member of the general public may obtain a copy of the results by getting in touch with the Secretary of SEPP. SEPP hopes this information will increase the knowledge of all breeders so that they may improve their programs with the goal of a better racing Siberian.

At every evaluation, there is a symposium or round-robin discussion at a dinner Saturday evening with speakers and/or a panel of evaluators and top drivers. During the entire weekend the teams are recorded on video tape. These tapes are also shown during the dinner. There is plenty of free time for discussion with top drivers and other racers. The weekends are informative and great fun for participants and spectators.

The purpose of SEPP is not to enhance the career of any individual dog or kennel. It is to provide a comprehensive

Top: Ch. Indigo's Saroja Cinsation, bred by David Qualls and M. Ravain, and owned by Jim and Melanie Babb and Ronald and Sandy James. *Bottom:* Ch. Tofchuks Solo of Aslanlar winning at a Mt. Ogden KC show. Owner, Sue Adams.

Ch. Sno-Fame Solo's Mr. J.W. Chips finished for his championship in 1982. The sire was Ch. Sno-Fame Chuka's Solo Odinok ex Donasha's Lady of the Wind. Bred by Ann M. Sullivan, he is co-owned by breeder and William and Linda Albright.

Top: Ch. Innisfree's Trademark, bred by Kathleen Kanzler and owned by Richard and Gayle Atkinson. Trademark is a Top Producer and being shown under Mildred Heald.
Bottom: Robin and Jim Abramowicz's Arahaz Bleska of Rostov. Bred and co-owned by R. Fischer.

Top: Talocon's Arctic Angel O'Ikon. "Angel" is winning at a 1984 show with Jack Austen handling for owners George and Yvonne Cooper of Boyarie Kennels. *Bottom:* AmCanMex Ch. Karnovanda's Sasha Groznyi and daughter winning at a show. Sasha is a Specialty winner, multi-Group winner and a Racing Dog award winner as well. Sasha is owned by Anne Bruder, Sunset Hills Kennels. Daughter Ch. Sunset Hill's Morning Glory is owned by Anne Dussetsledger of Texas.

examination of dogs, to further the knowledge of the owners and any other interested Siberian fancier or judge, for the purpose of improving breeding programs and understanding of the racing Siberian. Thus far, a number of breedings of the best dogs have resulted in several litters of promising puppies. SEPP sincerely hopes to continue the program with the support of those who value the workability of the Siberian Husky.

THE HIGHEST SEPP-RATED DOGS

In the first four evaluations for SEPP, the dogs receiving the highest SEPP rating of Superior/Excellent were Bandit, owned by Jerry and Arden LeVasseur; Critter, owned by Robert and Roberta McDonald; Pryde, owned by Edward and Caroline Burke; Rice and Rostov, owned by Linda Trinkaus; Jimmy, owned by Vincent Buoniello; and the only female, Tiko, owned by Paul Boudreau.

Top: Panda of Cornell Ave., winning at a 1975 dog show; bred and owned by R. Fischer. *Bottom:* At 10 years of age, Phyllis Castelton's Can Ch. White Fox's Kayakin of Anadyr, CD.

Top: Sno-mate Sakonnet's Tecihila winning at a 1986 show. Sire was Ch. Sno-mate's Celebration ex Ch. Sno-mate's Mariah. Owned by Leroy and Leslie Simons, Leighton, IA. *Bottom:* Cinnaminson's Niño d'Oro, bred by Sy Goldberg and owned by Walter and Nancy Kelknap of Alamogordo, NM. The sire was Ch. Cinnaminson's Jolly Rodger ex Cinnaminson's Sterling Silver.

Top: Winner of the 1984 National Specialty Show of the SHCA was Ch. Kadyak's Ms. Kishwin, bred and owned by Ardene Eaton; Al Lee, handler. Sired by Ch. Innisfree's Sierra Cinnar ex Chujack's Ms. of Marlytuk. The judge was Phyllis Brayton for the Golden Specialty of the parent club.
Bottom: Margaret Cook shows her Can Ch. Balcom's Teeco S. Taree Night at the Wampanoag KC Show in 1983, under Robert Thomas.

Top: Fra-Mar's Koala Diavol, winning Best of Winners; owned by Marie Wamser of Valley City. *Middle:* Ch. Frosty Aires Alcan King, an oldtimer great at his last show in December 1970, at age 11 years, 11 months. He is handled here by owner Marie Wamser. With him is AmCanBda Ch. Fra-Mar's Soan Diavol, another great dog from Marie's kennels. *Bottom:* AmCan Ch. Yeti's Baltic Vin, winning on the way to his Canadian championship at this 1981 show. He is the sire of Specialty Show winners and champions. Bred and owned by Joy Messinger, Verona, NJ.

Top: AmCan Ch. Bo-Gerick's Top of the Line. "Topper" was sired by Ch. Innisfree's Aazar Bit-A-Thor ex AmCan Ch. Innisfree's Ms. Cinnar. Owners are the Dalakians and the Douglas Hursts.
Bottom: AmCan Ch. Snoking's Snowdrift at the 1983 SHC of Delaware Valley Specialty Show. Owners, Richard and Janice MacWhade.

SEPP EVALUATION I–Passing Dogs

RATING	DOG	SEX	OWNER
Superior–Excellent	Bandit	M	LeVasseur, J & A
Superior–Excellent	Critter	M	McDonald, B & R
Superior–Excellent	Pryde	M	Burke, E & C
Superior	Allen	M	Trinkaus, L
Superior	Aries	M	Trinkaus, L
Superior	Paps	M	McDonald, B & R
Superior	Pepper	M	LeVasseur, J & A
Good–Superior	Dan	M	LeVasseur, J & A
Good–Superior	Puggy	M	LeVasseur, J & A
Good–Superior	Iroquois	M	Fogarty (Ryan), D
Good–Superior	Muttrina	F	Bailey, B & D
Good–Superior	Rocky	M	McDonald, B & R
Good–Superior	Slim	M	Tucker, R & S
Good–Superior	Sly	M	Kinne, J & C
Good	Ben	M	Tucker, R & S
Good	Bruno	M	Tucker, R & S
Good	Speckle	M	Tucker, R & S
Good	Tucker	M	Tucker, R & S
Good	Carbon	M	McDonald, B & R
Good	DJ	M	Haas, T
Good	Doc L	M	Bailey, B & D
Good	Mageik	M	Burke, E & C
Good	McKinley	F	Burke, E & C
Good	Nadya	F	Fogerty (Ryan), D
Good	Timber	M	Fogarty (Ryan) D

Ch. Setting Sun's Miss Parashinka with her breeder Kay Halcomb as winner of Oldest Bitch in the Parade of Champions at the 1984 SHCA National Specialty Show.

Ch. Tawny Hill's Gamyn, bred and owned by Adele M. Gray of Prospect, CT, winning under judge Lorna Demidoff at a 1973 show.

SEPP EVALUATION II– Passing Dogs

Rating	Dog	Sex	Owner
Superior–Excellent	Rice	M	Trinkaus, L
Superior–Excellent	Rostov	M	Trinkaus, L
Superior–Excellent	Tiko	F	Boudreau, P
Superior	Demon	F	Gilchrist, L & S
Superior	Garnet	M	Gilchrist, L & S
Superior	Gremlin	F	Gilchrist, L & S
Superior	Hustle	F	Gilchrist, L & S
Superior	Jowle	F	Gilchrist, L & S
Superior	Ni na	F	Gilchrist, L & S
Superior	Penny	F	Gilchrist, L & S
Superior	Raz	M	Gilchrist, L & S
Super ior	Tango	M	Gilchrist, L & S
Superior	Trapper	F	Gilchrist, L & S
Superior	Ember	F	Trinkaus, L
Superior	Oats	M	Trinkaus, L
Superior	Rascal	M	Bailey, B & D
Superior	Willow	F	Burke, E & C
Good–Superior	Bootia	M	Boudreau, P
Good–Superior	Tex	M	Boudreau, P
Good–Superior	Brownie	M	Bailey, B & D
Good–Superior	Lad	M	Gilchrist, L & S
Good	Black Knight	M	Hooker, D & R
Good	Earnest	M	Tucker, R & S
Good	Meadow	F	Hoh, B
Good	Missy	F	Weir, R
Good	Shoshone	F	Fitzgerald, D & W
Good	Tanaina	F	Fitzgerald, D & W

Ch. Indigo's Sweet Irth, bred by Dan and Leslie Haggard, and owned by the Indigo Kennels. This owner-handled Group winner also has many Group placements.

SEPP EVALUATION III– Passing Dogs

RATING	DOG	SEX	OWNER
Superior– Exc	Jimmy	M	Buoniello, V
Superior	Katy	F	Boudreau, P
Superior	Nadia	F	LeVasseur, J & A
Good–Excellent	Urich	M	LeVasseur, J & A
Good–Superior	Barron	M	Gilchrist, L & S
Good–Superior	Opal	F	Gilchrist, L & S
Good–Superior	Wylie	M	Gilchrist, L & S
Good–Superior	Nugget	F	Slocum-Stead, A
Good–Superior	Pete	M	Slocum-Stead, A
Good–Superior	Balto	M	Boudreau, P
Good–Superior	Desy	F	Boudreau, P
Good–Superior	King	M	Boudreau, P
Good–Superior	Sarah	F	Buoniello, V
Good	Gabe	M	Haas, T
Good	Martha	F	Tucker, R
Good	Silver	F	Gilchrist, L & S

SEPP EVALUATION IV– Passing Dogs

RATING	DOG	SEX	OWNER
Superior	Nugget	F	Slocum-Stead, A*
Superior	Nick	M	Wallace, T
Superior	Anya	F	Wallace, T
Superior	Heather	F	Wallace, T
Superior	Tok	M	Winder, J
Good–Excellent	Caribou	F	Bruce-Boehler, B
Good–Excellent	Lonely	M	Wallace, T
Good–Excellent	Blue	M	Wallace, T
Good–Superior	Cirque	M	Seablom, F
Good–Superior	Cascade	F	Seablom, F
Good–Superior	Geyser	M	Seablom, F
Good–Superior	Chancey	M	Slocum-Stead, A
Good–Superior	Otter	M	Slocum-Stead, A
Good–Superior	Tracks	M	Winder, J
Good–Superior	Bob	M	Wallace, T
Good–Superior	Tip	F	Wallace, T
Good	Koyuk	M	Moll, D
Good	Daiquiri	M	Wallgren, J

Ch. The Honey Bear of Troika, at 1 year of age, after taking a Best of Winners award. Owned and handled by Patty Jones. Kansas Bear finished championship with two 5-point majors.

Top: Ch. Innisfree's Fonzie, bred by K. Kanzler and owned by Richard and Gayle Atkinson. This multi-Best in Show winner has sired 6 champions out of Ch. Innisfree's Newscent's Niavar for the Indigo Kennels. *Bottom:* Turick's Final Conflict winning Sled Dog Class under judge Lou Harris at a 1984 show. Bred and owned by Carolyn Kaiser; handler, Leonard Bain. Conflict was by Turkick's Damien of Teso Pac ex Ch. Turkick's Tulik of Yeso Pac.

Top: Des-Mar's Susitna wins first place under judge Roland Lombard at the Cascade Sled Dog Match in 1984 in Oregon. Desmond Cole, breeder-owner handling.

Bottom: Ch. Kontiki's Natural Sinner and his 3½-month-old son, Karnovanda's Go For The Gold. The dam was Ch. Karnovanda's Twilight Time. Owner, Judith Russell.

Top: Komet's Traveller taking a Best of Breed win under Dr. Roland Lombard at the 1986 Nevada Dog Driver's Match in Sierra, NV. *Bottom:* The Torch Bearer of Troika at 9 months. Owners, Siberians of Troika.

Top: Ch. Innisfree's Standing Ovation, Group-placing bitch, finishing for her championship. Owner, James E. Babb. *Bottom:* Almaring's Heidi, by Ch. Almaring's Alai ex Almaring's Nikolashka, bred and owned by Ingrid Buccato.

Top: Ready and rarin' to go at the SEPP evaluation trials are Igloo Pak's Snow Bandit, owned by Jerry and Arden LaVasseur, and Iroquis, owned by Debra Fogarty. *Bottom:* Kortar's Kranberry Kaptain, CD, goes right from the racing team into the show ring in 1984.

Top: Ch. Aslanlar's Nefis Eshek winning the Breed at the 1974 Southern Oregon Show under Fred Young. Owned by Sue Adams. *Bottom:* Mr. and Mrs. William Creamer's Arahaz Kristi and Arahaz Ciara.

A pedigree represents something of value when one is dedicated to breeding better dogs.

To the novice buyer or one who is perhaps merely switching to another breed and sees only a frolicking, leggy, squirming bundle of energy in a fur coat, a pedigree can mean everything! To those of us who believe in heredity, a pedigree is more like an insurance policy—so always read it carefully and take heed.

For the more serious breeder who wishes to make a further study of bloodlines in relation to his breeding program, the American Kennel Club library stud books can and should be consulted.

THE BREEDING STOCK

Some of your first questions should concern whether the stud has already proven himself by siring a normal healthy litter. Also inquire as to whether the owners have had a sperm count made to determine just exactly how fertile or potent the stud is. Determine for yourself whether the dog has two normal testicles.

When considering your bitch for this mating, you must take into consideration a few important points that lead to a successful breeding. You and the owner of the stud will want to recall whether she has had normal heat cycles, whether there were too many runts in the litter and whether a Caesarean section was ever necessary. Has she ever had a vaginal infection? Could she take care of her puppies by herself, or was there a milk shortage? How many surviving puppies were there from the litter, and what did they grow up to be in comparison to the requirements of the breed Standard?

Don't buy a bitch that has problems in heat and has never had a live litter. Don't be afraid, however, to buy a

Left: **Phyllis Castelton's puppies out of her Blitzen dog, photographed in 1980 in Anchorage, AK.**

Pittsburg Pirate rooters Arahaz Kristi and Arahaz Ciara as pups.

healthy maiden bitch, since chances are, if she is healthy and from good stock, she will be a healthy producer. Don't buy a monorchid male, and certainly not a cryptorchid. If there is any doubt in your mind about his potency, get a sperm count from the veterinarian. Older dogs that have been good producers and that are for sale are usually not too hard to find at good, established kennels. If they are not too old and have sired quality show puppies, they can give you some excellent show stock from which to establish your own breeding lines.

The best advice used to be not to breed a bitch until her second heat. Today, with our new scientific knowledge, we have become acutely aware of such things as hip dysplasia, juvenile cataracts, and other congenital diseases. The best advice now seems to be aimed at not breeding your dogs before two years of age, when both the bitch and the sire have been examined by qualified veterinarians and declared, in writing, to be free and clear of these conditions.

The stud fee will vary considerably—the better the bloodlines and the more winning the dog does at shows, the higher the fee. Stud service from a top winning dog could run up to $500. Here again, there may be exceptions. Some breeders will take part cash and then, say, third pick of the litter. The fee can be arranged by a private contract rather than the traditional procedure

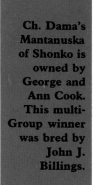

Ch. Dama's Mantanuska of Shonko is owned by George and Ann Cook. This multi-Group winner was bred by John J. Billings.

we have described. Here again, it is wise to get the details of the payment of the stud fee in writing to avoid trouble.

THE DAY OF THE MATING

Now that you have decided upon the proper male and female combination to produce what you hope will be, according to the pedigrees, a fine litter of puppies, it is time to set the date. You have selected the two days (with a one day lapse in between) that you feel are best for the breeding, and you call the owner of the stud. The bitch always goes to the stud, unless, of course, there are extenuating circumstances. You set the date and the time and arrive with the bitch *and* the money.

Standard procedure is payment of a stud fee at the time of the first breeding if there is a tie. For the stud fee, you are entitled to two breedings with ties. Contracts may be written up with specific conditions on breeding terms, of course, but this is general procedure. Often a breeder will take the pick of a litter to protect and maintain his bloodlines. This can be especially desirable if he needs an outcross for his breeding program or if he wishes to continue his own bloodlines, if he sold you the bitch to start with and this mating will continue his line-breeding program. This should all be worked out ahead of time and written and signed before the two dogs are bred. Remember that the payment of the stud fee is for the services of the stud— not for a guarantee of a litter of puppies. This is why is it so important to make sure you are using a proven stud. Also bear in mind that the American Kennel Club will not register a litter of puppies sired by a male that is under eight months of age. In the case of an older dog, they will not register a litter sired by a dog over 12 years of age, unless there is a witness to the breeding in the form of a veterinarian or other responsible person.

Many studs over 12 years of age are still fertile and capable of producing puppies, but if you do not witness the breeding there is always the danger of a "substitute" stud being used to produce a litter. This brings up the subject of sending your bitch away to be bred if you

Ch. Kiok's Sweet Kitu, CDX, bred, owned, and trained by Joe and Brenda Kolar, Astoria, OR.

cannot accompany her.

The disadvantages of sending a bitch away to be bred are numerous. First of all, she will not be herself in a strange place, so she'll be difficult to handle. Transportation, if she goes by air (while reasonably safe), is still a traumatic experience. There is always the danger of her being put off at the wrong airport, not being fed or watered properly, and so on.

Some bitches get so upset that they go out of season and the trip—which may prove expensive, especially on top of a substantial stud fee—will have been for nothing.

If at all possible, accompany your bitch so that the experience is as comfortable for her as it can be. In other words, make sure, before setting this kind of schedule for a breeding, that there is no stud in the area that might be as good for her as the one that is far away. Don't sacrifice the proper breeding for convenience, since bloodlines are so important, but put the safety of the bitch above all else. There is always a risk in traveling, since dogs are considered cargo on a plane.

THE ACTUAL MATING

It is always advisable to muzzle the bitch. A terrified bitch may fear-bite the stud or one of the people involved, and the wild or maiden bitch may snap or attack the stud to the point where he may become discouraged and lose interest in

the breeding. Muzzling can be done with a lady's stocking tied around the muzzle with a half knot, crossed under the chin and knotted at the back of the neck. There is enough "give" in the stocking for her to breathe or salivate freely and yet not open her jaws far enough to bite. Place her in front of her owner, who holds on to her collar and talks to her and calms her as much as possible.

If the male will not mount on his own initiative, it may be necessary for the owner to assist in lifting him onto the bitch, perhaps even in guiding him to the proper place. The tie is usually accomplished once the male gets the idea. The owner should remain close at hand, however, to make sure the tie is not broken before an adequate breeding has been completed. After a while the stud may get bored and try to break away. This could prove injurious. It may be necessary to hold him in place until the tie is broken.

We must stress at this point that, while some bitches carry on physically and vocally during the tie, there is no way the bitch can be hurt. However, a stud can be seriously or even permanently damaged by a bad breeding. Therefore, the owner of the bitch must be reminded that she must not be alarmed by any commotion. All concentration should be devoted to the stud and to a successful and properly executed service.

Many people believe that

breeding dogs is simply a matter of placing two dogs, a male and a female, in close proximity, and letting nature take its course. While this is often true, you cannot count on it. Sometimes it is hard work, and in the case of valuable stock it is essential to supervise to be sure of the safety factor, especially if one or both of the dogs are inexperienced. If the owners are also inexperienced, it may not take place at all.

ARTIFICIAL INSEMINATION

Breeding by means of artificial insemination is usually unsuccessful, unless under a veterinarian's supervision, and can lead to an infection for the bitch and discomfort for the dog. The American Kennel Club requires a veterinarian's certificate to register puppies from such a breeding. Although the practice has been used for over two decades, it now offers new promise, since research has been conducted to make it a more feasible procedure for the future.

Great dogs may eventually look forward to reproducing themselves years after they have left this earth. There now exists a frozen semen concept that has been tested and found successful. The study, headed

A beautiful veteran, Arahaz Miss Silver Tip, bred by R. Fischer.

by Dr. Stephen W.J. Seager, MVB, an instructor at the University of Oregon Medical School, has the financial support of the American Kennel Club, indicating that organization's interest in the work. The study is being monitored by the Morris Animal Foundation of Denver, Colorado.

Dr. Seager announced in 1970 that he had been able to preserve dog semen and to produce litters with the stored semen. The possibilities of selective world-wide breedings by this method are exciting. Imagine simply mailing a vial of semen to the bitch! The perfection of line-breeding by storing semen without the threat of death interrupting the

breeding program is exciting also.

As it stands today, the technique for artificial insemination requires the depositing of semen (taken directly from the dog) into the bitch's vagina, past the cervix and into the uterus by syringe. The correct temperature of the semen is vital, and there is no guarantee of success. The storage method, if successfully adopted, will present a new era in the field of purebred dogs.

THE GESTATION PERIOD

Once the breeding has taken place successfully, the seemingly endless waiting period of about 63 days begins. For the first ten days after the

Bouncing to Best in Show at Rubber City is Ch. Aazar's Sure Hit owned by Larry and Susan Govedich.

RUBBER CITY K.C.
BEST IN SHOW
BEST IN SHOW
RUBBER CITY
KENNEL CLUB SHOW
JUNE 1983
PHOTOS BY ALVERSON

BEST OF
WINNERS
TENNESSEE VALLEY
KENNEL CLUB
MARCH 1980
PHOTO BY BONNIE

Rosemary
Fischer
handles to Best
of Winners.

breeding, you do absolutely nothing for the bitch—just spin dreams about the delights you will share with the family when the puppies arrive.

Around the tenth day it is time to begin supplementing the diet of the bitch with vitamins and calcium. We strongly recommend that you take her to your veterinarian for a list of the proper or necessary supplements and the correct amounts of each for your particular bitch. Guesses, which may lead to excesses or insufficiencies, can ruin a litter. For the price of a visit to your veterinarian, you will be confident that you are feeding properly.

The bitch should be free of worms, of course, and if there is any doubt in your mind, she should be wormed before the third week of pregnancy. Your veterinarian will advise you on the necessity of this and proper dosage as well.

PROBING FOR PUPPIES

Far too many breeders are overanxious about whether the breeding "took" and are inclined to feel for puppies or to persuade a veterinarian to radiograph or X-ray their bitches to confirm it. Unless there is reason to doubt the normalcy of a pregnancy, this is risky. Certainly 63 days is not too long to wait, and why risk endangering the litter by probing with your inexperienced hands? Few bitches give no evidence of being in whelp, and there is no need to prove it for yourself by trying to count puppies.

ALERTING YOUR VETERINARIAN

At least a week before the puppies are due, you should telephone your veterinarian and notify him that you expect the litter and give him the date. This way he can make sure that there will be someone available to help, should there be any problems during the whelping. Most veterinarians today have answering services and alternative vets on call when they are not available themselves. Some veterinarians suggest that you call them when the bitch starts labor so that they may further plan their time, should they be needed. Discuss this matter with your veterinarian when you first take the bitch to him for her diet instructions, etc., and establish the method that will best fit in with his schedule.

Even if this is your first litter, I would advise that you go through the experience of whelping without panicking and calling desperately for the veterinarian. Most animal births are accomplished without complications; you should call for assistance only if you run into trouble.

When having her puppies, your bitch will appreciate as little interference and as few strangers around as possible. A quiet place, with her nest, a single familiar face, and her own instincts are all that is necessary for nature to take its course. An audience of squealing and questioning children, other pets nosing around, or strange adults should be avoided. Many a bitch that has been distracted in this way has been known to devour her young. This can be the horrible result of intrusion into the bitch's privacy. There are other ways of teaching children the miracle of birth, and there will be plenty of time later for the whole family to enjoy the puppies. Let them be born under proper and considerate circumstances.

LABOR

Some litters, and many first litters, do not run the full term of 63 days. Therefore, at least a week before the puppies are actually due and at the time you alert your veterinarian as to their expected arrival, start observing the bitch for signs of the commencement of labor. This will manifest itself in the form of ripples running down the sides of her body that will come as a revelation to her as well. It is most noticeable when she is lying on her side. She will be sleeping a great deal as the arrival date comes closer. If she is sitting or walking about, she will perhaps sit down

Top: Itaska's Mighty Max at just 6 weeks of age. Bred by the Itaska Kennels. *Bottom:* On the inside looking out. Arlington Kennels in Staten Island, NY.

James and Maureen Kent's first litter of future racing dogs.

quickly or squat peculiarly. As the ripples become more frequent, birth time is drawing near, and you would be wise not to leave her. Usually within 24 hours before whelping she will stop eating, and as much as a week before she will begin digging a nest. The bitch should be given something resembling a whelping box with layers of newspaper (black and white only) to make her nest. She will dig more and more as birth approaches, and this is the time to begin making your promise to stop interfering unless your help is specifically required. Some bitches whimper and others are silent, but whimpering does not necessarily indicate trouble.

The sudden gush of green fluid from the bitch indicates that the water or fluid surrounding the puppies has "broken" and that they are about to start down the canal and come into the world. When the water breaks, the birth of the first puppy is imminent. The first puppies are usually born within minutes to half an hour of each other, but a couple of hours between the later ones is not uncommon. If you notice the bitch straining constantly without producing a puppy, or if a puppy remains partially in and partially out for too long, it is cause for concern. Breech births (puppies born feet first instead of head first) can often cause delay or hold things up, and this is often a problem that requires veterinary assistance.

BREECH BIRTHS

Puppies are normally delivered head first; however, some are presented feet first or in other abnormal positions, and they are referred to as a "breech births." Assistance is often necessary to get the puppy out of the canal, and great care must be taken not to injure the puppy or the dam.

Aid can be given by grasping the puppy with a piece of turkish toweling and pulling gently during the dam's contractions. Be careful not to squeeze the puppy too hard;

merely try to ease it out by moving it gently back and forth. Because even this much delay in delivery may mean the puppy is drowning, do not wait for the bitch to remove the sac. Do it yourself by tearing the sac open to expose the face and head. Then cut the cord anywhere from one-half to three-quarters of an inch away from the navel. If the cord bleeds excessively, pinch the end of it with your fingers and count five. Repeat if necessary. Then pry open the mouth with your finger and hold the puppy upside down for a moment to drain any fluid from the lungs. Next, rub the puppy briskly with turkish or paper toweling. You should get it wriggling and whimpering by this time.

If the litter is large, this assistance will help conserve the strength of the bitch and will probably be welcomed by her. However, it is best to allow her to take care of at least the first few herself to preserve the natural instinct and to provide the nutritive values obtained by her consumption of one or more of the afterbirths as nature intended.

Occasionally the sac will break before the delivery of a puppy and will be expelled while the puppy remains inside, thereby depriving the dam of the necessary lubrication to expel the puppy normally. Inserting vaseline or mineral oil via your finger will help the puppy pass down the birth canal. This is why it is essential that you be present during the whelping so that you can count puppies and afterbirths and determine when and if assistance is needed.

CAESAREAN SECTION

Should the whelping reach the point where there is complication, such as the bitch's not being capable of whelping the puppies herself, the "moment of truth" is upon you and a Caesarean section may be necessary. The bitch may be too small or too immature to expel the puppies herself, her cervix may fail to dilate enough to allow the young to come down the birth canal, there may be torsion of the uterus, a dead or monster puppy, a sideways puppy blocking the canal, or perhaps toxemia. A Caesarean section will be the only solution. No matter what the cause, get the bitch to the veterinarian immediately to insure your chances of saving the mother and/or the puppies.

The Caesarean section operation (the name derived from the idea that Julius Caesar was delivered by this method) involves the removal of the unborn young from the uterus of the dam by surgical incision into the walls through the abdomen. The operation is performed when it has been determined that for some reason the puppies cannot be delivered normally. While modern surgical methods have made the operation itself reasonably safe, with the dam being perfectly capable of

"The Caesarean section operation . . . involves the removal of the unborn young from the uterus of the dam by surgical incision into the wall through the abdomen."

nursing the puppies shortly after the completion of the surgery, the chief task lies in the ability to spark life into the puppies immediately upon their removal from the womb. If the mother dies, the time element is even more important in saving the young, since the oxygen supply ceases upon the death of the dam, and the difference between life and death is measured in seconds.

After surgery, when the bitch is home in her whelping box with the babies, she will probably nurse the young without distress. You must be sure that the sutures are kept clean and that no redness or swelling or ooze appears in the wound. Healing will take place naturally, and no salves or ointments should be applied, unless prescribed by the veterinarian, for fear the puppies will get it into their systems. If there is any doubt, check the bitch for fever, restlessness (other than the natural concern for her young), or a lack of appetite, but do not anticipate trouble.

Even though most dogs are generally easy whelpers, any number of reasons might occur to cause the bitch to have a difficult birth. Before automatically resorting to Caesarean section, many veterinarians are now trying the technique known as episiotomy.

Used rather frequently in human deliveries, episiotomy (pronouced e-pease-e-ott-o-me) is the cutting of the membrane between the rear opening of the vagina back almost to the opening of the anus. After delivery it is stitched together, and barring complications, heals easily, presenting no problem in future births.

FALSE PREGNANCY

The disappointment of a false pregnancy is almost as bad for the owner as it is for the bitch. She goes through the gestation period with all the symptoms—swollen stomach, increased appetite, swollen nipples—and even makes a nest when the time comes. You may even take an oath that you noticed the ripples on her body from the labor pains. Then, just as suddenly as you made up your mind that she was definitely going to deliver puppies, you will know that she definitely is not! She may walk around carrying a toy as if it were a puppy for a few days, but she will soon be back to normal and will act as if nothing happened—and nothing did!

FEEDING THE BITCH BETWEEN BIRTHS

Usually the bitch will not be interested in food for about 24 hours before the arrival of the puppies, and perhaps as long as two or three days after their arrival. The placenta that she cleans up after each puppy is high in food value and will be more than ample to sustain her. This is nature's way of allowing the mother to feed herself and her babies without having to leave the nest and hunt for food during the first crucial days. In the wild, the mother always cleans up all traces of birth so as not to attract other animals to her newborn babies.

However, there are those of us who believe in making food available should the mother feel the need to restore her strength during or after delivery— especially if she whelps a large litter. Raw chopped meat, beef bouillon, and milk are all acceptable and may be placed near the whelping box during the first two or three days. After that, the mother will begin to put the babies on a sort of schedule. She will leave the whelping box at frequent intervals, take longer exercise periods and begin to take interest in other things. This is where the fun begins for you. Now the babies are no longer soggy little pinkish blobs. They begin to crawl around and squeal and hum and grow before your very eyes!

It is at this time, if all has gone normally, that the family can be introduced gradually and great praise and affection given to the mother.

THE TWENTY-FOUR HOUR CHECKUP

It is smart to have a veterinarian check the mother and her puppies within 24

Ch. Kontoki's Made in the Shade taking 3-point major for owner Thomas Oelschlager.

"The crucial period in a puppy's life occurs when the puppy is from 21 to 28 days old . . ."

hours after the last puppy is born. The veterinarian can check the puppies for cleft palates or umbilical herniae and may wish to give the dam—particularly if she is a show dog—an injection of Pituitin to make sure of the expulsion of all afterbirths and to tighten up the uterus. This can prevent a sagging belly after the puppies are weaned when the bitch is being readied for the show ring.

REARING THE FAMILY

Needless to say, even with a small litter there will be certain considerations that must be adhered to in order to insure successful rearing of the puppies. For instance, the diet for the mother should be appropriately increased as the puppies grow and take more and more nourishment from her. During the first few days of rest, while the bitch looks over her puppies and regains her strength, she should be left pretty much alone. It is during these first days that she begins to put the puppies on a feeding schedule and feels safe enough about them to leave the whelping box long enough to take a little extended exercise.

It is cruel, however, to try to keep the mother away from the puppies any longer than she wants to be because you feel she is being too attentive or to give the neighbors a chance to peek in at the puppies. The mother should not have to worry about harm coming to her puppies for the first few weeks. The veterinary checkup will be enough of an experience for her to have to endure until she is more like herself again.

A show puppy prospect should be outgoing (probably the first one to fall out of the whelping box!), and all efforts should be made to socialize the puppy that appears to be the most shy. Once the puppies are about three weeks old, they can and should be handled a great deal by friends and members of the family.

During the third week the puppies begin to try to walk instead of crawl, but they are unsteady on their feet. Tails are used for balancing, and they begin to make sounds.

The crucial period in a puppy's life occurs when the puppy is from 21 to 28 days old, so all the time you can devote to them at this time will reap rewards later on in life. This is the age when several other important steps must be taken in a puppy's life. Weaning should start if it hasn't already, and this is the time to check for worms. Do not worm unnecessarily. A veterinarian should advise on worming and appropriate dosage and he can also discuss with you at this time the schedule for serum or vaccination, which will depend on the size of the puppies as well as their age.

Exercise and grooming should be started at this time, with special care and consideration being given to the diet. You will find that the dam

Barrelful of future Siberian champions bred by Elsa Marchesano of Levittown, NY.

will help you wean the puppies, leaving them alone more and more as she notices that they are eating well on their own. Begin by leaving them with her during the night for comfort and warmth; eventually, when she shows less interest, keep them separated entirely.

By the time the fifth week arrives, you will already be in love with every member of the litter and desperately searching for reasons to keep them all. They recognize you—which really gets to you and they box and chew on each other, try to eat your finger, and have a million other captivating antics that are special with puppies. Their stomachs seem to be bottomless pits, and their weight will rise. At eight to ten weeks, the puppies will be weaned and ready to go.

SOCIALIZING YOUR PUPPY

The need for puppies to get out among other animals and people cannot be stressed enough. Kennel-reared dogs are subject to all sorts of idiosyncrasies and seldom make good house dogs or normal members of the world around them when they grow up.

The crucial age that determines the personality and general behavior patterns that will predominate during the rest of the dog's life are formed between the ages of three and ten weeks. This is particularly true between the 21st and 28th day. It is essential that the puppy be socialized during this time by bringing him into family life as much as possible. Walking on floor surfaces, indoor and outdoor, should be experienced; handling by all members of the family and visitors is important; preliminary grooming gets him used to a lifelong necessity; light training (such as setting him up on tables and cleaning teeth and ears and cutting nails, etc.) has to be started early if he is to become a show dog. The puppy should be exposed to car riding, shopping tours, a leash around its neck, children (your own and others), and in all possible ways, relationships with humans.

It is up to the breeder, of course, to protect the puppy from harm or injury during this initiation into the outside world. The benefits reaped from proper attention will pay off in the long run with a well-behaved, well-adjusted adult dog capable of becoming an integral part of a happy family.

SPAYING AND CASTRATING

A wise old philosopher once said, "Timing in life is everything!" No statement could apply more readily to the age-old question that every dog owner is faced with sooner or later—to spay or not to spay.

For the one-bitch pet owner, spaying is the most logical answer, for it solves many problems. The pet is usually not of top breeding quality, and therefore there is no great loss to the bloodline; it takes the pressure off the family if the dog runs free with children, and it certainly eliminates the problem of repeated litters of unwanted puppies or a

Vixen and Gypsy, the first Siberians at Deanna and Lou Gray's Grawyn Kennels in Woodstock, IL.

backyard full of eager males twice a year.

But for the owner or breeder, the extra time and protection that must be afforded a purebred quality bitch can be most worthwhile—even if it is only until a single litter is produced after the first heat. It is then not too late to spay; the progeny can perpetuate the bloodline, the bitch will have been fulfilled—though it is merely an old wives' tale that bitches should have at least one litter to be "normal"—and she may then be retired to her deserved role as family pet once again.

With spaying, the problem of staining and unusual behavior around the house is eliminated, as is the necessity of having to keep her in "pants" or administering pills, sprays, or shots, of which most veterinarians do not approve anyway.

In the case of males, castration is seldom contemplated, which to me is highly regrettable. The owners of male dogs overlook the dog's ability to populate an entire neighborhood, since they do not have the responsibility of rearing and disposing of the puppies. When you take into consideration the many females the male dog can impregnate, it is almost more essential that the males rather than the females be taken out of circulation. The male dog will still be inclined to roam but will be less frantic about leaving the grounds, and you will find that a lot of

An attentive Husky smile.

wanderlust has left him.

When considering the problem of spaying or castrating, the first consideration after the population explosion should actually be the health of the dog or bitch. Males are frequently subject to urinary diseases, and sometimes castration is a help. Your veterinarian can best advise you on this problem. Another aspect to consider is the kennel dog that is no longer being used at stud. It is unfair to keep him in a kennel with females in heat when there is no chance for him to be used. There are other, more personal, considerations for both kennel and one-dog owners, but when making the decision, remember that it is final. You can always spay or castrate, but once the deed is done there is no return.

Index

For the reader's convenience, all prefixes and suffixes have been eliminated from titled dogs.